Columbine, 20 Years Later and Beyond

Columbine, 20 Years Later and Beyond

Lessons from Tragedy

Jaclyn Schildkraut and Glenn W. Muschert

Foreword by Frank DeAngelis
Former Columbine High School Principal

 PRAEGER™

An Imprint of ABC-CLIO, LLC
Santa Barbara, California • Denver, Colorado

Library of Congress Cataloging-in-Publication Data

Names: Schildkraut, Jaclyn, author. | Muschert, Glenn W., author.
Title: Columbine, 20 years later and beyond : lessons from tragedy / Jaclyn
    Schildkraut and Glenn W. Muschert ; foreword by Frank DeAngelis.
Other titles: Columbine, twenty years later and beyond
Description: Santa Barbara, California : Praeger, 2019. | Includes
    bibliographical references and index.
Identifiers: LCCN 2018041881 (print) | LCCN 2018043649 (ebook) | ISBN
    9781440862533 (eBook) | ISBN 9781440862526 (hardcopy : alk. paper)
Subjects: LCSH: Columbine High School Massacre, Littleton, Colo., 1999. |
    School violence—United States. | School violence—United
    States—Prevention. | Schools—United States—Safety measures.
Classification: LCC LB3013.33.C6 (ebook) | LCC LB3013.33.C6 S34 2019
    (print) | DDC 371.7/82—dc23
LC record available at https://lccn.loc.gov/2018041881

ISBN: 978-1-4408-6252-6 (print)
      978-1-4408-6253-3 (ebook)

23 22 21 20 19   1 2 3 4 5

This book is also available as an eBook.

Praeger
An Imprint of ABC-CLIO, LLC

ABC-CLIO, LLC
147 Castilian Drive
Santa Barbara, California 93117
www.abc-clio.com

This book is printed on acid-free paper ∞

Manufactured in the United States of America

To Cassie Bernall, Steven Curnow, Corey DePooter, Kelly Fleming, Matthew Kechter, Daniel Mauser, Daniel Rohrbough, Rachel Scott, Isaiah Shoels, John Tomlin, Lauren Townsend, Kyle Velasquez, and William "Dave" Sanders—this book is dedicated to your memory, 20 years later and beyond. May your lives and your losses never be forgotten.

To the Columbine community, we remember.

All author royalties from the sale of this book are being donated to the Columbine Memorial Foundation in honor of the victims and survivors of April 20, 1999. For more information on the foundation or to make your own contribution, please visit www.columbinememorial.org.

Contents

Foreword

I've learned in my journey over the past 20 years that living in the aftermath of a tragedy like Columbine is a marathon, not a sprint. On April 20, 1999, my community and I became members of a club that no one wants to join. We had to redefine normal—a lesson I now share with other communities that have shared in similar tragedies when they ask, "When does it get back to normal?" For us, normal changed that day.

The shooting not only affected the four classes of students (1999, 2000, 2001, and 2002) who were in the building that day but also impacted anyone who had ever gone to Columbine. Our school opened its doors in 1973, with the first class graduating in 1975. When those shots were fired, there were people who saw their school in the media and were saying, "That's *my* school. Those are *my* teachers." They took it personally, even though they were not in the building when the shooting happened.

After the shooting, we had to pull our community together. We needed to stick together. That evening and in the days following, I realized that the one thing we needed to do was to build on the outstanding tradition that had been established at Columbine since it opened its doors. We have always been family. I had to build on that. There was so much negativity occurring. I'd come to believe that we needed to not dwell on the negative but rather build on the positive.

One of the things I had come up with at my first assembly as principal back in 1996 was the phrase, "We are Columbine." Of course, there was the normal Columbine pride that our students and alumni had. After the shooting, that phrase took on a whole new meaning. We all came together—not just the students, past and present, or the faculty, staff, and administrators but also the parents, grandparents, and others. It took all of us to rebuild the community. We came together as one, almost like a phoenix rising up from the ashes. We did not allow this horrendous act to separate us. We were always strong, but this tragedy made us an even stronger and more tight-knit community.

Columbine will always represent a time to remember and a time to hope. We will always represent the 13 who lost their lives and the 24 who were injured, as well as all the people who were affected by the events of that horrific day. But Columbine represents so much more than that one day. It represents hope—a hope that we used to build on the memories of the beloved 13 and that led us down the long road to recovery.

As a community, we faced a lot of challenges that first year after the shooting. Carla Hochhalter, the mother of one of the students injured on April 20, committed suicide. One of our students took his own life. Two others were murdered at a local restaurant. It seemed like every time we took a step forward, something would happen, and we would have to take steps back. This is why I say that it is a marathon, not a sprint.

We had each other, and we had systems in place to help us. It was difficult, but we had each other. We also had the 13 families—of the 12 students and of my dear friend Dave Sanders. They were so inspirational to all of us, and that definitely helped us to work to rebuild the community. They were so supportive too, and that certainly helped us as we continued to heal.

Someone once told me, "You can't determine what happens to you, but you can determine how you respond." There are a few reasons I'm where I am today: my faith, family, and friends. It was two days after the tragedy, and I went down to my church, St. Frances Cabrini. The priest, Father Ken Leoni, said to me at that point, "Frank, you should have died, but God saved you. He spared you for a reason. Now, you do need to rebuild that community. . . . You will not have to walk that journey alone; he will be there every step of the way. . . . You must lead by faith and not by sight." Well, I took these messages to heart, and they guided me and continue to do so today.

I can remember the day after the shooting, on April 21, first telling everyone that I promised to be there until the class of 2002 graduated. I think as a staff, we all had made that commitment. There was very little turnover between 1999 and 2002.

As we got closer to 2002—it was actually in the fall of 2001—I was thinking that I had not fulfilled that promise to rebuild the school, even though the freshmen (on the day of the shooting) were ready to graduate the following spring. Our community was not where it needed to be, and that day, I said I was going to be there until every kid who was in an elementary school in the Columbine area graduated. So I stuck to that promise, which took me to 2012. Then, of course, someone—a parent—came up and said, "You can't leave, because my kid was in the first year of a two-year preschool program, so you need to stay longer." So I stayed until 2014, when I finally retired.

I think my greatest accomplishment is that I fulfilled what Father Leoni had asked me to do. When I left 15 years after the shooting, for all the kids who walked across that stage, if they were in school on that horrific day, I was their principal. I gave them their diplomas, and I was there to support them throughout their four years at Columbine. I think that's the thing that I can probably be most proud of—that I fulfilled that promise to help rebuild our community.

I needed Columbine more than it needed me. Being there for my kids helped me. They gave me a support system, but so did my faith and counseling. When there were people saying that counseling was a sign of weakness, and I'd better not tell anyone that I talked to a counselor because I would be deemed unfit, I did not listen. I went to counseling. I'm still in counseling. What I share when I go out and speak, what I share in my book, is that individuals affected by these tragedies need to find that support system.

People who are affected by these tragedies may not necessarily go through a Columbine. It's not a competition of who suffers more, but people are going to go through tragedy. They're going to go through tough times in their lives. It's finding that support system in place. For me, it was not just faith; for me, it was the counseling too. For me, I had family in place. Along with that, along with all the positive support that came in, it took its personal toll on me as far as relationships. I went through a divorce, unfortunately. It strained my relationship with my daughter, though I am working on that. I faced challenges, and I had every reason to quit. But I was not going to allow that to happen. I truly, truly believe—actually, I don't believe this, I know this for a fact—that I am much stronger today than I was prior to Columbine.

Many people think that Columbine was the first of its kind. It wasn't. Before us, there was Pearl, Mississippi; Paducah, Kentucky; Jonesboro, Arkansas; Springfield, Oregon. The media brought Columbine into people's living rooms, and I truly believe that's the reason we're still talking about it 20 years later. It becomes a noun, and it becomes a verb. But that's also the reason so many shooters after ours reference Columbine and the two killers— Red Lake (Minnesota), Virginia Tech, Sandy Hook, and Chardon (Ohio), to name a few. And it's not only at schools—there was a lot of comparison between the Aurora movie theater shooting and Columbine. Columbine is on people's minds, not just here in the United States but also across the world.

Every community that is affected by one of these shootings is going to share similarities to our tragedy. On April 20, when I found myself as the newest member of the club no one wanted to be a part of, Bill Bond, who was the principal of Heath High School in Paducah, Kentucky, reached out to me, offering advice and guidance. I would call him when I needed help, and he would call to check in on me. He wasn't an expert on dealing with tragedy, and neither am I, but we were able to learn about what worked and what didn't.

Today, I find myself in a similar role, working with communities as they navigate the waters of their own shootings and aftermath. I share with them what it was like for me, my experience. These are things that people who do not go through similar situations would never think about—but things that I can identify with. I also share with them about preparing for the marathon instead of trying to run the sprint. Over the years, I have talked to many principals, superintendents, and parents. I tell them, "I can't give you what's going to happen five years from now, 10 years from now. Let's talk baby steps. Where are you going to be a month from now, three months from now, and then a year from now?" These are the same considerations I had to work through after April 20, and I think being able to talk to someone who has actually walked in their shoes is helpful.

Columbine was a fantastic school prior to April 20 and after April 20, and it will continue to be in the future. What is really impressive to me is that we have 25 former students who are now teachers at Columbine. Five of those individuals were students when the shooting happened. I've seen former students who are now young adults move back to the area because they want their own children to attend Columbine. Even the students who walk the halls of the school today are part of that Columbine legacy. "They Stretch for Excellence." It's the tradition. It's that Rebel pride. We are Rebels for life, and no one ever can take that away from us. We are a strong community in every sense of the word.

We will never forget what happened on that horrific day. Again, I can't stress enough, we'll always remember what happened, but Columbine also provides hope—hope for others, for other communities, for other schools that go through something similar. We were able to build up the memories of the 13, and we were able to build ourselves up into a community that I really believe is stronger than what we were. No matter how dark the day may seem, there's always light.

The book *Columbine, 20 Years Later and Beyond: Lessons from Tragedy* does such a great job of giving the historical perspective of the tragic event while also debunking some of the myths that have been out there for the last 20 years. It talks about things that were done right, as well as things that were done that needed to be improved upon, and it gives a comprehensive story of the Columbine tragedy. It covers the role of the media. It covers threat assessment. It covers post-traumatic stress disorder. It covers all the key components of questions asked in the aftermath of Columbine that 20 years later, we're still talking about.

People will always say to me, "Well, Frank, these shootings continue to happen." I tell them, "You're right, they continue to happen. We read about them, but how many have been stopped? How many lives have been saved because of things that we have in place now?" That's what this book does. It gives people the information on things that are being done so we can continue to work to save lives.

If people say, "This happens in other places; it does not happen here," they are living in a fantasy world because it can happen anywhere on any given day. This book alerts people to that, and it gives them a valuable resource. This book appeals not only to educators but also to law-enforcement personnel, psychologists, and parents. It's a must-read.

Frank DeAngelis
Former principal, Columbine High School

Preface

The inscription below sits etched in the Wall of Healing at the Columbine Memorial, located adjacent to the school in Clement Park. Of all the quotes featured in the Wall, it is these words that form the foundation for this book. Given that mass violence, both in and out of schools, continues to be a topic of concern in the public discourse even 20 years after the Columbine shooting, such a question is of particular importance, especially because, in order to prevent further attacks from occurring, we have to learn from past errors that allowed events like Columbine to happen. Accordingly, this book focuses on answering the latter part of the inscription—"what have we learned?"—to identify not only how far we as a society have come since April 20, 1999, but

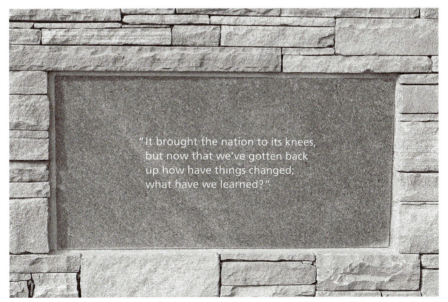

An inscription in the Wall of Healing at the Columbine Memorial. (Author photo)

also how far we still have to go in improving both our responses to these events and our prevention of future attacks. Moreover, were the answer to this pertinent question "nothing," the 13 lives lost that day and the countless others changed forever would have been in vain. We offer these lessons not only to help prevent others from sharing the same fate but also to honor the legacies of the victims, their families, the survivors, and the Columbine and Jefferson County communities as a whole.

The events of April 20, 1999, have permeated the national discussion about school safety and mass shootings and continue to do so, even 20 years later. A large focus of that discussion has been on the two perpetrators. Some people have sought to understand why they committed their acts; others have immortalized them, turning them into martyrs and folk heroes. Regardless of which side of the discussion people find themselves on, the fact remains that the shooters' names have become somewhat household terms. This book does not seek to contribute to such continued infamy.

Instead, we utilize a No Notoriety (www.NoNotoriety.com) approach in this book, one in which the shooters are not named and their images are not shown. There is ample information available through a multitude of sources should a reader be interested in learning more about them. We have elected, however, not to confound the lessons learned or the victims' memories by highlighting these two individuals. As you read, you will find that we refer simply to them as the shooters or, in the event that they are discussed individually, Shooter H and Shooter K (linking to their last names). While we understand that this might be a nontraditional approach to telling the story of the Columbine shooting and its aftermath, we believe it is the best approach to achieve our aims of focusing on what has been learned in the last 20 years and areas in which more information is needed. By focusing on these lessons and the individuals affected rather than on the shooters themselves, it is our goal to refocus the narrative where it needs to be instead of continuing to perpetuate a misguided narrative that began 20 years ago.

Acknowledgments

A very special thank-you must first go to Frank DeAngelis, Rick and Sue Townsend, Coni Sanders, Heather (Egeland) Martin, Zachary Cartaya, Amy Over, Anne Marie Hochhalter, and others in the Columbine community for providing us with an unfettered insight into April 20, 1999. Your candidness and willingness to share your experiences have made this project what it is.

Thank you to our research assistants—Courtney Baxter, Alexandra Bergin, Korine Clark, and Brian Monahan—for all your help on the project. Your support and hard work mean everything and have facilitated an amazing finished product. We also appreciate the insight and feedback from Dr. Hunter Martaindale and Dr. James Knoll in their respective areas of expertise.

Finally, to our editor, Jessica Gribble, thank you for the opportunity to make this project a reality. You have never been short of enthusiasm, support, or words of encouragement. Thank you for believing in us and our vision and helping us see it through to fruition.

CHAPTER ONE

April 20, 1999

It seemed like any other day for Columbine High School in Jefferson County, Colorado. This community of 500,000 residents, nestled in the foothills of the Rocky Mountains southwest of Denver, appeared an ideal place to raise a family, with its close community ties and lots of opportunities, including good schools. That spring day, as people awoke and went about their morning routines, more than 1,900 teenagers in the community headed to Columbine High School, an impressive building of 250,000 square feet located on Pierce Street just south of Bowles Avenue. (Though the mailing address for

The east entrance of Columbine High School. (Author photo)

Columbine places the school in Littleton, it actually sits in an unincorporated part of the county. Littleton is an adjacent city of approximately 40,000 residents in neighboring Arapahoe County.)

Aside from its physical size, Columbine was (and continues to be) impressive in many other ways. At the time of the shooting, the school had a 92% on-time graduation rate (Austin, 2003), with more than 88% of students continuing to college (DeAngelis, 2018). Nearly half of the students participated in advanced placement curriculum (U.S. News and World Report, n.d.), and one in four earned scholarships for higher education (DeAngelis, 2018). Like many schools, Columbine prided itself on championship athletics, with many of its teams' accomplishments proudly displayed in trophy cases lining the hallways (Assael, 1999; Larkin, 2007). The school had a positive reputation within the community, yet it also had the normal "aches and pains" of high school, including cliques, concerns over bullying, and a social hierarchy.

On the morning of April 20, 1999, students entered the school as normal and headed to their various classes. Two students, however, never attended their classes that day. Instead, they arrived at the school around 11:00 a.m., parking in adjacent lots (creating a cross-triangulated pattern), and entered the school with two 20-pound propane tank bombs concealed in large duffle bags. The timers on the bombs had been set to detonate at 11:17 a.m. local time, the time at which the two students previously had determined that the cafeteria, where the devices were planted, would be at its highest capacity—nearly 500 individuals. The pair then retreated back to their vehicles to wait for the explosion. On the way back to his car, Shooter H encountered student Brooks Brown, whom he knew, and subsequently told him to leave the school; Brooks was seen a short time later walking along Pierce Street.

In addition to the two bombs placed in the cafeteria, the pair had dozens of additional improvised explosive devices (IEDs; e.g., pipe bombs, Molotov cocktails), two sawed-off shotguns, a semiautomatic rifle (Hi-Point 995 9-millimeter [mm] carbine), a semiautomatic pistol (Intratec TEC-DC9), additional rounds of ammunition, and seven knives. Two other bombs, set for the same time as the cafeteria devices, had been placed in a field three miles from the school, designed to divert law enforcement away from the school when they exploded, thereby giving the shooters more time without interference. Both of their cars had been rigged with explosives and also contained napalm (a form of jelled gasoline) to enhance any explosion; additionally, the substance later was found on the shooters' bodies (Columbine Review Commission, 2001; Jefferson County Sheriff's Office, 2000).

The students' plan had been to shoot any survivors fleeing the building after the bombs detonated. Due to an issue with the alarm clocks used as the timing devices, however, the bombs never exploded—the hammers that rang the alarms were made of plastic and did not create the spark necessary to detonate them. When they realized that their original plan was not going to come to fruition, the pair decided to improvise. At 11:19 a.m., they approached the school on the west side of the building, moving up the exterior steps to an entrance on the upper level. Once there, witnesses reported that one of the shooters yelled "Go! Go!" They both then retrieved their shotguns from duffle bags they were carrying (the rifle and pistol were concealed underneath their black trench coats) and began shooting (Columbine Review Commission, 2001; Jefferson County Sheriff's Office, 2000).

Students Rachel Scott and Richard Castaldo, who had been eating lunch outside on a grassy area, were the first struck. Rachel was killed; Richard survived but was paralyzed permanently from his injuries. The shooters continued firing toward students who were near the cafeteria exits. Shooter H fired his weapon at students Lance Kirklin, Sean Graves, and Daniel Rohrbough. Daniel was hit in the leg and struck two more times by shooter H—once in the chest and once in the abdomen—and as he fell to the ground, he died almost instantaneously (El Paso County Sheriff's Office, 2002). Lance tried to catch Daniel as he fell, but he also was shot (El Paso County Sheriff's Office, 2002). Students Michael Johnson and Mark Taylor also were wounded by the gunfire. Shooter K then walked down the stairs back toward the cafeteria entrance and approached Lance, shooting him again, this time in the face. Sean was hit by Shooter K six times in the abdomen, back, and leg as he was running; his legs subsequently gave out, and he collapsed near the cafeteria, partially paralyzed (Columbine Review Commission, 2001; Jefferson County Sheriff's Office, 2000; The Denver Post, 2009).

Shooter K briefly entered the cafeteria, stepping on Sean before returning outside and continuing to fire. Student Anne Marie Hochhalter was struck several times by Shooter H before being pulled to safety by a friend; she also was paralyzed in the attack. The shooters were overheard saying "This is what we always have wanted to do. This is awesome!" as they lit several of the IEDs and pitched them onto the school's roof, into the parking lot, and onto the grassy area where Rachel and Richard had been sitting. By this point, students inside the school, who initially had thought the sounds of gunfire were part of a senior prank, began to understand the gravity of the situation. At 11:24 a.m., teacher Dave Sanders and school custodians Jon Curtis and Jay Gallatine entered the cafeteria and ordered students to seek shelter. As surveillance video footage captured Dave retreating back up to the second level of the school, students began to emerge from their hiding places under the tables and flee the cafeteria. At approximately the same time, Jefferson County Sheriff's Office (JCSO) Deputy Neil Gardner, who served as the school resource officer, was making his way back to the school from neighboring Clement Park after receiving two calls, the first directing him to the rear parking lot and the second notifying him of a student—later identified as Anne Marie—who had been shot and appeared to be para-lyzed (Columbine Review Commission, 2001; Jefferson County Sheriff's Office, 2000).

By this time, the shooters had approached the school's west entrance dou-ble doors. Art teacher Patti Nielsen, having heard the commotion and also believing that it was a prank, had gone to the same entrance to investigate and tell the students to stop. As she approached the doors, Shooter H fired his gun, shattering the glass entryway; the broken glass wounded Patti and student Brian Anderson, who was standing with her. The shooters then entered the building, continuing to fire at students they saw and detonating IEDs. Deputy Gardner arrived on scene around this time, distracting the shooters and allowing Patti and Brian to retreat to the library, where she called 911; JCSO dispatchers put out the first radio calls advising of the shots fired at 11:25 a.m. Shooter H turned his weapon toward the deputy, firing approximately 10 rounds before the weapon jammed. Deputy Gardner returned four shots, missing Shooter H, who, after unjamming his weapon, fired several more rounds before retreating back into the school (Columbine Review Commission, 2001; Jefferson County Sheriff's Office, 2000).

Two additional JCSO deputies, Paul Smoker and Scott Taborsky, arrived at the scene just after the shooters entered the school through the west entrance. Once there, they began trying to help two wounded students near the ball fields just up the hill. Leaning through one of the broken entryway windows, Shooter H fired at the officers. Deputy Smoker returned several shots before Shooter H retreated back into the school. The shooters walked down the north hallway, a main corridor of the building, continuing to fire their weap-ons at fleeing students and deploy IEDs both upstairs and by throwing them down onto the lower level (near the cafeteria). They also fired down the adja-cent library hall, which ran perpendicular to the main corridor and con-nected with areas like the cafeteria, auditorium, and science classrooms (Columbine Review Commission, 2001; Jefferson County Sheriff's Office, 2000).

As the shooters turned down the hallway from the main corridor, they encountered Dave Sanders, who was passing by the library with another student. Seeing the shooters, Dave and the student turned around to head back toward the area they had just come from. As they neared the hallway leading toward the science wing, Dave was struck twice by shotgun blasts from Shooter H—once in the back and once in the neck. The shots missed the student, who made it into a science room and urged others to hide. After falling face-first to the floor, Dave was able to pull himself to the sci-ence corridor, where teacher Richard Long helped him into a nearby class-room. Students in the room, including two Eagle Scouts, began to administer first aid and tried to help make him comfortable, showing him photos of his children that they found in his wallet and talking with him about his family (Columbine Review Commission, 2001; Jefferson County Sheriff's Office, 2000).

Inside the library, teacher Patti Nielsen remained on the line with 911. The audio recordings indicated that the shooters spent approximately three minutes in the hallway outside the library, firing their guns and detonating IEDs. Two of those devices were thrown into the downstairs cafeteria and were captured igniting by the surveillance camera. At approximately 11:29 a.m., the shooters entered the library. In addition to Patti, 56 students and 3 other staff members (another teacher and 2 library employees) had sought shelter in various parts of the library. Many of the students had taken cover under the library tables; Patti took cover in a cupboard near the front counter she had been hiding behind, the other teacher hid in the periodicals room, and the two library employees secured themselves in the adjoining television studio (Columbine Review Commission, 2001; Jefferson County Sheriff's Office, 2000).

The shooters demanded that everyone stand up. They also ordered the student athletes—primarily identifiable by their white hats—to rise. When no one complied, Shooter H fired two rounds from his shotgun at student Evan Todd, who was standing near the front counter, after noticing him. Evan was struck in his back with several pieces of buckshot as he scrambled over the counter. Kyle Velasquez, who had been seated at one of the computer stations near the west windows, was shot and killed by Shooter K, who then fired toward a table where Makai Hall, Patrick Ireland, and Daniel Steepleton were hiding, wounding each of them. Witnessing the two other boys being shot, Patrick tried to crawl out from under the table and flee when he was shot in the back of the head and blacked out. Also hiding under computer desks nearby were students Kacey Reugsegger and Steven Curnow. Shooter H fired his weapon at both of them, critically wounding Kacey in the shoulder and killing Steven. He then moved to another table where student Cassie Bernall was hiding, slapped the top twice while saying "Peek-a-boo," and fired, killing her. The shotgun then recoiled, breaking Shooter H's nose (Columbine Review Commission, 2001; Jefferson County Sheriff's Office, 2000).

Student Bree Pasquale was the next to encounter Shooter H, who asked her if she wanted to die. Before she could answer, Shooter K called him over to another table where students Matthew Kechter and Isaiah Shoels were hiding. As Isaiah begged for his life, Shooter K responded by calling him racial slurs. Shooter H then fired his shotgun at Isaiah, killing him; Shooter K fired his weapon at Matthew, mortally wounding him. The two shooters then continued through the library, detonating IEDs. One device landed near Makai Hall, who was able to throw it away from himself and the others to an area where it detonated without harming anyone (Columbine Review Commission, 2001; Jefferson County Sheriff's Office, 2000).

Shooter K continued to fire his weapon, first striking student Mark Kitgen and then wounding students Lisa Kruetz and Valeen Schnurr. Another student who had been hiding with them, Lauren Townsend, was fatally shot. Shooter H fired under another table, wounding students Nicole Nowlen and John Tomlin. As John crawled out from under the table, Shooter K shot him a second time, killing him. Shooter H shot and killed another student, Kelly Fleming, before returning to where Lisa and Valeen were hiding. He fired, striking them each again and wounding student Jeanna Park. As Shooter H approached another table, he ordered the student hiding to identify himself. The student, John Savage, complied and was recognized by Shooter K, whom he had known. John asked Shooter K what he was doing; he replied, "Oh, just killing people." The shooters then ordered John to leave the library when he asked if they also were going to kill him, which he did immediately (Columbine Review Commission, 2001; Jefferson County Sheriff's Office, 2000).

The shooters continued through the library, taunting students and firing their weapons. Students Jennifer Doyle and Austin Eubanks were wounded while Corey DePooter and Daniel Mauser were killed. After spending seven and a half minutes in the library, during which time 10 students were killed and another 12 were wounded, the shooters left and went back toward the commons (Columbine Review Commission, 2001; Jefferson County Sheriff's Office, 2000).

After leaving the library, the shooters returned to the west entrance doors, where they again exchanged fire with responding officers, including Deputies Gardner and Smoker. They then retreated back into the building and headed toward the science wing. Though everyone who was in the school now was secured in a classroom or had evacuated when the opportunity arose, leaving the hallways empty, the shooters continued to randomly fire their guns and ignite IEDs. At 11:44 a.m., they descended back to the first level of the school into the cafeteria, where they made several unsuccessful attempts to detonate the propane tank bombs by both shooting at them and throwing a pipe bomb near the devices. All of this was caught on the surveillance camera (Columbine Review Commission, 2001; Jefferson County Sheriff's Office, 2000).

Over the next 16 minutes, the shooters wandered through the school. They headed back upstairs toward the main office area on the upper level before heading back down to the cafeteria. Around noon, they returned to the library, where they exchanged fire with responding law enforcement officers through the broken-out west-facing windows. The officers were providing cover to paramedics who had arrived on scene and were attempting to evacuate Sean Graves, Anne Marie Hochhalter, and Lance Kirklin. At 12:06 p.m., the first SWAT team entered the school through the main entrance on the east side of the building and began clearing the scene room by room.

At approximately 12:08 p.m., nearly 50 minutes after the rampage began, the shooters retreated further into the library where, after detonating a Molotov cocktail, they committed suicide by self-inflicted gunshot wounds to their heads (Columbine Review Commission, 2001; Jefferson County Sheriff's Office, 2000).

Throughout the ordeal, students had, when possible, fled the school; some had evacuated to nearby Clement Park while others left the area completely. Still, by the time the shooting had ended, many still were trapped inside the building along with faculty and staff. As law enforcement officers swept the school, they worked to evacuate the students, who subsequently were transported to nearby Leawood Elementary School for reunification with their families. At approximately 2:15 p.m., a SWAT officer positioned on the roof of a nearby residence noticed a sign in one of the west-facing windows that said "1 bleeding to death"; this later was determined to be the science classroom where Dave Sanders was with 30 students and their teacher, who were trying to keep him alive (Columbine Review Commission, 2001; Jefferson County Sheriff's Office, 2000).

Patrick Ireland, one of the wounded students in the library, had been slipping in and out of consciousness since he had been shot in the head several hours earlier. As police were clearing the school, he was able to make his way to the west window of the library that had been shot out when the perpetrators exchanged gunfire with responding law enforcement. At 2:38 p.m., he was able to climb out of the window, falling into the arms of SWAT officers who were atop an armored vehicle that had pulled up to help him. Lisa Kruetz, another wounded student in the library, was rescued by police nearly an hour later (Columbine Review Commission, 2001; Jefferson County Sheriff's Office, 2000).

Four minutes after Patrick was rescued, SWAT officers reached the science room where Dave Sanders was located and called for medical assistance. Two members of the SWAT team took over administration of first aid and tried to keep Dave talking until he no longer could speak. Approximately 30 minutes later, a paramedic finally was able to reach the room where Dave was located, but he determined that Dave had no pulse. It had been more than three hours since he had initially been shot, and Dave Sanders was the last person to die at Columbine High School that day (Columbine Review Commission, 2001; Jefferson County Sheriff's Office, 2000).

By 4:45 p.m., law enforcement had completed their sweep of the school, and it had been declared secured. Dr. Christopher Colwell, the attending physician from Denver Health Medical Center's emergency room, was brought in to make the official death pronouncements. In total, 13 people were killed in the school. An additional 24 were injured, all of whom were transported to area hospitals for medical attention and subsequently survived (Columbine Review Commission, 2001; Jefferson County Sheriff's

Office, 2000). The events that transpired that spring day at Columbine
High School transformed not only a community but the nation at large.

* * *

Twenty years later, the physical reminders of the damage done on April
20, 1999, to Columbine High School are largely gone. The window that Patrick Ireland climbed to safety through has long since had new panes
installed. The library where he and others were injured and where 10 students lost their lives was demolished. In its place, the ceiling of the
cafeteria—which received a facelift of its own after the damage caused,
including new tables, chairs, flooring, and paint—was raised to create a two-
story atrium. A quick glance up reveals a mural of aspens and evergreens,
species found all across Colorado, with a special reminder of the victims of
the shooting: 13 clouds.

Just off the west entrance doors, where the shooters first made entry into
the school, additional changes have been made. The entryway has been
extended out, encapsulating the area where Rachel Scott and Richard
Castaldo had been eating lunch when they were shot. In addition to new
lockers, the renovated entryway also features a butterfly embedded in the
flooring to signify where Rachel's life was cut tragically short. A new library

The Hope Columbine Memorial Library, built with money raised by the 13 families who lost their loved ones during the shooting. (Author photo)

sits just off the entryway, built with funds raised by the families of the 13 people killed on April 20 (Associated Press, 2001). Opened June 9, 2001, the Hope Columbine Memorial Library was designed not only to provide students with a new learning space but also to honor the lives lost on April 20. A plaque bearing the names of the victims adorns the library's entryway.

In Loving Memory
Of
Cassie Bernall
Steven Curnow
Corey DePooter
Kelly Fleming
Matthew Kechter
Daniel Mauser
Dan Rohrbough
Dave Sanders
Rachel Scott
Isaiah Shoels
John Tomlin
Lauren Townsend
Kyle Velasquez
April 20, 1999

The legacy of the Columbine High School shooting, however, has far outlasted the time it took to rehabilitate the physical damaged caused to the building that day. In fact, just the name "Columbine" has transcended April 20, 1999, shifting the shooting from a historical moment to a cultural event. As one *Denver Post* reporter so aptly noted around the time of the shooting's tenth anniversary:

A plaque bearing the names of the 13 victims of the shooting adorns the entrance of the new Hope Columbine Memorial Library. (Author photo)

> This is Columbine. The school whose very name has been co-opted into a cultural icon for the worst that kids can do and the worst that parents can imagine. The name itself morphs into virtually every form of speech—none of them good: It's an adjective, as in "Hey, don't go all Columbine here." It's a noun, as in "Authorities said the suspects had planned another Columbine." Columbine is a touchstone, an event, a heartbreak. (Augé, 2009)

Additionally, each time another mass shooting occurs, the events of April 20 resurface in the discourse. Columbine provides a point of reference against which to draw comparisons (Schildkraut, 2014, 2016). It provides an anchor upon which to ground the conversation about how to respond and what to do next—the same conversation that has been recycled after each shooting for the last 20 years. In some ways, it even provides a way to make sense of the seemingly senseless by normalizing these acts of violence.

* * *

There have been many lessons learned from Columbine over the last 20 years—some in the immediate aftermath of the shooting, others that took longer to come to fruition. While a considerable body of scholarly literature exists on school shootings (see, generally, Muschert & Schildkraut, 2015, for a compiled list of journal articles and other references), many of which highlight or even specifically focus on Columbine, there is no single resource that unites these lessons. Yet, given the multifaceted nature of events like Columbine, such a source is needed to synthesize all of the information generated since the attack. That is the overarching goal of this book.

Each chapter of this book has two aims. First, we examine the lessons learned in the aftermath of April 20, 1999, as they relate to that chapter's focal topic. Second, we consider how such information gleaned from the attack has—or has not—led to change and what progress in that particular area needs to be made as we move forward into the next 20 years. Together, this allows us not only to see how Columbine changed a single community but also to assess how it has changed the nation.

This first chapter has recounted the events of that fateful day. We have done this not to retraumatize a community but to provide a necessary foundation and understanding from which to build upon. Columbine has become what researchers (Larkin, 2007, 2009; Muschert, 2002) call a "watershed" moment; therefore, understanding the event is central to understanding why it serves as a turning point. In Chapter 2, we consider how the shooting transcended a community and a single day to become a cultural event that is ingrained in the collective conscience. Central to this shift from historical to cultural event has been the media coverage, which we assess further in Chapter 3.

Once the groundwork to truly understanding Columbine has been laid, we turn our attention to identifying areas of concern highlighted by the shooting and how our society has worked to overcome them since the attack. Chapter 4 explores how practices for law enforcement and other first responders have changed based on what was learned from Columbine. Similarly, Chapter 5 considers the warning signs that the two perpetrators—and, subsequently, other school and mass shooters—displayed and how the concept of threat assessment can and should be used to prevent future attacks. Chapter 6 examines the securitization of schools in the aftermath of Columbine, including attention to the host of security products and technologies that have been introduced to combat the issue of mass shootings.

While many of the changes discussed in the aforementioned chapters take place at the local or state levels, other developments have come on a broader scale. Central to understanding this larger response is public opinion, which is discussed further in Chapter 7. In Chapter 8, we examine the legislative responses offered in the aftermath of Columbine and consider why most have failed. We also explore what measures have been successful and how additional changes at the federal level may be possible.

Knowing the participants is central to understanding any event. When it comes to events like Columbine, the focus is often on those who are killed, their families, and individuals who are injured and survive—and rightfully so. Often forgotten, however, are the other survivors—the people who were present on April 20, 1999, and who, while they may not bear physical scars from that day, live with other wounds, such as psychological trauma. We consider the broader social and psychological footprint of Columbine and similar events in Chapter 9.

As noted at the beginning of the book, the two killers have become household names. While it is not our intent to give them any more fame, we would be remiss if we did not explore how they became folk (anti)heroes, martyrs, and models for other school and mass shooters. Thus, in Chapter 10, we consider their lasting impact, irrespective of the footprint left by the event itself. Building from there, Chapter 11 explores attempts made to profile school and mass shooters and why such efforts have caused more problems than they have solved in providing insight into these individuals.

In the two remaining chapters, we revisit the notion of Columbine as a cultural event. In Chapter 12, we explore how the shooting has transcended beyond a historical event to one that is not just cultural in nature but that has been cemented as an icon within popular culture. Finally, we examine how to move the Columbine Effect forward in Chapter 13 by not only summarizing the information laid out in the previous chapters but also synthesizing the information into a revised lesson plan to facilitate forward progress in the aim to combat episodes of mass violence. Both independently and collectively, the information contained in these chapters will help readers differentiate between Columbine as a single day and Columbine as a legacy.

CHAPTER TWO

The Columbine Legacy

Columbine disrupted the everyday life of the nation. The particularly shocking and brutal events stirred an immense expression of emotions, including sadness, anger, fear, and confusion. The shooting became a topic of conversation not only among journalists but also around water coolers and kitchen tables across the nation. Similar discussions also were held at town hall meetings, by school boards, in places of worship, at meetings with police, in academic settings, and in gatherings of local, state, and federal policy makers. What began as a collective sense of shock to a previously unprecedented crime continued to ripple outwards in so many areas of social life. Indeed, this is the legacy of Columbine: how one event has significantly influenced not only our understanding of youth-related social problems but also the policy responses to such issues.

The upwelling in the social system was similar to a geologic upheaval, or, as Charles Darwin (1906) wrote in reference to his experience of an earthquake, "one second of time has created in the mind a strange idea of insecurity, which hours of reflection would not have produced" (p. 289). This is precisely the social reaction the Columbine shootings provoked: a shock to the individual and collective American psyche. Vulnerabilities in the social system were exposed as the firm foundations on which social existence rested seemed to lose their stability. In its time, Columbine created a sense of social angst, the type that left people questioning everything they thought they knew. It is a lasting legacy of the shooting that this insecurity has not faded entirely, even 20 years later. In fact, we continue to use this event as a cultural referent, and even those born after the shooting, who have no direct knowledge of Columbine, move through the halls of schools nationwide aware that the memory of April 20 looms large.

Indeed, the legacy of Columbine has developed into something deeper and broader in the collective psyche of America, and it is this chapter that lays a foundation for how this terrible tragedy shook the nation ultimately becoming a point of departure for new social developments and a catalyst for those already in progress. In this book, we concern ourselves more with the trends set in motion by the Columbine shooting than we do specifically with the details of the event. Specifically, we are interested in exploring how this event has morphed from a specific historical event into a generalized cultural touchstone. We provided a detailed description of the Columbine event in Chapter 1; however, we do so primarily to provide a foundation on which to build. Consequently, if the discussion of Columbine moves away from the historical event, what we are left with is the question of what the meaning of the shooting has become and how the legacy of the attack continues in contemporary life. The images of the Columbine shooting, as shocking as they are, nonetheless blur with the passage of time. What remains prominent, however, is the unsettling quality brought by the notion of the pervasiveness of such violence. Thus, we examine how the shooting has become firmly entrenched in American cultural memory, how this recollection of these past events and their meanings have influenced trends in the past two decades, and how they are likely to carry into the future.

The "Columbine Effect"

The shooting transcended a historical moment to become a cultural milestone, ultimately dubbed the "Columbine Effect," or the tendency for Columbine and subsequent high-profile shootings to capture public attention and to drive antiviolence policies in schools (Muschert & Peguero, 2010; Muschert, Henry, Bracy, & Peguero, 2014). We use the term "Columbine" in a metaphorical sense to discuss the cultural history of youth crime and social problems over the past two decades. Sociologists studying collective memory have suggested that watershed events come to define generations, as they are among the rare moments in our highly individuated and disparate lives when the majority of the population experiences a high level of emotional consensus (Schuman & Rodgers, 2004; Schuman & Scott, 1989). Compare, for example, a person's recollection of April 20, 1999 (when he or she first heard about Columbine) to nearly every other day in the same year. Compared to other days, most people can recall what they were doing and where they were when they heard about the attack at Columbine. The same goes for similar events that mark turning points in history. Among those milestones for American culture are the Japanese attack on Pearl Harbor in 1941, the assassination of President John F. Kennedy in 1963, and the September 11, 2001, terror attacks on the World Trade Center and Pentagon buildings.

There is something unifying and solidifying about the common, shared experiences of these noteworthy events.

These historical references also come to define eras, such as the "post-Columbine" and "post-9/11" eras. Similarly, generations can be defined by such watershed events, and we have heard references not only to the "Columbine kids," meaning the shooters, but also to the "Columbine generation," meaning those youth who have come up through the school system in the past two decades since the attack (see, for example, Toppo, 2018; Vila, 2018). The wider usage of the term "Columbine" also is suggestive of its presence as a cultural touchstone, as it can be used as a noun (e.g., "What we are seeing is another Columbine"), as a verb (e.g., "We have suspected that he could go Columbine"), and as an adjective (e.g., "We have received reports of another Columbine-style event"). Few terms have become as broadly adapted as a cultural referents, as even for those born after the 1999 shootings, the term has salience and is used as an expression of generalized anxiety about the possibility of mass violence in schools. As time has passed, what we mean by the term "Columbine" also has evolved: its use often has little connection to the historical specifics of the event but instead is employed to express a generalized sentiment or concern about some social issue stemming from the shooting.

Of course, a historical event known as the Columbine High School shootings did take place on April 20, 1999; the massacre has been discussed in the previous chapter and in detail elsewhere (see Brown & Merritt, 2002; Cullen, 2009; Kass, 2010; Larkin, 2007). For those who directly experienced the horrific events, life was changed instantly, and those in the Columbine community and surroundings continue to live with the fallout (see, generally, Chapter 9). These individuals' experiences have become a reference point for a string of other communities nationwide that also have experienced similar tragedies in the aftermath of Columbine. Whenever another mass shooting (either in or out of schools) occurs, those discussing the event (frequently, the news media) tie back to Columbine in describing contemporary episodes such that the past is leveraged to make sense of present developments. Further, in some instances, the comparison back to Columbine in the discussion of a current attack may be used to predict what may take place in the future.

The connection to Columbine, however, is not limited only to those who have been directly affected by mass violence in school settings. Instead, the Columbine legacy is something that remains broadly tangible. It raises the question as to how it is possible that so many Americans, the vast majority of whom have not been affected directly by mass violence, became connected in an emotional sense with what happened 20 years ago at Columbine. Moreover, how has this impact been so lasting that that it continues to resonate with them now, 20 years later, and foster the belief that a similar event is possible in their own community? Before the Columbine shooters carried out their attack, such a series of events was nearly unthinkable and certainly hardly expected. Since then, a Columbine-style attack has always been within the realm of possibilities, a perception reinforced by a seemingly endless string of shootings paraded across the headlines of news media.

Thus, "Columbine has become a keyword for a complex set of emotions surrounding youth, risk, fear, and delinquency in early 21st century United States" (Muschert, 2007b, p. 365). The public spectacle and outpouring of grief and concern about Columbine and similar events (now more or less expressed as a sending of "thoughts and prayers") are emotional forms of social outrage—which may, in some way, ironically suppress practical efforts at prevention, response, and post-event restoration. While professionals in many fields—including (but certainly not limited to) sociology, criminology, psychology and counseling, and criminal justice—certainly have acknowledged time and again the suffering and anguish such events cause to their victims and communities, what often is lacking in public discourse is the sober assessment and discussion of associated social problems, which have been indicated to contribute not only to school shootings but also to broader issues of violence in society. Case studies of school shootings (e.g., Langman, 2015; Newman, Fox, Harding, Mehta, & Roth, 2004) and meta-analyses (e.g., Muschert, 2007a; 2010) have suggested that school shootings rarely have simple origins and instead are sparked by complex sets of contributing factors that cannot be addressed with simple, ready-made solutions.

The Spread of Angst about Mass Violence in Schools (and Beyond)

To understand the development and extent of this generalized anxiety, it is worth understanding the context in which the Columbine story emerged, noting how so many people have been affected indirectly as reports of the shooting spread widely (and quickly) via mainstream media outlets. Columbine did not happen in a vacuum but rather within a cultural context. It is perhaps not surprising that before Columbine, American culture already had concerned itself with youth (or subgroups of youth) as a social problem generally, and specifically with concerns about levels of juvenile violence. In the political context of the 1970s and 1980s, there already had been a move to unravel the government's role in New Deal-era social policies and to re-exert the legitimacy of the government by embracing a crime-control or order-maintenance function. From the mid-1980s to the mid-1990s, Americans became increasingly concerned about the emergence of a new generation of youth known as juvenile superpredators (Spencer, 2011). Such youth were characterized as holding little or no respect for human life as they prowled the most urban neighborhoods of the underclasses. Criminologists discussed the years of 1993 and 1994 as foreshadowing an explosion of youth violence (see Muschert, 2007b).

Thus, Columbine emerged in a cultural context that included a political mandate to "get tough" on crime (including young offenders), to wage a "War on Drugs," and what in retrospect can be defined as the early years of the contemporary age of mass incarceration in America. A noted irony of this "get tough on crime" trend is that subsequent data indicated that it developed at a time when rates of crime and delinquency were on the decline (Conklin, 2002; Sacco, 2005). Indeed, that trend has continued to into the present, such that the era of crime reduction observed in the United States in the last quarter century strongly overlaps what we now call the post-Columbine era (see Muschert et al., 2014; Spencer, 2011).

From the first-person perspectives of those living in turn-of-the-21st-century America, however, there indeed seemed a crisis of youth social problems and the question was where to direct interventions. The primary institutions of socialization for youth in the contemporary era continue to be families, peer groups, and schools. Perhaps it is an irony that, despite the constant discourse about families, whether structured as its decline or inadequacy, politicians and policy makers generally avoid interference in the private realm of the family. Similarly, aside from the most aggressive of juvenile criminal gangs, policy makers also consider intervention into youth peer groups and their social dynamics largely off-limits. Hence, so many of the policy concerns about youth social problems tend to center around schools, which increasingly are called upon to fill a variety of social needs—from socializing youth, to serving as central institutions within communities, to serving as surrogate parents and providing security for youth.

Of course, this begs the question as to the extent to which schools fulfill their primary pedagogical roles. Schoolteachers and administrators often feel powerless to achieve such broad sets of goals amid public anxieties for schools to improve (or at least not to decline) in educational performance and in the face of potentially counterproductive policies (see Muschert et al., 2014, for a broad discussion of school antiviolence policies and their possible contradictions). Certainly, youth and schools were already of concern before Columbine and the apparent trend of school shootings that started in the late 1990s, but the events of April 20, 1999, further focused discussions about what is right and wrong with schools, often accelerating changes that were already under way well before the attack.

Clearly, school violence in any and all forms is undesirable, and it does require preventative actions and the development of adequate plans to handle events when they do happen. School shootings are very rare events and, as examples of violence in the educational setting, they occupy the most extreme end of the continuum. Despite their rarity, they exert large influence on how we think about the problem of school violence. These rare events also are heavily influential in people's conceptions of school violence and youth social problems more generally. In the case of youth social problems generally or even school violence more specifically, the tendency to think of Columbine-style attacks as in any way typical of the broader issue potentially diverts attention away other aspects of the problem, such as bullying, simple assaults in schools, and cases of sexual misconduct. What researchers generally have observed in the past two decades has been the tendency for intense fear and public concern about school shootings disproportionately to drive the development and expansion of school antiviolence policies, a trend termed the "Columbine Effect" (see Muschert & Peguero, 2010; Muschert et al., 2014).

School shooters have become the inaccurate poster children for violent youth offenders, and school antiviolence policies often address these worst-case scenarios while potentially ignoring more common, typically less severe forms of school violence, such as bullying, assault, and sexual misconduct. Though not exclusively so, control responses in the United States tend to be punitive and appear in the form of zero-tolerance policies, police presence, and installation of surveillance. In comparison, responses in the European contexts tend to be more integrative, including the establishment of mediation programs, conflict resolution, and antibullying programming. Those who criticize the U.S. tendency to use punitive measures in schools claim that such measures may do more harm than they prevent, add a prison-like atmosphere to schools, and may damage primary pedagogical goals for which schools are created (Muschert & Peguero, 2010).

The response to Columbine—and, indeed, the shooting's continuing relevance—has less to do with the event itself and more to do with the fact that this event sparked a wider search for meaning (or to understand why the attack occurred). Despite the fact that a similar discourse occurs every time another mass shooting tragedy occurs, such discussion has yet to find a satisfying resolution. The lack of resolution about the meaning of mass shootings is as much of an aspect of the short attention span of the media and general public toward social problems as it is in fact the case that the issue itself is complicated. For example, the search for the meaning of the Columbine story opened up questions about a wide variety of social changes, including the emergence of new communication technologies (including, in particular, the Internet and mobile phones), issues of race, concerns about masculinity, the social role of evangelical Christianity (a theme that arose when it was reported that victim Cassie Bernall was killed when she said yes after being asked by the shooters if she believes in God), issues of responsibility and blame, the desirability/feasibility of gun control, issues around individual mental health, the role of nonstop news coverage, the continued potency of white supremacist ideologies, and concerns about violent media. Given this laundry list of related issues, it is not surprising that the public discourse falls short of supplying needed answers and is further clouded by the sheer emotionality of bloody images and public displays of grief associated with the victims.

In essence, the Columbine shootings provided the news media with more points of intrigue and emotional power than any nonfiction writer might have dreamed up. What makes the story so immediately impactful to a broad segment of the population is the perception that this type of event is too close to home and could possibly occur in one's own community (Schild-kraut, Elsass, & Stafford, 2015; see also Chapter 7 for a discussion on public opinion related to Columbine). Although much of the Columbine story might have had the qualities of a drama, this narrative served as more than just intrigue; instead, it shook American society to its very foundation. It is per-haps apt to compare Columbine and its social reverberations as a sort of earth-shaking seismic event, a social disruption or disaster.

Although most people are familiar with earthquakes' immense power to roil the earth, causing fear, panic, and destruction, what has been examined less consistently is that some social and historical events (such as Colum-bine) shake the normative foundations of society, causing similar levels of alarm, anxiety, and, ultimately, social devastation. An earthquake is the physical release of energy that has accumulated in the form of friction as tectonic plates move in relation to one another. Earthquakes generally are identified by their epicenter, or the surface location closest to the middle of the seismic event. Frequently, the location of the epicenter becomes the name of the earthquake, such as Northridge or Loma Prieta. Earthquakes, how-ever, have their origins well under the surface and take place deep under-ground (the hypocenter), where the foundations of the earth move. It is, subsequently, the human-centered view of this phenomenon that associates it with the surface where we live. In reality, tectonic plates attempt to slide past one another, and the resistance to movement builds up strain and causes tension at levels deep underground. While it is mostly the surface manifesta-tions of earthquakes that concern humans—destruction of buildings, tsuna-mis, and just the terror of the earth shaking under one's feet—the deep study of these natural disasters requires the long-range, deep understanding of movements in the earth's crust.

Similarly, the Columbine shooting was the epicenter of a normative earth-quake, one that seemed to shake the foundations on which social life rests. Here, we use the metaphor of an earthquake to indicate that social conflicts and culture wars build up over time as segments of the population differ in their vision of how society should be organized. A massive expression of emotion, such as that observed after Columbine, does not emerge suddenly but rather reflects deep conflicts within the society. At the time of the shoot-ing, the United States already had ongoing dissonance regarding many of the issues raised by Columbine, including the extent to which youth are prob-lematic (for example, as potential victims and/or perpetrators of violence), a tension between religious and secular visions of society, disagreement regarding the line between individual and collective responsibilities, and of course the role of firearms in a democratic and open society. Such issues, then, did not emerge from a vacuum, and of course we can understand Columbine as a catalyst for ongoing discussion rather than the origin of such social conflicts. Thus, Columbine can be understood as a precipitating event that exposed deep social tension that had been accumulating for some time.

In a social sense, tension tends to accumulate along the fault lines where competing value systems come into contact with one another. The Columbine shootings sparked a release of energy that resonated through the social system, disrupting the normal day-to-day flow of life and bringing a large portion of Americans into a similar socioemotional experience. Social conflicts already festered below the surface of day-to-day life, and before Columbine, the culture wars about broader issues had built up considerable tension that lay just below the surface of public life, including gun rights, race relations, concerns about masculinity, and religious tensions. Whereas the energy released in an actual earthquake is physical in nature, the energy expressed in a normative earthquake is behavioral and takes the form of observable social actions. The media coverage of Columbine may be of interest in itself (it is the topic of the following chapter); however, the real focus of research on the event is much more abstract, investigating deep and often hidden social processes. Like its tectonic counterpart, a normative earthquake does not just happen on its own. Rather, it would have been building up tension for some time, and that increase would have occurred deep in the normative structures of society, often in subtle ways.

Columbine in Its Broader Contexts

As contemporary life continues to be characterized by fears and anxieties (note the present-day relevance of xenophobia, fear of terrorism, concerns over economic insecurity, the decline of civility, and the decay of social institutions; see, generally, Beck, 1992, 1999; Furedi, 2005), Columbine remains an important point of reference in conversations about youth social problems. In the global perspective, we find the Columbine Effect in schools to be an iteration of the "Shock Doctrine" (Klein, 2007), in which otherwise unpopular control policies have been imposed by capitalizing on the fear and disorder that ensues in the aftermath of massive collective tragedies, such as wars, terrorist attacks, mass migrations, and disasters. In a similar manner, the shooting at Columbine High School (in particular but not exclusively, as one must not ignore similar events which preceded and followed the attack) generated such a degree of fear nationwide that educators, who traditionally have been characterized as among the caring and nurturing professions in society, have yielded to the calls for punitive discipline, advanced surveillance, and securitization of schools (which is discussed further in Chapter 6).

As we survey the legacy of April 20, 1999, two decades later, it seems that the Columbine Effect is still very much with us. In this chapter, we have described this trend as the tendency for extreme events to heavily influence policies that deal with youth-related social problems and therefore to concentrate on addressing the potential for extreme violence. This turns the focus away from less extreme (though more likely) aspects of youth violence. From this point forward, we examine the legacy of the shooting in more specific terms relating to a variety of the concrete responses within the social institutions that participated in the post-Columbine discussion and response to school violence. These trends, as appearing in schools and related environs, are discussed at length in the remaining chapters of this book and address a broad set of topics, including policing, prevention, security, legislation and policy development, and calls for positive social change.

CHAPTER THREE

We Interrupt This Program to Bring You Breaking News

Despite the fact that school and mass shootings are perceived to be commonplace in U.S. society (Schildkraut & Elsass, 2016), the reality is that just a small fraction of the nation's population is affected directly by these events. The broad reach of mass shootings, however, comes at the hands (as well as computers, microphones, and camera lenses) of the media, whose reporting on such events provides access and information to millions more people (Schildkraut, Elsass, & Meredith, 2018). Researchers (Graber, 1980; Surette, 2015) estimate that for up to 95% of the general population, the media serve as their main source of information about crime news, and school and mass shootings are no exception. In general, the news often is skewed toward stories about crime (Chermak, 1995; Graber, 1980; Maguire, Sandage, & Weatherby, 1999; Surette, 2015), with a greater emphasis on violent cases such as these that have the necessary salience to keep audiences interested (Gruenewald, Pizarro, & Chermak, 2009; Meyers, 1997; Paulsen, 2003).

Events like Columbine contain so many sensational elements and various narratives—including the villains (the shooters), innocent victims, and emerging heroes (Muschert, 2002, 2007)—that prioritizing them is an almost guaranteed way to capture viewers and boost ratings. There are, of course, important considerations that must be factored in with pursuing such an avenue of reporting. Gladwell (2008) asserts that "we learn more from extreme circumstances than anything else . . . [and] it's those who lie outside ordinary experience that have the most to teach us" (p. 6). Given the statistically rare nature of mass shootings (Schildkraut & Elsass, 2016) and the lack of context offered when reporting on these attacks (Schildkraut,

2016), a disproportionate focus on such events by the media can distort perceptions, thereby influencing public opinion (which we discuss further in Chapter 7) and demands for response (as covered in Chapter 8) in an equally skewed manner.

Cohen (1963) has noted that the media "may not be successful much of the time in telling people what to think, but it is stunningly successful in telling people what to think *about*" (p. 13). The story of the Columbine shooting is no exception to this rule. In this chapter, we explore how the media events unfolded as April 20, 1999, progressed, both during and beyond the shooting. The sheer volume of coverage generated by the attack is considered, as is—perhaps even more importantly—how the content was presented. We consider how the process of frame changing, which emphasizes the "where" (space) and the "when" (time) facets of a story, was used to provide audiences with new content to keep them interested well after the shooting had stopped. We also examine how the two most commonly asked questions—the "who" and the "why"—were answered through the media coverage, creating narratives that persist 20 years later. In essence, this chapter is meant not only to explore how the Columbine story unfolded in the media, but also how the coverage laid a foundation for journalists and the public alike to discuss this and subsequent shootings.

The Media Circus of April 20, 1999

The shooting at Columbine High School began around 11:19 a.m. Mountain Standard Time. At 11:32 a.m. local time, Jefferson County Sheriff's Office public information officer, Steve Davis, was dispatched to the scene. He arrived a short time later to find that several local news stations had beaten him there (Jefferson County Sheriff's Office, 1999). Just before noon, CNN—then the leading cable news network—interrupted its current programming to break the story live from the scene. Drawing from several local affiliate networks, CNN's coverage continued for more than six hours (Muschert, 2002). Locally, stations like KUSA broke in with warnings to residents about the events unfolding, though they soon returned to regular programming as the information was limited (Shepard, 2000). Twenty minutes after the initial information was shared on KUSA, they pushed their regular programming off the air and remained live for the next 10 hours, with other local stations soon following suit (Shepard, 2000).

The initial coverage showed the chaos taking place at the school: unedited images of students running from the building with their hands over their heads. Video of police—upward of 250 officers at the height of the response—arriving on scene. SWAT teams descending on the building behind the protection of an armored truck (Birkland & Lawrence, 2009). Dramatic images looped across television screens for audiences both near and far (Leavy &

Maloney, 2009; Muschert, 2002). It was what Charles Gottlieb (1999) called "point-shoot-and-air journalism" (para. 3).

During the early coverage, eyewitness accounts, mainly from students who had escaped from the school, provided the majority of the information and content. Students described what they saw—two (or three, an early false narrative) shooters dressed in all black, firing indiscriminately on their classmates. Some reported what they had witnessed directly, while others shared what they had heard from their friends (Shepard, 2000). Speculation came out early in the coverage about the role of the Trench Coat Mafia, a group of gothic-dressed outcast students who became an early cause for concern. As students were evacuated to nearby Leawood Elementary School, the news cameras captured their dramatic reunions with their parents (Muschert, 2002).

On April 20, news crews had been staged in nearby Boulder, Colorado, covering the developing grand jury investigation into the murder of child beauty queen Jon-Benet Ramsey. When the shooting broke out, they abandoned their post and began the 40-mile drive to Jefferson County. Over the next hours and even days, more outlets arrived. The Jefferson County Sheriff's Office (1999) estimated that, at the peak of media interest, upward of 500 reporters were on the scene—including at least 20 news crews from other countries—along with between 75 and 90 satellite news trucks and 60 television cameras. They set up camp in the 285-acre Clement Park, situated adjacent to the school. Still, given the media spectacle that was forming in real time, these outlets accounted for only a fraction of the attention the sheriff's office had to deal with (Jefferson County Sheriff's Office, 1999).

At 1:30 p.m., a little more than two hours after the shooting had erupted, Deputy Davis held his first press conference for the media, providing them with updates that had become available. On both the day of the shooting and the day after, these briefings came every hour. Aside from assembling information between briefings to inform the updates, which he did from a command post established in the Columbine Public Library at Clement Park, Deputy Davis also provided on-camera interviews for a number of outlets. In fact, across those two days, he gave 134 interviews in addition to his hourly updates (Jefferson County Sheriff's Office, 1999).

With each of these updates, new details emerged: Information about the injured students and about the gunmen, some of which was correct and other that was erroneous. The coverage also continued to broaden. More eyewitness accounts from glassy-eyed students and teachers trying to make sense of what they had just been through. Remarks from political leaders, including then-Colorado Governor Bill Owens and President Bill Clinton. Images of Patrick Ireland falling to safety from the library window. Then, during the 4:00 p.m. briefing, Deputy Davis and Sheriff John Stone updated reporters on the newest developments, including finding two gunmen deceased in the library and providing the first—although later amended—victim count of as many as 25 dead that spread like wildfire through the media. An hour later, the Sheriff's department indicated in a briefing that all students (except those who were deceased inside) had been evacuated from the building; few updates followed during the remainder of the evening (Jefferson County Sheriff's Office, 1999). CNN abandoned its uninterrupted coverage, instead opting, like many other outlets, to break in with new information as it became available (Muschert, 2002). At 9:45 p.m., the shooters finally were identified (Muschert, 2002).

Despite the hourly updates that had been provided by the Sheriff's office, much of the information being circulated still was from eyewitness accounts, even the next day. Pieced together using these information subsidies (Wigley & Fontenot, 2009), the news organizations were able to provide a composite look of how the events had unfolded. This narrative first was aired on *Good Morning America* and CNN's *Early Edition* on the morning of April 21. Students joined hosts live from the media city in Clement Park, providing their accounts of what had happened during the shooting. Then came the commentary about potential causal factors of the attack and how these issues should be addressed to prevent future attacks, as well as broader concerns such as school safety (Muschert, 2002).

By the middle of the third week, the Sheriff's department ceased holding daily briefings, but the media's presence in the Columbine community persisted. Every facet of the aftermath of the shooting was covered through a camera lens or a reporter's pen. The funerals for those killed. The surviving students' return to school at nearby Chatfield High School. The graduation of the class of 1999, including several of the survivors. All of these events played out in the media while they continued to report on every breaking facet of the investigation. Eventually, however, the media moved on once another story captured their interest (Kass, 2010).

Given the rapid speed at which the Columbine story unfolded, many inaccuracies plagued the coverage from the very moment the news broke. In fact, by the fall of 1999, a number of pieces of information—including the role of the Trench Coat Mafia in the shooting—already had been refuted (Kass, 2010). By then, however, it was too late; the information was engrained in the American consciousness, and the myths persisted, despite attempts to correct them. As Keith Coffman of the *Denver Post* later summarized in conjunction with the tenth anniversary of the shooting, "The Columbine massacre of a decade ago was one of the most widely—if inaccurately—reported crime stories in American history" (in Kass, 2010, para. 14).

Just How Much Coverage Was There?

The shooting at Columbine almost instantly became what Kellner (2003, 2008a, 2008b) calls a "media spectacle" (see also Birkland & Lawrence, 2009). The intense public interest in the attack required news organizations to churn out story after story—and, in exchange for ratings, they willingly complied. CNN, for example drew in more than two million viewers on the afternoon of the shooting, almost three times as many as the Tuesday the week before (Gottlieb, 1999). Other news outlets, including Fox News (a newer entity at the time, having been established just three years before the shooting; see Ray, 2011) and MSNBC, also generated nearly double their regular afternoon ratings (Gottlieb, 1999). Beyond the live, breaking coverage from the scene that had been witnessed by television audiences both locally and nationally, pervasive coverage of the shooting continued across all media, including television, newspaper and other print publications, and even radio.

After the initial breaking coverage that had captured the attention of news consumers across the nation, CNN continued to augment its reporting on the shooting. In fact, Muschert (2002) found that in the month following the shooting (including the original six-hour report), 114 separate segments about Columbine were aired on six different shows. CNN's *Early Edition* and its weekend counterparts, *CNN Saturday Morning* and *CNN Sunday Morning*, included 44 different reports in its coverage; an additional 34 stories were found to be aired under the *CNN Live Event/Special* heading. A further 18 stories were aired on *CNN Worldview* and its weekend counterparts, *CNN Saturday* and *CNN Sunday*, while *Larry King Live* and its corresponding weekend program featured 10 segments, and *CNN Newsday* broadcasted 7 (Muschert, 2002). For CNN, Columbine became the seventh-highest rated story of the decade behind other newsworthy events such as Operation Desert Storm in 1991 and the O. J. Simpson car chase in 1994 and trial verdict in 1995 (Muschert, 2002).

The intense coverage was not limited solely to cable news outlets. Robinson (2011), for example, determined that Columbine was the most covered story on evening news broadcasts in the year of the shooting, with 319 stories aired. In just the first week after the shooting (including the day of the attack), Maguire, Weatherby, and Mathers (2002) found that ABC, CBS, and NBC collectively aired 53 stories about Columbine on their evening newscasts, totaling nearly four hours of coverage. By comparison, 13 other school shootings that occurred in close temporal proximity to Columbine (between 1996 and 2000) had garnered just slightly more coverage than the Littleton attack when combined (Maguire et al., 2002). Columbine was also the lead story on all of the newscasts broadcast the week it occurred on these stations and, on certain days, accounted for more than 80% of the total airtime, excluding commercials and promotions (Maguire et al., 2002; see also Consalvo, 2003). More broadly, for up to a month after Columbine, these same three networks devoted approximately half of their evening news broadcasts to covering the shooting (Robinson, 2011). In total, extending beyond just evening news broadcasts, ABC aired 112 stories over the same 30-day period, with the majority coming during *Good Morning America* (57 segments) and *World News Tonight* with its weekend counterparts (32 pieces; Muschert, 2002).

Given the timing of Columbine, coupled with the nature of news cycles, few print sources (the *Rocky Mountain News* in Denver being a notable exception) were able to report on the attack on the day it occurred as many publications already had completed the post-press process (Muschert, 2002). Still, in the days and weeks following, and even beyond, a considerable number of stories were published on the shooting. Newman (2006), for example, found that in the year after the shooting, more than 10,000 articles were published in the nation's 50 most circulated newspapers. Among these, 170 stories appeared in the *New York Times* alone (Chyi & McCombs, 2004; see also Muschert & Carr, 2006; Schildkraut & Muschert, 2014). Compared to eight other school shootings occurring between 1997 and 2001, Columbine again eclipsed the coverage of these other attacks, even when they were combined, with nearly 50% more stories for the single incident (Muschert & Carr, 2006). Even highly salient cases occurring later, such as the 2012 Sandy Hook Elementary School shooting, failed to eclipse the coverage of Columbine (Schildkraut & Muschert, 2014). *USA Today*, another nationally circulated newspaper, also published a considerable number of stories on the shooting (Kupchik & Bracy, 2009).

News magazines also contributed to the share in coverage of the shooting (Consalvo, 2003). *TIME*, a weekly publication, printed 25 separate stories about Columbine in the month after the shooting (Muschert, 2002). The May 3, 1999, edition highlighted the shooting on its cover, juxtaposing the two perpetrators' images against those of their 13 victims (*TIME*, 1999a). A second cover of the magazine was devoted to the shooting later that year. In its December 20, 1999, issue, the publication highlighted its access to the Basement Tapes, a series of videos the perpetrators had made prior to their attack, and featured a still of the gunmen from the cafeteria surveillance footage (*TIME*, 1999b; see also Gibbs & Roche, 1999). Another weekly magazine, *Newsweek*, also devoted 19 articles to the shooting over the 30 days following the attack (Muschert, 2002). Like *TIME*, *Newsweek* also featured the shooting on its May 3, 1999, cover (Verger, 2014). Instead of showing the gunmen, however, the magazine chose to highlight the students as they fled from the school (Verger, 2014). Even popular entertainment magazines, such as *People*, followed suit, featuring students affected by the shooting on its May 3, 1999, cover (Hewitt, 1999).

It's Not Just about the Quantity . . .

It would be nearly impossible to suggest that the sheer volume of coverage of the Columbine shooting did not have some impact on news consumers (see, for example, Chapter 7 for a further discussion on public opinion and related perceptions about the attack). In order to understand such an impact, however, consideration must be given not only to how much was shared but *how* the content was being presented. News producers make conscious decisions about how they frame such stories, in terms of both the format and the content. Both independently and together, such decisions can have a considerable impact on how audiences make sense of the information they are provided.

In respect to the structuring of the story, there are two key features that can be used to understand how the salience of a piece or a broader story is measured. First, a story features a headline—a stand-alone unit whose primary function is to draw news consumers to that particular piece (Muschert, 2002). Some researchers contend that the headline is the single most influential component of any news story (van Dijk, 1988) and that it also can shape how consumers interpret the content (Cerulo, 1998). Second, each piece of news also contains a lead—the initial part of the story that both introduces and summarizes the overall story that then follows (Muschert, 2002, 2009). Other researchers (e.g., Bell, 1991; Cerulo, 1998; Muschert, 2009) contend that the lead is the most important part of the story as it provides an overview of the key themes of the piece. Despite these differences of viewpoint as to which feature of a news story is the most important, agreement exists that both should be considered for understanding how the piece is presented (Muschert, 2002).

In his examination of the coverage of Columbine, Muschert (2002) found that both the headlines and the leads of the stories analyzed were most likely to focus on the reactions to the shooting, whether from inside or outside the community, from the police, or through a broader ideological lens. Moreover, the greatest focus was on the ideological theme, with specific attention paid to exploring the potential causes for the shooting (Muschert, 2002). To a lesser extent, commentary about the attack (e.g., placing the story in some type of context, evaluations from politicians), framing the event as terror, and discussing the consequences stemming from the shooting (both *real*, such as the death or victim toll, and *possible*, regarding how much worse it could have been) served as prominent themes in both the headlines and leads (Muschert, 2002; see also Leavy & Maloney, 2009). Collectively, Muschert's (2002) findings illustrate how media outlets were able to hook news consumers by structuring the stories' abstracts (comprised of the headlines and leads) in a way that led to greater consideration about *why* the shooting had happened and a desire to learn the potential answers within the pieces themselves.

In order to keep said consumers, however, news organizations had to find a way to maintain the freshness of the content. To do so, they employed a process known as frame-changing. First introduced by Erving Goffman (1974), the concept of framing more broadly is used to explain how individuals make sense of the world around them. When applied to media and agenda setting—a process by which claims makers (such as politicians and news

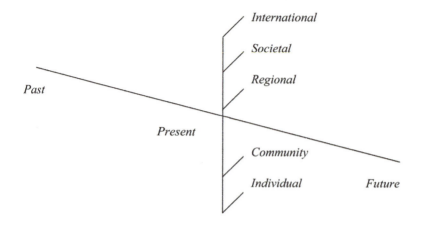

Figure 3.1 Two-Dimensional Measurement Scheme. (Adapted from Chyi & McCombs, 2004)

organizations) select and prioritize one issue or event over others (McCombs & Shaw, 1972; see also Entman, 2007; McCombs, 1997, 2005; Weaver, 2007)—the concept of frame changing is a tool for breaking down complex social issues and presenting them in a way that is both relatable and accessible to audiences (Gans, 1979; Scheufele & Tewskbury, 2007). The media frame itself has been described as "a central organizing idea for news content that supplies context and suggests what the issue is through the use of selection emphasis, exclusion, and elaboration" (Tankard, 2001, pp. 100–101). As different media frames surface in the news coverage, thereby emphasizing certain facets of a particular story, it can shape the "reality" of the story for the audience (Reese, 2007). In the end, the coverage can be skewed as the content has become biased (Entman, 2007; Reese, 2007).

To better understand how the Columbine story was framed and how the coverage shifted over time, Chyi and McCombs (2004) analyzed the *New York Times*'s coverage of the shooting for 30 days. Creating a two-dimensional model (see Figure 3.1), the researchers suggested that when analyzing frame changing of a news event, the where (space) and when (time) were the two most important attributes to consider. As illustrated, both exist on a continuum. Space frames emphasize who specifically is affected by the event and range from micro-level (the individual) to a more macro focus (international). Time, also existing on a continuum, considers when the story takes place—either past (focusing on the backstory leading up to the event), present (considering the short-term implications), or future (assessing the long-range impact).

Chyi and McCombs' (2004) analysis yielded a number of important findings related to how the media framed the Columbine story. In the context of space, the articles were more likely to be focused on the broader societal impact as compared to the individual- or community-level effect and to consistently maintain that focus over the full coverage period examined. When considering the time dimension, the articles were most likely to be framed in the present, thereby considering the immediate impact of the shooting. In the first 15 days of the coverage, the past dimension was found to be more likely to be used over the future dimension, thereby emphasizing the backstory of the case leading up to the shooting itself. In the second half of the coverage period, the framing shifted to the future dimension, thereby allowing for long-term consideration about the meaning of Columbine.

Several other studies have replicated the work of Chyi and McCombs (2004) in order to compare frame changing of other mass shootings to the coverage of Columbine. Muschert and Carr (2006) compared eight other school shootings, all of lesser media (and public) interest, which occurred around the same time period (three years either before or after Columbine). Schildkraut and Muschert (2014) later compared Sandy Hook—which is perhaps the closest shooting to Columbine in terms of media and public interest—to the 1999 attack. In both studies, the researchers found that the framing patterns clearly departed from those employed in the Columbine coverage (Muschert & Carr, 2006; Schildkraut & Muschert, 2014). Specifically, whereas Columbine had elicited a consideration of a broader societal impact, a smaller proportion of the articles for the other shootings prioritized that dimension, instead focusing more on either the individual or community frames (Muschert & Carr, 2006; Schildkraut & Muschert, 2014). Moreover, while all three studies found that the present dimension of the time frame was used considerably more frequently than either past or future, the Columbine coverage was more likely to use the latter (Muschert & Carr, 2006; Schildkraut & Muschert, 2014), suggesting that no other shooting—either before or after it occurred—elicited the long-term speculation about its meaning and impact.

The Remainder of the Five Ws

Though Chyi and McCombs (2004) suggest that, in the context of framing, the where and when are the two most important attributes of a story, the reality is that for journalists covering events like Columbine, these details are largely already answered. While the spatial component of framing may allow for consideration as to who is affected by the shooting, it also is easily answered from a content perspective by identifying the scene of the crime—in this case, Columbine High School and (incorrectly) Littleton, Colorado. The temporal component (when it happened) is also is quickly determined by the date of the event. Similarly, the "what" is answered when the news breaks—a school or mass shooting. Thus, when news producers are constructing their stories, they are more likely to focus on the remaining two W's of journalistic practice—the who and the why.

The Who

Once the identities of the perpetrators and their victims were made public through the media, coverage almost instantaneously shifted to learning more about who they were. The initial coverage of the perpetrators focused on detailing how they died (Muschert, 2002). Soon after, however, the media began to delve more into who they were, with some outlets trying to piece together a portrait or profile of the killers (Muschert, 2002). Depending on the story, they were cast either as normal youths (Muschert, 2002) or deviants or monsters (Consalvo, 2003; Frymer, 2009; Muschert, 2002). By casting the shooters as the latter, the media were able to separate them from more "normal" individuals who could never commit such an act and, perhaps more importantly, from their victims (Consalvo, 2003).

The shooters' backgrounds were picked apart: where they had grown up, what their family life was like, who their friends were, what their high school experiences had been like, and other similar considerations (Muschert, 2002). The media reported that they were members of a group of students known as the Trench Coat Mafia, who, even though the shooters had never been full members and had distanced themselves from the clique sometime earlier, still were guilty by association (Consalvo, 2003; Frymer, 2009; Lickel, Schmader, & Hamilton, 2003; Ogle, Eckman, & Leslie, 2003; Springhall, 1999; Weatherby, Luzzo, & Zahm, 2016). Other stories suggested that they worshipped the devil, listened to satanic music (including Marilyn Manson, a claim that also was later refuted), and took large quantities of drugs (Frymer, 2009; Ogle et al., 2003; Springhall, 1999), despite that the medical examiner's toxicology report indicated that there were no illicit substances in their systems at the time of the shooting (Muschert, 2002). (It should be noted, however, that while no substances were discovered during their post-mortem toxicology reports, investigatory documents showed that both shooters previously had experimented with drugs and alcohol; see, for example, Jefferson County Sheriff's Office, 1999.) With each new detail, the two shooters—who came to embody the term "superpredator"—became archetypal examples of youthful offenders and the issue of juvenile delinquency as a whole (Muschert, 2007).

Juxtaposed against the two perpetrators were the 13 individuals whose lives they had taken. As they were identified, profiles about the victims were incorporated into the coverage in order to capture additional interest from news consumers (Leavy & Maloney, 2009; Muschert, 2002). Their pictures were accompanied by discussion about their interests and achievements, future plans, and their goals that never would come to fruition (Muschert, 2002). Initially, the sketches were short; as more details became available, the tributes to the victims also expanded (Muschert, 2002). Several of the funerals, including those of teacher Dave Sanders and students Cassie Bernall and Isaiah Shoels, were heavily covered by the media (Leavy & Maloney, 2009; Muschert, 2002, 2007). The coverage of the victims, however, began to wane two weeks after the shooting as the discussion shifted toward responses and prevention of future incidents (Muschert, 2002).

The coverage of the victims revealed two noticeable trends. First, as compared to the shooters, the victims received less attention by both the local and national press (Weatherby et al., 2016). In fact, Weatherby and colleagues (2016) found that in *The Denver Post*, the local paper, the shooters received just over twice as many mentions as the victims. At the national level, as depicted by *The New York Times*, for every one reference made to one of the shooting's victims, the gunmen received nearly six and a half mentions on average (Weatherby et al., 2016).

Second, despite the fact that 13 lives were taken on April 20, not all victims received equitable coverage. Muschert (2007) found that Dave Sanders was covered more than any other victim. Isaiah Shoels, the only black student killed in the attack and who was believed to have been targeted for his race, was the second most covered. Students Rachel Scott and Cassie Bernall, who often were highlighted for their religious beliefs, were the third and fourth most covered, respectively. Comparatively, the remaining nine students received less media attention, with Kyle Velasquez receiving the least of any victim (Muschert, 2002, 2007). The pattern of prioritizing the shooters over the victims and certain victims over others has been found to carry through to the coverage of other school and mass shootings (see, for example, Schildkraut, 2012a).

The Why

There is perhaps no greater question left unanswered, even 20 years later, than why. Since the moment the shooting broke out, members of society—both those directly affected by the tragedy and those who experienced it indirectly via the media—have sought to make sense of the events of April 20, 1999, and answering this question would be a critical first step in doing so. With the perpetrators dead, it was uncertain whether such answers would be found. In December 1999, it seemed that answers might soon be available when *TIME*, which had been provided viewing access along with several other outlets, wrote a story about a series of videos, called the Basement Tapes, that the killers had left behind (Gibbs & Roche, 1999; see also Larkin, 2009). Described by Larkin (2009) as the only definitive way to explain the shooters' motivations, the tapes originally were sealed by the Jefferson

County Sheriff's Office until 2026 (Schildkraut, 2012b) because they were so graphic that it was believed that making them public would provide a template for other would-be shooters (Mink, 2006; Schildkraut & Elsass, 2016). In 2011, however, JCSO destroyed the tapes along with other pieces of evidence collected during the investigation (Prendergast, 2015), thereby denying anyone a direct answer as to why.

In the absence of definitive answers, fingers started pointing in every direction. As Scharrer, Weidman, and Bissell (2003) noted, a cultural marker of Western society is to think of events like Columbine in terms of cause and effect. As such, Columbine is, according to Birkland and Lawrence (2009), "an event so dramatic in its effects [that] 'must,' . . . have identifiable causes" (p. 1407). It was this very search for causes that led to what Frymer (2009) has described as "a series of simplified answers, answers that soon became objectified myths about the motivations about the shooting" (p. 1393).

Much of the discourse about causal factors centered upon what Schildkraut and Muschert (2013) call the usual suspects: guns, mental health, and violent media. People wanted to know how the shooters had gotten their weapons, particularly as their journal entries revealed they had them in their possession before either turned 18 (Schildkraut & Elsass, 2016; see also Springhall, 1999). The media speculated that the shooting ultimately was a result of inadequate gun legislation (Haider-Markel & Joslyn, 2001; Lawrence & Birkland, 2004; Leavy & Maloney, 2009) and the availability of firearms (Rocque, 2012). In doing so, the media effectively stoked an already raging political fire burning between the gun control and gun rights camps (for further discussion, see Chapter 8). When it was revealed that one of the shooters had been prescribed Luvox, a drug typically used to treat obsessive-compulsive disorder that also doubles as an antidepressant (Columbine Review Commission, 2001), mental health entered the discussion (Schildkraut & Elsass, 2016).

Popular forms of entertainment media, including movies, music, and computer and video games, also found themselves at the center of the debate (Rocque, 2012). Movies like *The Matrix* and *The Basketball Diaries* faced backlash as promoting real-life violence (Birkland & Lawrence, 2009; Leavy & Maloney, 2009; Springhall, 1999), though it was Oliver Stone's *Natural Born Killers*—with the acronym NBK, which the Columbine shooters used to describe their act—that garnered the most criticism (Cullen, 2009; Consalvo, 2003; Larkin, 2007). Goth-rock music also was perceived to be correlated with the shooting after it was revealed that German bands like Rammstein and KMFDM were preferred by the perpetrators (Ogle et al., 2003; Powers, 1999; Schildkraut & Muschert, 2013; Springhall, 1999). Musical artist Marilyn Manson, however, faced considerable backlash when it was reported that the shooters also had listened to his music (Frymer, 2009; Leavy & Maloney, 2009; Springhall, 1999), an inaccuracy that later was brought to light but a myth that persists to this day (Cullen, 2009; D'Angelo, 2011; Willis, 2015). Violent video games, including the *Doom* and *Quake* computer games played by the shooters, were perceived to have contributed to the attack (Consalvo, 2003; Cullen, 2009; Schildkraut & Elsass, 2016; Springhall, 1999), even though recent research does not find a causal relationship between mass shootings like Columbine and video game violence (Ferguson, 2014; Ferguson & Olson, 2014; Fox & DeLateur, 2014; Markey, Markey, & French, 2014). Some even criminalized the mass media itself and its preoccupation with violence as causal factors (Lawrence & Birkland, 2004), though most news organizations absolved themselves of any responsibility for the shooting by diverting the blame elsewhere (Scharrer et al., 2003).

Beyond the usual suspects, a host of other potential causal factors for the shooting were raised. Many suggested that the social hierarchy of the school, which prioritized jocks as elite, created the conditions that led to two marginalized individuals believing they were reclaiming their rightful places (Consalvo, 2003; Larkin, 2007; Lewin, 1999; Ogle et al., 2003; Springhall, 1999). In the same vein, bullying emerged as one of the leading causal factors for the shooting (Brown & Merritt, 2002; Consalvo, 2003; Cullen, 2009; Muschert, 2007; Rocque, 2012), despite later reports indicating that the shooters, who were liked and had a strong friend group, actually had bullied other students themselves (Larkin, 2007). Some suggested that the shooters possessed a hatred for racial minorities that led to them targeting certain students (Consalvo, 2003; Frymer, 2003). Other proposed causal factors for the shooting included lack of parental involvement (Frymer, 2009; Leavy & Maloney, 2009; Lickel et al., 2003; see also Schildkraut & Elsass, 2016, for a discussion of legal action taken against the shooters' parents), general social strain and status frustration (Levin & Madfis, 2009), a lack of religion (Brooks, 2007; Seelye, 1999), a crisis of masculinity (Consalvo, 2003; Kalish & Kimmel, 2010; Kimmel & Mahler, 2003; Rocque, 2012), and even the environmental design of suburban communities like the one where Columbine is located (Hamilton, 1999). Despite all of the directions fingers pointed when trying to explain why the shooting had happened, the one place they failed to point was at the perpetrators themselves (Schildkraut & Elsass, 2016; Schildkraut & Muschert, 2013).

Breaking the Mold and Creating a New One

When the story of Columbine broke, the traditional guidelines of journalism went out the window. Information went live on the air without fact-checking or editing (Gottlieb, 1999; see also, generally, Lipschultz & Hilt, 2011). People who pretended to be linked to the event were placed on air without a second thought, further perpetuating the inaccuracies that were running rampant on April 20 (Gottlieb, 1999). Filler information was looped in to fill time and space so as not to lose the audience, which instead created more confusion (Gottlieb, 1999). In the end, much of the context and the meaning were lost (Gottlieb, 1999), and the day produced many myths and misconceptions that persist to this day.

The problem was that at the time of the Columbine shooting, there was really no mold on *how* to report on these types of stories. As a result, in an attempt to create a coherent story, the media created a format that Gottlieb (1999) calls "crisis coverage" (para. 5; see also Graber, 2006). Graber (2006) views this format as a three-stage process. First, there is "a flood of uncoordinated bulletins announcing the extraordinary event" as the media race to the scene and begin reporting on the event (Graber, 2006, p. 130). Once the information is out there, members of the media then transition to the second stage, where they "try to correct past errors and put the situation into proper perspective," though such efforts may not always be successful (Graber, 2006, p. 133). Finally, Graber (2006) notes that the media must shift to place "the crisis into a larger, long range perspective and to prepare people to cope with the aftermath" (p. 134). Not only did the coverage of Columbine exemplify the crisis coverage process, it subsequently created a mold by which all other mass shootings could be—and subsequently have been—reported through. Though not all mass shootings receive equitable coverage or even any media attention (Schildkraut et al., 2018), the perpetual crisis coverage of those that do has become nothing if not predictable and differs little in structure from that which was witnessed on April 20, 1999.

The coverage of Columbine had another unintended consequence: it turned the shooters into celebrities, folk heroes, and martyrs (which we discuss further in Chapter 10). In doing so, it created the potential for copycat attacks—other attempted or completed rampages in which the perpetrators model their actions after the Columbine shooters in an attempt to gain similar rewards, namely media attention, fame, and notoriety. More recently, researchers (e.g., Garcia-Bernardo, Qi, Schultz, Cohen, Johnson, & Dodds, 2017; Kissner, 2016; Towers, Gomez-Lievano, Khan, Mubayi, & Castillo-Chavez, 2015) have found that the first two weeks after a highly covered school or mass shooting can create a contagion period, during which time the likelihood of copycat shootings is greater. Following the February 14, 2018, shooting at Marjory Stoneman Douglas High School in Parkland, Florida, for example, threats and incidents of school violence increased 300% in just 30 days; the majority of events came within the first 12 days (Klinger & Klinger, 2018), when media coverage also was the most pervasive. Others (Lankford & Tomek, 2017) have suggested that, as illustrated by the Columbine shooting, a longer-term copycat effect is more likely than a short-term contagion.

Regardless, there are potentially lethal consequences for perpetuating the use of the crisis coverage model. Accordingly, what the coverage of Columbine highlights is the need to change this model in order to help eliminate the rewards for other would-be perpetrators that can potentially reduce the number of school and mass shootings in the United States. One of the most promising approaches is the adoption of a No Notoriety policy that asks the media to limit the use of the perpetrators' names and images in the coverage of these events (NoNotoriety.com, n.d.; see also DontNameThem.org, n.d.; Lankford & Madfis, 2018; Meindl & Ivy, 2017). Founded by Tom and Caren Teves after their son, Alex, was murdered in the 2012 movie theater shooting in nearby Aurora, Colorado, the No Notoriety protocol also recommends that media outlets refuse to publish manifestos or other materials left behind by the killers or promote data from relevant experts; instead, they should prioritize the victims, survivors, and heroes of these tragedies (NoNotoriety.com, n.d.).

In sum, the way the Columbine shooting was covered—both in the immediate aftermath and in the years since—has provided many valuable lessons. In one sense, it created a "how-to" model of reporting for news outlets to follow when reporting on similar crises. Absent a set of guidelines on how such stories should be covered, Columbine effectively wrote the script for crisis coverage reporting. Conversely, the collateral effects of such coverage show that while Columbine may have created the mold, perhaps the greatest lesson stemming from the shooting is that the reporting practices need to change, as lives literally are depending on it.

CHAPTER FOUR

Police Responses, Then and Now

The events of April 20, 1999, identified many issues in responding to school and mass shootings, with police responses being just one of these areas. On the day of the shooting, police did "exactly what they had been trained to do" (Columbine Review Commission, 2001, p. 60). Doing so, however, led to the identification of a number of opportunities for the improvement for other agencies and jurisdictions that might one day face a similar situation. As one SWAT trainer from the Los Angeles Police Department testified before the Columbine Review Commission (2001), the lessons learned from Columbine effectively "reverse[d] what officers [had] been taught for twenty years" before the shooting (p. 66, footnote 164). In short, Columbine not only broke the mold for law enforcement response to school and mass shooting events, but the lessons learned in the aftermath also rewrote the playbook.

In this chapter, we explore the evolution of practices of first responders related to active shooter events since April 20, 1999. We begin with an overview of the police response to Columbine on the day of the shooting. Aside from the material presented in this chapter, additional information on the step-by-step responses of various teams and agencies can be found in the Columbine Review Commission's (2001) report on the shooting, though it bears noting that a critical piece of information—details from the Jefferson County Sheriff's Office—are largely missing as the agency was directed not to testify due to pending litigation at the time of the inquiry. Their account of the responses, however, also has been made available through the release of investigatory materials (see Jefferson County Sheriff's Office, 2000).

From there, we consider what key issues were identified and how, based on the lessons learned from these responses, police practices have changed since.

This discussion is centered on two key ideas: stop the killing and stop the dying (Blair, Nichols, Burns, & Curnutt, 2013) and is explored through consideration of changing active shooter response protocols for law enforcement, the implementation of tactical first aid practices, and the employment of rescue task forces. We also review the protocols and trainings offered by the Advanced Law Enforcement Rapid Response Training (ALERRT) Center, which serves as the national standard for active shooter training. Finally, we consider how these different techniques can be synthesized into a broader lesson on improving survivability in a school or mass shooting event.

Law Enforcement Response on April 20, 1999

By the time the scene had been secured, more than 1,000 officers and emergency medical professionals from a number of agencies across the greater Denver metropolitan area had responded to Columbine (Columbine Review Commission, 2001). The response to the shooting began, however, with one person: school resource officer and Sheriff's Deputy Neil Gardner. Armed with a handgun, Deputy Gardner had exchanged fire with one of the gunmen, which likely provided valuable time for those within the school to take cover. Working against him, however, was the fact that he was not wearing his prescription glasses, and he engaged with the shooter from approximately 60 yards away—a distance that made it nearly impossible to take out the gunman with the .45 caliber semiautomatic pistol he was carrying under the best of circumstances (see, generally, Chick, 2007; Columbine Review Commission, 2001).

Minutes after the shooting had begun, a student called in to 911, reporting that another student was down in the parking lot (this person later was identified as Anne Marie Hochhalter). Deputy Gardner radioed in to dispatch three minutes later—at 11:26 a.m.—once the shooter he was engaged with retreated inside the building. In the coming minutes, more and more officers arrived on scene. A command post was set up by a Jefferson County SWAT commander on the east side of the school (near the corner of Pierce and Leawood Streets) approximately 10 minutes after Deputy Gardner placed his call (Columbine Review Commission, 2001).

At 11:51 a.m., approximately 30 minutes into the attack, SWAT officers were given authorization to immediately enter the school, although the first team did not do so for another 15 minutes—two minutes before the gunmen committed suicide. When they made entry, they did so on the east side of the school; the majority of the activity, however, had occurred on the west side. SWAT teams from additional agencies also responded and soon had entered the building. One team from Jefferson County, led by Sergeant Barry Williams, entered through the faculty lounge on the lower west side of the building (adjacent to the cafeteria) at 1:09 p.m.; they reached Dave Sanders at 2:30 p.m.

and entered the library nearly an hour after that (Columbine Review Commission, 2001). At 3:39 p.m., the scene was turned over to the bomb technicians; around the same time, SWAT teams began a second sweep of the school.

Key Issues Identified

Looking retrospectively at how the events unfolded on April 20, 1999, has provided law enforcement agencies across the nation with opportunities to improve their tactics. Central to being able to make such improvements, however, are the invaluable lessons that were learned that day. Drawing from the Columbine Review Commission's (2001) investigation into the shooting, as well as other examination of law enforcement's actions on the day of shooting (e.g., Police Executive Research Forum, 2014), three key areas of improvement were identified: entry into the school, knowledge of the building, and communication.

On the day of the shooting, responding police officers from all across Denver descended on Columbine High School and did exactly what they were trained to do in the case of a hostage situation: establish a perimeter and wait for the SWAT team (Blair et al., 2013; Columbine Review Commission, 2001; Police Executive Research Forum, 2014). The SWAT teams, as the Police Executive Research Forum (2014) explains, have received special tactical training and are better equipped than routine patrol officers (see also Blair et al., 2013). (A concern about the differential in firepower between school resource officer Deputy Neil Gardner and the shooters was raised by the Columbine Review Commission [2001].) On the day of the shooting, two perimeters actually were established: an "inner" perimeter designed to prevent the gunmen from escaping and an "outer" perimeter to provide law enforcement with a buffer (Columbine Review Commission, 2001). The result was that it was more than 30 minutes before any law enforcement officer entered the building (Police Executive Research Forum, 2014), leaving the perpetrators with virtually unchallenged access to the entire school (Columbine Review Commission, 2001).

Once SWAT officers did make entry, they were further challenged by their unfamiliarity with the building's layout. Many of the responding officers were from outside Jefferson County, meaning they likely would not have entered the building prior to the day of the shooting. Of the seven agencies from within the county that responded, most had an inaccurate understanding of where key locations within the building (such as the library) were located, due, in part, to major renovations that had taken place throughout the years. Without a map or blueprint of the school, the SWAT teams had only those diagrams that were quickly sketched by local officers from memory and students and school officials who had escaped from the building.

This may have contributed, at least in part, to why SWAT teams entered the building on the east side when the majority of the carnage—outside the school and in the library—was on the west end of the school (Columbine Review Commission, 2001).

Also complicating the situation were numerous communication issues, which have been considered to be among the greatest challenges for law enforcement. The first of these issues stemmed from the radios. Much like the challenges faced by first responders on 9/11 two years later (e.g., Dwyer, Flynn, & Fessenden, 2002; Roberts, 2004), all of the responding law enforcement agencies' radios operated on different bandwidths and therefore were incompatible for communicating with one another. Once inside the building, this issue was exacerbated; at times, responding officers were unable to communicate with other members of their own team. Additionally, given Columbine's enormous size, which interfered with radio signals, these teams could not communicate back out to the incident command center. The blaring fire alarm, which rang out for more than six hours after being activated, presented further challenges; visual communications also were impaired due to the residual smoke from incendiary devices detonated by the shooters (Columbine Review Commission, 2001).

In sum, the issues that law enforcement and other first responders faced on April 20, 1999, inevitably made it more difficult to quickly bring the rampage to an end and secure the scene. These challenges also potentially cost at least one person—teacher Dave Sanders—his life, as medical assistance did not reach him in time. Since then, agencies have worked to institute policies and practices aimed at addressing these very issues in the event that a similar attack were to happen in their jurisdiction. These are discussed further in the following sections.

Forging New Strategies

Many in the Columbine and Jefferson County communities, as well as across the nation, criticized first responders for what they perceived to be inaction during the shooting, despite the fact that the police were doing exactly what they were not only trained but also authorized to do at the time (Blair et al., 2013). For the law enforcement community, Columbine also was a turning point for them in many ways (Fletcher, 2016; Frazzano & Snyder, 2014; Jacobs, Wade, et al., 2013; Smith & Delaney, 2013; Smith, Iselin, & McKay, 2009). As Blair and colleagues (2013) noted, the shooting had identified three important points: (1) not every situation allows for an officer to wait for SWAT; (2) patrol officers must be provided with tactical training; and (3) these same first responders must be able to stop an active shooter on their own (p. 13). Accordingly, across the nation, active shooter trainings, policies, and procedures, as well as the equipment that patrol officers were being provided with, were drastically overhauled (Blair et al., 2013; see also Police Executive Research Forum, 2014).

One of the first steps to achieve these revisions was to utilize existing SWAT members as trainers (Blair et al., 2013). Naturally, these individuals have the necessary tactical training and expertise to pass along, but they also have former experience as patrol officers that should be helpful in tailoring the material to their earlier positions. Still, when training patrol officers in SWAT-based techniques for active shooter situations, there are challenges that must be addressed. These include (but certainly are not limited to) the need to teach tactics to individuals who have no experience with them, the importance of teaching and empowering patrol officers in dynamic decision-making processes, employing scenario-based training, and ensuring that the principles are taught in a manner that can be easily recalled when the officer is under extreme stress (Blair et al., 2013).

Two other considerations also must be taken into account when creating a training protocol for patrol officers. First, the trainers must be mindful of the limited equipment that first responders are issued and adapt their instruction to account for the differences in available supplies (Blair et al., 2013). While SWAT teams, for example, are supplied with ballistic shields, these devices are not provided to officers on routine patrol. Accordingly, Blair and colleagues (2013) suggested that patrol officers and other first responders be better equipped with specific types of tactical gear. Such critical supplies should include patrol rifles, which are found to be more accurate in neutralizing a threat than a standard-issue pistol; "go bags" that hold extra ammunition and medical supplies (discussed further in the next section); and rifle-grade body armor in the form of plate-carrying vests that also could hold additional provisions (Martaindale & Blair, 2019).

The second consideration is that, unlike SWAT teams, patrol officers do not work in fixed teams that always train together (Blair et al., 2013; Martaindale & Blair, 2019). Instead, at any given time—as discussed earlier in this chapter—officers from numerous jurisdictions may respond to a call and, subsequently, must work together in their response. Not only must this challenge be addressed in theory, it also must be implemented in practice. One such approach is the employment of team training, whereby officers from multiple agencies train together to understand how others operate. By doing so, the fluidity of their interactions is markedly improved in the event they have to respond to a shooting together (see, generally, Matthews, 2018; Paul, 2018).

Beyond the training considerations, changes also have been observed in how law enforcement responds during an actual event. After Columbine, law enforcement began responding in teams (Martaindale & Blair, 2019; see also Smith et al., 2009). The first officers on scene would team up, stage in some type of predetermined formation—either a diamond, triangle, or T pattern to allow for maximum visibility of a potential threat (Blair et al., 2013; Paul, 2018)—and move together as a unit toward the sound of gunfire (Fletcher, 2016). This protocol, while overcoming the issues of the "create a perimeter and wait for SWAT" training identified in the Columbine response review, still presented numerous challenges—mainly how much ground could be covered and how quickly the response could be carried out (Fletcher, 2016).

Accordingly, as time is always of the essence when a shooting is in progress (Smith & Delaney, 2013), protocols again adapted to use either solo or two-officer entry teams (Fletcher, 2016; Martaindale & Blair, 2019; Paul, 2018; Police Executive Research Forum, 2014). Using these smaller teams provides several benefits. First, using solo entries allows for a quicker response time. A drawback of the larger teams is that an officer who arrives on scene must wait for the requisite number of people to establish the formation before entering, thereby wasting precious seconds that can be used to neutralize the threat (Fletcher, 2016; see also Paul, 2018). Second, having individual officers make solo entries into a building at the same time through different access points also can help to cover more ground quicker than can a team of officers making entry through a single entryway. Further, using this type of "swarm" technique (approaching a target from multiple directions) actually may cause the shooting to end more quickly through either the surrender or suicide of the perpetrator. In one study by the National Tactical Officers Association, it was found that 63% of active shooter incidents were stopped by a single officer; an additional 30% were ended by a response from two officers (Fletcher, 2016). In sum, the evolution of training protocols since Columbine to today's use of solo- and dual-officer entries has proven not only to save time but likely lives.

The changing of law enforcement protocols in both the short- and long-term aftermath of Columbine represents an adherence to the first of two goals for active shooter responses: stop the killing (Blair et al., 2013; see also Smith et al., 2009). Ideally, stopping the killing involves the neutralization of the offender. Often, the perpetrators actually neutralize themselves before or just after police arrive on scene, either through leaving the location, committing suicide (which occurs in approximately half of mass shootings; see Schildkraut & Elsass, 2016), surrendering, or being stopped by law enforcement by being shot or subdued. If neutralization is not an option, the next best strategy is to isolate the perpetrator from their intended targets, which often is accomplished when they self-barricade in a separate area. If this self-barricading occurs where others are present, as it did in the June 12, 2016, shooting at the Pulse nightclub in Orlando, Florida, law enforcement's response must shift to hostage situation protocols, including containing and establishing communication with the perpetrator, bringing in specialized units as needed (such as hostage negotiators), and determining what the response will be to resolve the situation if the shooter does not hold until a tactical team arrives. The final option is to distract the shooter, which inevitably happens in conjunction with or separate from the first two responses (Blair et al., 2013). The faster first responders can stop the killing, the more lives will be saved and the quicker those who need medical attention can receive it.

Tactical First Aid

While the primary objective of law enforcement officers is to stop the killing, the second goal of active shooter response is to stop the dying (Blair et al., 2013). As Smith and Delaney (2013) point out, "every minute with uncontrolled injury increases the death rate" (para. 13). In other words, the more quickly someone wounded in a school or mass shooting can be treated, the greater their likelihood for survival (International Association of Chiefs of Police, 2013; Pearce & Goldstein, 2015; Smith & Delaney, 2013). Given that law enforcement officers usually are the first responders on scene, providing them with training on basic emergency medical care and providing them with the necessary tools to tend to the injured once they have stopped the killing can mean the difference between life and death for some (Blair & Martaindale, 2013; Blair et al., 2013; International Association of Chiefs of Police, 2013; Jacobs, Wade et al., 2013; Pearce & Goldstein, 2015). Time, as has been noted, is critical to saving lives (Smith et al., 2009), and preventable deaths always should be eliminated (Callaway et al., 2011).

The International Association of Chiefs of Police (2013) has recommended that every law enforcement officer receive tactical medical training, including, but not limited to, hemorrhage control and rapid evacuation of victims to a casualty collection site outside of the building (see also Blair et al., 2013). These recommendations follow training protocols used by the U.S. military, which requires that every soldier have basic lifesaving skills that can be deployed quickly and efficiently when it is tactically feasible for them to do so (Smith & Delaney, 2013). The training should focus on stabilizing the victim until EMS can enter the scene or the law enforcement officer can evacuate them to the casualty collection point (Blair & Martaindale, 2013; Blair et al., 2013), with the overarching priority to get the wounded individual to a hospital for definitive care (Pearce & Goldstein, 2015; see also International Association of Chiefs of Police, 2013).

A shared commonality between victims on the battlefield and those injured during school and mass shootings are the types of injuries they sustain. Specifically, there are three types of injuries that are typical of both scenarios: exsanguination, tension pneumothorax, and suffocation (Callaway et al., 2011; Pearce & Goldstein, 2015; Smith et al., 2009). *Exsanguination* refers to the process of losing blood, usually from some type of wound to an extremity. *Tension pneumothorax* concerns penetrating or blunt injuries to the chest, such as a gunshot or stab wound, which can lead to a collapsed lung and subsequent breathing issues as air cannot escape the body. *Suffocation* in these situations arises when fluids or the injured person's tongue block the airway.

Without treatment, death is imminent in a matter of minutes for any one of these conditions (Pearce & Goldstein, 2015; Smith et al., 2009). If left untreated, a person can bleed out from exsanguination in one to three minutes. If an airway is compromised, causing inadequate oxygenation and subsequent suffocation, the person has five minutes or less to live. Untreated tension pneumothorax can lead to death in approximately 10 minutes. Though extremely serious and life-threatening, each of these can be treated in the field with proper training (Meenach, 2015; Pearce & Goldstein, 2015; Smith et al., 2009).

Certain actions, when taken quickly, can stabilize the person until he or she receives additional medical care and, ultimately, can prevent death (Smith et al., 2009). For conditions involving exsanguination, tourniquets are emphasized as a quick and effective way to control the hemorrhaging. These devices can be applied immediately to stop the bleed and also can be quickly de-escalated once the patient arrives at the hospital for additional care. When removed within several hours, the odds of the extremity being saved are particularly high. In areas where hemorrhaging occurs but a tourniquet cannot be used, such as the neck or another arterial bleed, hemostatic agents such as combat gauze or wound-packing granules may be used; they also may be used in conjunction with a tourniquet for better injury management (Smith et al., 2009; see also Blair et al., 2013; Callaway et al., 2011; Jacobs, Rotondo et al., 2013; Meenach, 2015; Rescue Essentials, n.d.).

When addressing suffocation or other airway control issues, nasopharyngeal airways (rubber tubes that are inserted in one's nose down to the jaw) are preferred over intubation for helping to keep the passage open (Smith et al., 2009). The rubber tubes are easy to use, fast to deploy, and tolerated by most individuals regardless of gag reflexes. They also have been found to be better tolerated in victims who are more alert (Nasopharyngeal Airway, n.d.). Conversely, intubation techniques require more equipment and time to deploy, among other challenges (Callaway et al., 2011; Smith et al., 2009).

Tension pneumothorax can be particularly difficult to identify in these situations because it may be confused with other forms of respiratory distress (Smith et al., 2009). Early management of the issue, however, is emphasized as it is critical to help re-establish the integrity of the chest wall to improve breathing. Depending on the available supplies, this may be accomplished one of two ways. The first is to use an adhesive occlusive chest seal (Blair et al., 2013; Meenach, 2015; Sideras, 2011; Smith et al., 2009). These dressings create an airtight seal over the wound that closes the opening in the chest wall, thereby allowing air to follow through its normal route

(Meenach, 2015). The second way to stabilize the injured party is to use a chest needle decompression (Callaway et al., 2011; Pearce & Goldstein, 2015; Sideras, 2011). A large-bore needle catheter is inserted into the chest on the side where the wound is located and should subsequently release the trapped air, providing relief to the injured party (Sideras, 2011).

Given the success of these techniques in stabilizing injured persons in the field, it is now recommended (and, in some cases, required) that law enforcement officers carry tactical medical kits in their vehicles (Jacobs, Rotondo et al., 2013; Pearce & Goldstein, 2015; Smith & Delaney, 2013). These "go bags" or medical kits should include tourniquets, occlusive chest seals, hemostatic gauze, compression dressings, and needle catheters (Blair et al., 2013; Pearce & Goldstein, 2015; Smith & Delaney, 2013; see also Smith et al., 2009, for a full list of specific recommendations for each of these products). Blair and colleagues (2013) also note that other basic medical supplies, including gauze, shears, and latex gloves, should be included in the kits. Still, it is not sufficient simply to purchase the supplies and assemble the kits. Instead, training in how to use each of these tools is necessary to ensure that they are deployed correctly in times of crisis (Blair et al., 2013; Jacobs, Wade et al., 2013).

Rescue Task Forces

Empowering law enforcement officers with tactical first aid is an important step in helping to stop the dying. Its necessity, however, comes as a result of two other standard practices that are integrated within these types of emergency responses. The first centers on emergency care training. Historically, law enforcement, fire, and EMS have trained independent of one another (Frazzano & Snyder, 2014; Rogers, 2018). This can be problematic during times of crisis when roles overlap and a coordinated effort is a necessity (Frazzano & Snyder, 2014; see also Jacobs, Wade et al., 2013).

The second concerning practice was the "stage until safe" approach (Frazzano & Snyder, 2014). Under this model emergency personnel, such as fire and EMS, would be staged off-scene and held until police were able to secure the scene and declare it safe for entry (Blair & Martaindale, 2013; Smith & Delaney, 2013; Smith et al., 2013). As a result, getting medical care to the injured was delayed. Subsequently, those who were seriously wounded but ultimately survivable were left to continue to bleed and possibly hemorrhage to death (Blair & Martaindale, 2013; Smith & Delaney, 2013; Smith et al., 2013). Given that all first responders—police, fire, and EMS—share the same goal of saving lives (Frazzano & Snyder, 2014), a protocol was needed that facilitated these agencies working together to provide more immediate care to injured victims (Ivanson, 2015).

The Rescue Task Force (RTF) concept was initially introduced to address this gap as a joint collaboration between Arlington County's (Virginia) police and fire departments (Smith et al., 2009; see also Frazzano & Snyder, 2014). The goal of the RTF is to improve medical response times and get necessary resources and care to injured parties as quickly as possible (Ivanson, 2015; Smith et al., 2009). More importantly, to achieve rapid stabilization of injured individuals, the RTF works to bring EMS onto the scene more quickly—minutes rather than hours—instead of leaving medical care to police while other first responders are staged away from the incident (Smith et al., 2009). In order to meet these goals, the RTF model has adapted the main principles of military model of medicine (Tactical Combat Casualty Care, or TCCC) to civilian EMS (Frazzano & Snyder, 2014; Smith et al., 2009).

Rather than waiting until the scene is declared secure by law enforcement, the RTF protocol works to bring medics into areas that have been designated by the officers as *warm zones* (Smith et al., 2009; see also Frazzano & Snyder, 2014; Ivanson, 2015; Mechem, Bossert, & Baldini, 2015; Mueck, 2017; Rogers, 2018; Smith & Delaney, 2013). Warm zones are areas that have been cleared by police, who now provide 360-degree protection for fire and EMS workers to be able to render medical aid (Ivanson, 2015; Mueck, 2017; Smith et al., 2009). The Arlington County RTF initially comprised four members: two police officers, who provided front and rear coverage, and two paramedics, who used the TCCC principles to help stabilize any injured person (Smith et al., 2009). It should be noted that the primary goal, at least in the initial moments, of the medics on the RTF team is to stabilize as many people as quickly as possible—primarily stopping any bleeding and ensuring victims can breathe (see also Ivanson, 2015; Mechem et al., 2015; Mueck, 2017). Once the acute life-threatening injury (as discussed earlier) has been stabilized, the RTF leaves that person where he or she is for the time being and moves on to the next. As more first responders arrive on scene and more RTF units are established, the process of evacuating all injured parties to central casualty points located outside the location begins. Once evacuated, the injured party is turned over to traditional EMS services and transported to local hospitals and trauma centers for definitive care (Mechem et al., 2015; Mueck, 2017; Smith et al., 2009).

The right equipment is necessity for RTF members. Like police, both EMS and fire need to be equipped with ballistic vests and helmets to ensure their protection and mitigate any potential risks (Smith et al., 2009; see also Ivanson, 2015; Mueck, 2017). They each should have "go bags" or medical kits similar to those discussed earlier for police officers. At the very least, they are expected to carry enough supplies to be able to help multiple people. The Arlington County RTF structure also provides for a supply depot to be established near the entry point of the building. This enables RTF teams to restock their supplies without having to go all the way back to their vehicles (Smith et al., 2009).

As noted earlier in this chapter, communication issues were highlighted by the Columbine Review Commission (2001) as problematic on the day of the shooting. The integrated concepts within the RTF model also help to address such challenges. Jacobs, Wade et al. (2013a), for example, called for a standardization of basic operational terms to bridge the gap between police and other first responders. Not only does the RTF communication structure achieve such an end, it also delineates information sharing responsibilities by assigning different tasks to each team member. The initial contact teams that go in ahead of the RTF (those tasked with neutralizing the threat) report back to the incident commander about those needing treatment and where they are located (Smith et al., 2009). The police officers on the RTF also communicate back to the incident commander, providing them with the team's location in the building and relaying back any additional critical information, such as the presence of a threat. The medics on the RTF communicate back with the fire commander, reporting back the number of victims and types of injuries so that the EMS personnel on the outside can prepare at the casualty collection point. In sum, the two-way dual message structure of the RTF helps to improve communications and ensure that necessary information is making it to the appropriate channels in real time (Smith et al., 2009).

Before an incident ever occurs, ongoing training remains a critical component of the RTF model. As noted, police, fire, and EMS each used to train independent of one another (Rogers, 2018). With the introduction of RTF, however, they now all train together as part of the protocol (Rogers, 2018). This allows increased coordination and cooperation between multiple agencies, not only during drills but also during rapid deployment when people who are under stress naturally will revert to what they have been trained to do (Frazzano & Snyder, 2014). Moreover, training provides all members of the RTF with additional lifesaving skills. All members are trained on first aid with an emphasis on hemorrhage control (Rogers, 2018). At the same time, despite that police still are tasked with providing security during the rescue operation, fire and EMS team members still receive basic training in law enforcement maneuvers and tactics to help increase their safety (Smith & Delaney, 2013). As Frazzano and Snyder (2014) aptly summarize, "A culture of interdependence and resource sharing must be stimulated in a training environment in order to be inculcated in an operational environment" (p. 4).

The RTF concept has been well-received in police departments across the nation (Martaindale & Blair, 2019). Police and fire departments in Philadelphia, Pennsylvania, for example, collaborated on their own version of an RTF, termed the Rapid Assessment Medical Support (RAMS) team, which is based off the same guiding TCCC principle (Mechem et al., 2015). Other similar programs have been instituted across the nation (see, generally, Cattafi, 2018; Dunn, 2017; Mayo, 2018; Shoup, 2018). Additional support for such programs also has been offered by the International Association of

Chiefs of Police (2018), International Association of Fire Chiefs (n.d.), International Association of Fire Fighters (n.d.), and the International Public Safety Association (2017; see also Fabbri, 2014).

Still, even though RTFs address many of the concerns raised in the aftermath of shootings like Columbine, they are not without their criticisms. Smith and Delaney (2013) note that a common argument against the use of RTFs is that fire and EMS personnel are not necessarily entering a secure scene, even though it has been cleared, thereby suggesting it is too great of a risk for the first responders to assume. In reality, however, very few first responders have been injured or killed when responding to a school mass shooting, and of those killed, all have been police officers, not fire or EMS personnel who were providing care. A second concern for RTFs is the potential for a delayed ambush from a second perpetrator, a common belief that emerges when active shooter scenes are still hot (Smith & Delaney, 2013). In reality, just over 2% of school or mass shooting events involve multiple perpetrators (Schildkraut, Formica, & Malatras, 2018); therefore, these concerns are not necessarily supported by the data. Accordingly, given that the benefits of the RTF model clearly outweigh any potential drawbacks that could be proposed, particularly as such concerns are largely unsupported by the evidence, municipalities should continue to integrate this protocol into their training regimen.

A New Standard

As noted, after Columbine, police and SWAT teams across the country began to reflect within their departments about practices they would use should a similar event happen in their own communities. A similar discussion was taking place in Hays County, Texas, nestled between Austin and San Antonio. Recognizing that their community was equally at risk of an attack similar to Columbine, the Hays County Sheriff's Office, along with the San Marcos (Texas) Police Department, partnered with Texas State University in 2002 to create the Advanced Law Enforcement Rapid Response Training (ALERRT) Center. Those involved applied for a grant for local training and soon a sought-after active shooter program for first responders had been created (ALERRT, n.d.a.; Martaindale & Blair, 2019).

Since its inception, the ALERRT Center has been awarded more than $50 million in financial support at both the state and federal levels to continue to support their training initiatives, including 13 separately funded first-responder courses. These courses include, but are not limited to, active shooter incident management, breaching, exterior response, and standard active shooter response training (ALERRT, n.d.d.). Using a "train-the-trainer" model, ALERRT's (n.d.a.) curriculum has been administered to more than 130,000 police and fire personnel across the nation. Police departments in major cities nationwide, including New York City, Miami, Atlanta, Dallas, and San Antonio, all have adopted the ALERRT curriculum in their training (ALERRT, n.d.a.). Their course catalog also includes active shooter training protocols for civilians (ALERRT, n.d.d.) and has been delivered to more than 200,000 U.S. citizens (ALERRT, n.d.a.).

With a growing reputation for quality instruction, the ALERRT Center was approached by the FBI in 2013 to form a partnership. Subsequently, the FBI named ALERRT as its national standard for active shooter training protocols. As part of this partnership, FBI Special Agents also help to deliver the ALERRT training across the nation and throughout U.S. territories. Beyond the protocols themselves, ALERRT is committed to evidence-based practices—each new training it rolls out is based upon studies conducted in its state-of-the-art facilities and through the in-house research department. ALERRT also conducts research with the Behavioral Analysis Unit through its partnership with the FBI (ALERRT, n.d.a.).

Law Enforcement Responses Today

Following the 2012 shooting at Sandy Hook Elementary School, members of public safety organizations (including law enforcement, fire, military, trauma care, and prehospital care) joined together to determine what strategies could improve survivability in the event of another mass casualty attack (Jacobs, Wade et al., 2013a; Jacobs, Rotondo et al., 2013b; see also Federal Bureau of Investigation, 2018; Pons et al., 2015). The result of these efforts came to be known as the Hartford Consensus. Like the approaches discussed previously in this chapter, the Hartford Consensus model draws from the military and TCCC perspectives. In addition to recommendations regarding

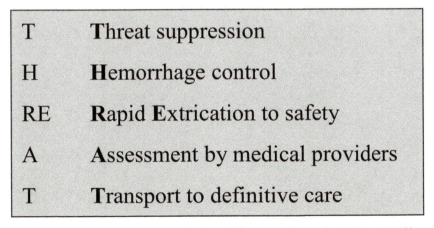

T	Threat suppression
H	Hemorrhage control
RE	Rapid Extrication to safety
A	Assessment by medical providers
T	Transport to definitive care

Figure 4.1 THREAT Acronym. (Adapted from Jacobs et al., 2013a, 2013b)

command structures and communication systems, the Hartford Consensus's main contribution is its proposal to respond to mass shooting events.

The group's proposal is summarized by a simple acronym: THREAT (see Figure 4.1). Threat suppression refers to the role of the contact team in neutralizing the perpetrator. Equally important is hemorrhage control (plus tending injuries that have caused tension pneumothorax or suffocation), which must be done as quickly as possible to save lives. As discussed, this may be accomplished by law enforcement with tactical first aid training or through the deployment of RTFs. Once stabilized, the injured parties are evacuated from the scene to a central casualty care point outside the building, where waiting EMS teams will triage the situation and assess each individual's current condition. Finally, injured parties are transported to hospitals and trauma centers, often with the most critical victims going first, for definitive care. Through a coordinated response that is both planned and rehearsed through drills ahead of time, this collaborative initiative can help to increase survivability through faster response times (Jacobs, Wade et al., 2013a; Jacobs, Rotondo et al., 2013b; see also Pons et al., 2015, for a proposed training course layout). When it means the difference between life and death, every second matters.

CHAPTER FIVE

Piecing Together the Past

When a shooting like Columbine happens, a parallel question to "why" that often enters the discourse is "how"—how could this happen? How were the shooters able to commit such an act? How could no one have known? How could this event have been prevented? In the search for answers to these and other similar questions, a pervasive myth has surfaced: that school and mass shooters, like the two perpetrators at Columbine, simply snap and that such events are sudden and impulsive (Levin & Madfis, 2009; Meloy, 2014; Reddy et al., 2001; Vossekuil, Fein, Reddy, Borum, & Modzeleski, 2004).

The reality is that school and mass shooters almost never snap (O'Toole, 2000). Instead, these perpetrators make a conscious, rational decision that they will engage in this type of action (Nicoletti, 2017; Wike & Fraser, 2009). As Knoll and Meloy (2014) explained, "the violence of the mass murderer is not sudden and explosive; but instead, planful, methodical, instrumental, and largely devoid of emotion" (p. 238; see also Borum, Fein, Vossekuil, & Berglund, 1999; Meloy et al., 2004; Vossekuil et al., 2004; White & Meloy, 2017). Though motivations for these attacks may differ somewhat based on the perpetrator, the reality is that these individuals all follow the same general pathway toward becoming mass shooters (Knoll & Meloy, 2014; Meloy, 2014; O'Toole, 2000; White & Meloy, 2017). Understanding this provides an opportunity to prevent these events before they happen—if people know what to look for (Doherty, 2016).

In this chapter, we explore the actions of the Columbine perpetrators as they transitioned from high school students into mass murderers to better identify and understand how this tragedy could have been prevented. We first examine the pathway-to-violence model to better understand how individuals progress toward carrying out a school or mass shooting. Once these stages and key behaviors in each are identified, we consider how threat

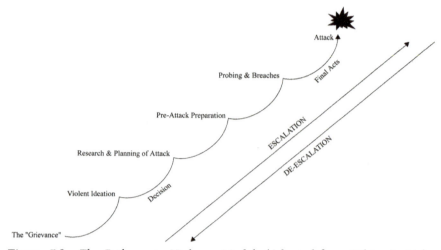

Figure 5.1   The Pathway to Violence Model. (Adapted from White & Meloy, 2017)

assessment protocols introduced in the aftermath of Columbine can be used to identify and disrupt such behaviors before the attack can come to fruition. Additionally, we consider lessons learned from successfully averted rampages that can be used to continue prevention efforts needed to save lives.

The Pathway to Violence

As noted, perpetrators like the Columbine shooters typically follow the same trajectory toward their intended act of violence. The pathway-to-violence model presented in Figure 5.1 has been introduced as a way to conceptualize the distinct steps that take such an offender from violent ideation to final act (Calhoun & Weston, 2003; Fein, Vossekuil, & Holden, 1995; White & Meloy, 2017). Understanding each of these phases, both individually and collectively, provides additional opportunities to disrupt these events before they ever happen, thereby potentially saving countless lives.

From "Grievance" to Decision

For all school and mass shooters, their pathway begins at the same place: the grievance. Grievances may fall into one of two categories. The first—real—refers to hardships like a significant loss (e.g., a job, divorce, financial) or some other type of personal failure (Vossekuil et al., 2004). The second category of grievances are those that are perceived. Individuals with perceived grievances may exhibit paranoid thinking or believe themselves to be inadequate in some way (Knoll & Meloy, 2014). They also may express feelings of being bullied, persecuted, socially rejected, or attacked by others (Knoll & Meloy, 2014; Larkin, 2009; Vossekuil et al., 2004).

Once an initial grievance sets in for the would-be mass shooter, so too does the violent ideation that follows. In this stage, the perpetrator abandons the idea of resolving the injury in a pro-social manner, instead determining that retribution through violent means is a more realistic approach (Knoll & Meloy, 2014; White & Meloy, 2017). The anger stemming from the grievance merges with a disregard for the consequences of one's actions and a lack of coping skills, leading the perpetrator to believe that violent means are the only way of remedying the injury (Knoll & Meloy, 2014; Vossekuil et al., 2004). As a result, the perpetrator subsequently makes the decision to move forward with the violent act. As Knoll and Meloy (2014) noted, in making this decision, the perpetrator prioritizes a revenge fantasy over nonviolent resolution of the grievance, compromise, or seeking outside assistance to help address the issue.

Research, Planning, and Preparation

After the decision to commit mass murder has been made, the perpetrator then begins researching and planning the attack. In the research phase, plans for how to carry out the attack are developed (Borum et al., 1999; Meloy et al., 2004). The perpetrator may look to previous mass shootings for inspiration (Meloy, Mohandie, Knoll, & Hoffmann, 2015) or develop a plan that is completely unique to their circumstances. The planning of the attack can last for days, weeks, or, in the most extreme cases, months (Borum et al., 1999; Meloy, 2014; Meloy et al., 2004; Silver, Simons, & Craun, 2018).

Once a perpetrator has developed a plan of action, he or she then moves into pre-attack preparation, which includes four key behaviors (White & Meloy, 2017). The first of these behaviors is armament—the gathering of weapons (Dietz, 1986; Meloy, Hoffmann, Roshdi, & Guldimann, 2014; Twemlow, Fonagy, Sacco, O'Toole, & Vernberg, 2002; White & Meloy, 2017). This can happen in a number of ways, depending on the situation. The majority of perpetrators acquire their firearms through legal means, following the mandated requirements for purchasing their weapons, either expressly for the shooting or sometime predating the attack (Silver et al., 2018). A smaller number secure firearms through theft, borrowing from a friend or acquaintance, or an illegal purchase (Silver et al., 2018).

A second form of "attack-related behaviors" perpetrators exhibit is improving their skill set (Borum et al., 1999, p. 329; see also White & Meloy, 2017). Oftentimes, perpetrators will practice using their weapons in order to familiarize themselves with them and to become more proficient (Meloy et al., 2015). In rare instances, perpetrators may use simulation through computer or video games to practice their attacks (Meloy et al., 2015). The perpetrators also may engage in a third category of preparation: probing and boundary pushing (White & Meloy, 2017). In this phase, these individuals push the limits to see how much they can get away with, in some instances even practicing bringing their weapons onto the intended scene without getting caught, or engaging in logistical planning (Borum et al., 1999), such as mapping out their attacks. Perpetrators also may go to multiple locations, scouting which is the best for their attacks (Silver et al., 2018).

The fourth behavior that is part of pre-attack preparation is leakage (White & Meloy, 2017; see also O'Toole, 2000; Meloy & O'Toole, 2011; Reddy et al., 2001; Twemlow et al., 2002). Prior to an attack, perpetrators broadcast their ideas and intentions to others (Knoll & Meloy, 2014; Meloy, 2014; White & Meloy, 2017). Leakage may occur verbally (Cullen, 2009; Daniels, Royster, & Vecchi , 2007), through social media outlets (Nicoletti, 2017), or through other modes of communication (Borum et al., 1999), such as letters, diaries, emails, journals, and voice mails (Daniels et al., 2007; Meloy & O'Toole, 2011; O'Toole, 2000). They also may broadcast their intentions through multiple outlets simultaneously, but in any case, according to Nicoletti (2017), they almost always make their intentions known somehow (see also Meloy et al., 2014). As Silver and colleagues (2018) noted, however, multiple concerning behaviors—leakage being just one—typically predate an attack. Others may include mental health–related concerns and problematic interpersonal interactions, such as conflicts with friends, family, or colleagues at work or school (Silver et al., 2018).

Implementation

If left unaddressed, the aforementioned pre-attack behaviors subsequently culminate in the perpetrator's final act: the shooting itself (White & Meloy, 2017). By the time the threat has escalated to this event threshold, it requires a reactive strategy to minimize the loss of life and end the attack as soon as possible (Nicoletti, 2017). Emphasizing the escalation of the perpetrator within the pathway, however, provides the opportunity for others to engage in de-escalation or even an eradication of the threat before it becomes an actual shooting (Nicoletti, 2017; White & Meloy, 2017). This requires a proactive, rather than reactive, strategy, one that is accomplished through threat assessment, as we discuss later in this chapter.

Tracking Columbine through the Pathway to Violence

Documents like the Columbine Review Commission (2001) report and the evidence and investigation information released by the Jefferson County Sheriff's Office (2000) provide opportunities to better understand the shooting—and, more specifically, what led up to it—through the pathway to violence.

As the model indicates, the desire to commit the attack began earlier with a grievance. For both of the shooters, their grievances stemmed from not fitting in and feeling rejected by their peers (Columbine Review Commission, 2001; Jefferson County Sheriff's Office, 2000). How these grievances manifested, however, was different for each. Shooter H, who was more the leader of the pair, expressed a hatred for mankind, a passion for his own anger, and feelings of superiority (Cullen, 2009; Jefferson County Sheriff's Office, 2000; Schildkraut, 2012b). For Shooter K, the follower, his hatred was more of himself, interwoven between bouts of depression, feelings of isolation, and thoughts of suicide (Columbine Review Commission, 2001; Cullen, 2009; Jefferson County Sheriff's Office, 2000; Schildkraut, 2012b), another important behavioral marker found in school and mass shooters (Meloy et al., 2014). As time progressed, their grievances festered, soon bolstered by violent ideations of exacting revenge on the people they perceived to have wronged them (Jefferson County Sheriff's Office, 2000). By early 1998 (though potentially sooner), they had made the decision to exact revenge by killing those they perceived to be their enemies (Columbine Review Commission, 2001; Jefferson County Sheriff's Office, 2000).

Following this decision, and more than a year before the shooting, the perpetrators began the development of "NBK"—the name they gave to their plan after the movie *Natural Born Killers*. Given that Columbine often is (incorrectly) perceived to be the first of its kind, the shooters did not have much to go off of in terms of learning from previous perpetrators. Instead, they concocted a plan completely unique to their situation. As noted at the onset of this book, Columbine never was intended to be a school shooting but rather a bombing designed to kill hundreds of people. Still, the pair realized that there might be survivors from the blast and subsequently planned to shoot them as they fled. All told, the investigation into the shooting revealed that the planning had begun more than a year before the attack (Columbine Review Commission, 2001; Jefferson County Sheriff's Office, 2000; Larkin, 2009).

Similarly, the perpetrators also began their pre-attack preparation a considerable amount of time before the shooting took place. Their armament process was twofold. First, they acquired four separate weapons—the two shotguns (on which they subsequently sawed the barrels down to six inches in length to increase the spray of the buckshot), the rifle, and the semiautomatic handgun—as well as a considerable amount of ammunition. Their writings indicated, however, that all weapons were acquired before either of the perpetrators had turned 18, meaning that additional planning had to be conducted about how to secure their weaponry (for a detailed discussion of this, see Chapter 8; see also Schildkraut & Hernandez, 2014). The second part of the armament process centered on their arsenal of explosives. Including the two propane tank bombs, the pair had constructed 99 different explosive devices in the time leading up to their attack (Columbine Review Commission, 2001; Jefferson County Sheriff's Office, 2000).

As with the pathway to violence, the shooters did not just acquire their weapons; they also practiced to become more proficient at using them. In a video left behind titled *Rampart Range*, the pair practiced firing the shotguns off in the woods, aiming both at trees and also bowling pins to simulate the human form (Columbine Review Commission, 2001; Jefferson County Sheriff's Office, 2000; Schildkraut, 2012b). The sawing off of the shotguns had made the recoil even greater and required the shooters to practice with them to be able to control the weapons and fire them repeatedly during the actual attack (Jefferson County Sheriff's Office, 2000). They also engaged in planning and preparation (though fantasy did continue through these more logistical steps). Every detail of the day of the attack was intentional: how they intended to suit up, where their weapons and ammunition would be carried on their persons, a series of hand gestures to signal different actions during the rampage, and a step-by-step timeline of the hours leading up to it (Jefferson County Sheriff's Office, 1999). Other writings further indicated that they had spent time surveying the cafeteria's traffic to determine when it would be at its highest capacity—the precise moment at which (11:17 a.m.) they had set the timers on the propane tank bombs to detonate to cause maximum death and injury (Columbine Review Commission, 2001; Jefferson County Sheriff's Office, 1999).

The perpetrators also engaged in a considerable amount of leakage. In addition to their journals, which subsequently were made public during the investigation and detailed more than a year of meticulous planning (Jefferson County Sheriff's Office, 1999; Meloy & O'Toole, 2011), numerous other indicators of their intentions were available. In one class project, Shooter H created a business plan for a hitman and protection services company (Jefferson County Sheriff's Office, 1999). A video production made in conjunction with the project, called *Hitmen for Hire*, showed the perpetrators, dressed in their trench coats, acting out killing scenes with weapons that resembled those used later in the shooting (Larkin, 2009; Schildkraut, 2012b). In a separate class paper submitted two months before the shooting, Shooter K wrote a paper about observing a Columbine-like attack. The paper alerted his teacher, who contacted his parents; she also left a note on his paper: "You are an excellent storyteller, but I have some problems with this one" (Jefferson County Sheriff's Office, 1999, p. 26,523). At one point, Shooter H had showed the *Rampart Range* video—filmed with Columbine's own equipment—to other students in the school's video studio (Columbine Review Commission, 2001). He also chronicled his hatred for mankind generally and his classmates more specifically on his website (Jefferson County Sheriff's Office, 2000).

By the time April 20, 1999, arrived, the shooters had fulfilled nearly every distinct step of the pathway to violence. Their behavior had escalated, as had their actions. The morning of the shooting, they engaged in their final steps: leaving behind video messages to their parents (what Simons and Meloy [2017] called "legacy tokens"), absolving them of any wrongdoing or knowledge of what was to come (Schildkraut, 2012b). It was the only sign of remorse about the attack the two ever would show. Their attack several hours later provided for the completion of the pathway.

The Importance of Threat Assessment

Identifying how the Columbine perpetrators progressed through the pathway to violence allows for a better understanding of when and how opportunities to disrupt the shooting presented themselves. Following the attack, senior FBI profiler Mary Ellen O'Toole (2000) offered a threat assessment perspective to identify other would-be mass shooters based on the lessons learned on April 20, 1999. Threat assessment has been defined as "a fact-based process emphasizing an appraisal of observed (or reasonably observable) behaviors to identify potentially dangerous or violent situations, to assess them, and to manage/address them" (Deisinger, 2016). Since the report was published, other researchers have added to this necessary and growing body of research to help schools and other agencies identify threats and help disrupt these tragedies before they are able to occur. The process of threat assessment involves three critical processes that are separate yet interrelated: (1) identification of the threat, (2) assessment of its risk, and (3) intervention with the individual who has made the threat (Doherty, 2016; Fein & Vossekuil, 1999; Simons & Meloy, 2017). Once the intervention has been put into place, follow-up also must be conducted to assess its effectiveness (Deisinger, 2016).

There are three important principles that underlie the idea of threat assessment (Borum et al., 1999; see also Hinman & Cook, 2001). The first is that acts of targeted violence, like school and mass shootings, are neither spontaneous nor impulsive. They result from a clear process of thinking and behavior. Second, violence is both situational and contextual. It results from a convergence of the potential perpetrators with a target, prior stressors, and the current situational context. Finally, "attack-related" behaviors must be identified in the threat assessment process. These behaviors, which move across a continuum (as illustrated by the pathway-to-violence model discussed earlier), are central to the detection, investigation, and resolution of a threat before the attack occurs (Borum et al., 1999).

Understanding the "Threat" in Threat Assessment

O'Toole (2000) has indicated that one of the most important clues that foreshadows an event like Columbine is leakage, which she notes happens when "a student intentionally or unintentionally reveals clues to feelings, thoughts, fantasies, attitudes, or intentions that may signal an impending violent act" (p. 16). In other words, leakage occurs when an individual communicates their intent to do harm to a third party (Meloy & O'Toole, 2011). Such comments may be *specific* in the details (e.g., time and place of attack), *generalized* (no concrete details offered), or *mixed* (a combination of specific and generalized; Hempel, Meloy, & Richards, 1999).

In her study, O'Toole (2000) identified three types of threats that are used by school shooters (a fourth—the *conditional* threat—was included but is more commonly applied to extortion cases). The first type is *direct* (O'Toole, 2000) and aligns with the specific threat identified by Hempel and colleagues (1999). It is delivered in an overt, straightforward, and explicit fashion and identifies a definitive act and target (O'Toole, 2000): "I am going to shoot up my school on Friday" (see also Meloy, 2014). It is important to note that a direct threat is different than leakage, and both technically can occur in a given scenario. Further, whereas researchers find that leakage occurs in a large majority of cases, only a fraction of the perpetrators actually use direct threats (Fein & Vossekuil, 1999; Hempel et al., 1999; Meloy, 2014; Nicoletti, 2017; Simons & Meloy, 2017). When there is a specific intended target, however, the proportion of direct threats is higher (Silver et al., 2018).

A second and more commonly used type of threat is *indirect*, meaning that the threats likely are covert, unclear, vague, or ambiguous (Meloy, 2014; O'Toole, 2000), much like the generalized threat described by Hempel and colleagues (1999). Indirect threats mask specific details by framing the plot as something that could—but not necessarily *will*—occur (O'Toole, 2000): "If I wanted to, I could kill every student in this school." Finally, threats may be *veiled*: "It would be a shame if something happened at this school." The threat is coded and leaves room for interpretation by the recipient; though it may suggest violence is possible, the message does not contain any explicit intentions (O'Toole, 2000). Regardless of which type is employed, Meloy, Sheridan, and Hoffmann (2008) underscore the importance of taking all threats seriously as action may follow.

Assessing the Threat

Once a threat has been identified, its credibility also must be determined in order to understand what actions must be taken. Accordingly, a starting point is to classify the threat as either *transient* or *substantive* (Cornell et al., 2004). Transient threats are those that lack a legitimate intent to harm another person, such as with careless jokes or statements that are the product of anger (Cornell et al., 2004; Cornell, Sheras, Gregory, & Fan, 2009). Conversely, substantive threats are more serious in nature and center on genuine harm intended for another individual (Cornell et al., 2004, 2009). Moreover, whereas transient threats often are easily resolved at the time they occur, those that are substantive require prolonged protective action to ensure that the danger does not come to fruition (Cornell et al., 2009). When doubt arises as to whether a threat is transient or substantive, it will be treated as the latter to err on the side of caution (Cornell et al., 2004, 2009).

When seeking to identify those threats that are substantive in nature, Cornell and colleagues (2004) suggest that there are five specific indicators that should be considered. First, a threat must have specific and credible details, such as who is the target, where and when the attack may occur, and how it is expected to be carried out (Cornell et al., 2004; O'Toole, 2000). Next, the threat will have been repeated over time or directed toward multiple individuals (Cornell et al., 2004). Further, planning of the attack has taken place or some type of plan has been articulated (Cornell et al., 2004; O'Toole, 2000). Additionally, the plotter will have tried to recruit others to participate in the attack, either as accomplices or witnesses (Cornell et al., 2004). Finally, physical evidence of the attack, such as a weapon, intended victim list, or other written plans, will be present (Cornell et al., 2004; O'Toole, 2000). O'Toole (2000) further contends that when identifying the type of threat an individual has made, the emotional content of the statement, which can provide valuable insight to the individual's mental state, should be considered, as should precipitating stressors that may serve as a provocation for them to act.

Upon report of a threat, information derived from answering a series of questions as part of a triage process is used to determine the imminence of the risk (Deisinger, Randazzo, & Nolan, 2014). Such questions can include (but certainly would not be limited to) whether the individual has developed or implemented plans to harm him- or herself or others, whether other people who know the individual are concerned about possible acts of violence, whether the individual has access to weapons, and if he or she has exhibited any behavior such as the "last resort warning behavior" that signals desperation or distress, either through words or through action, coupled with a necessity of violence (Deisinger et al., 2014; Meloy et al., 2015; see also Doherty, 2016). The information that is gathered subsequently can be used to determine the level of risk an individual may pose (Simons & Meloy, 2017).

O'Toole (2000) suggests that threats will fit into one of three levels of risk: low, medium, and high. *Low-level threats* are vague, indirect, and lack credibility; as such, they pose a minimal risk to public safety because the individual in question is not likely to take action. *Medium-level threats* have the potential of being carried out but are unlikely to be as they lack concrete preparation. Individuals who make these types of threats show signs of consideration about how they would carry out their threat but have failed to take steps toward doing so. Finally, *high-level threats* are those that are direct, credible, and likely imminent. Individuals who make these threats have taken steps toward preparing to carry out a specific plan that poses a serious danger to others (O'Toole, 2000; see also Twemlow et al., 2002).

Table 5.1 Differences between Threat and Risk Assessment

Threat Assessment	Risk Assessment
• Case-specific	• Population-specific
• Target-specific	• Utilizes a structured clinical approach
• The scenario usually is not clinical	
• Goal: protect the target, apprehend the perpetrator	• The scenario is clinical
• Procedure: threat management plan	• Goal: "predict" the likelihood of action and reduce the risk of occurrence
	• Procedure: risk assessment and treatment plan

(Adapted from Borum et al., 1999; Hinman & Cook, 2001; Turner & Gelles, 2003)

Twemlow and colleagues (2002) point out that "assessing threat is not the same as assessing potential for violence" (p. 476). In other words, threat assessment is qualitatively different from risk assessment (a summary of these differences is illustrated in Table 5.1). Accordingly, the overarching goal of the threat assessment process is to identify and subsequently disrupt any act of violence before it is able to come to fruition (Meloy et al., 2011; Simons & Meloy, 2017). Aside from assessing the credibility of a given threat, the means, motive, and method by which an individual could carry out their plan also must be evaluated (Twemlow et al., 2002). The threat assessment process should determine whether the individual in question has access to weapons, has expressed any changes in emotions or interests, has experienced victimization by peers or social groups, or if others have raised concern about the individual's behavior (Twemlow et al., 2002). As Fein and colleagues (2002) assert, "the central question of a threat assessment is whether a student *poses* a threat, not whether the student *made* a threat" (p. 36, emphasis in original). In reality, there are three possibilities in relation to a threat: (1) an individual made a threat but does not pose a threat; (2) an individual made a threat and *does* pose a threat; and (3) no threat has been made but the individual does pose a threat (Borum et al., 1999).

Experts suggest that the best approach to threat assessment is one that involves multidisciplinary teams rather than individuals (Doherty, 2016; Knoll & Meloy, 2014; Simons & Meloy, 2017; Twemlow et al., 2002). These teams should involve school administration (or, in the case of workplaces, human resource departments), law enforcement, mental health professionals, legal services, and other vested stakeholders (Cornell et al., 2004; Doherty, 2016; Simons & Meloy, 2017). Team members work together to determine the level and immediacy of the threat, the person of concern's propensity for violence, and what intervention or response (e.g., gathering more information, deploying a lockdown, arrest) is needed based on the situational factors (Deisinger et al., 2014; Simons & Meloy, 2017). Some school districts, led by the efforts of Virginia, use a two-level system: Level 1 teams (which can include principals or other administrators, school psychologists or counselors, school resource officers, and staff who know the student in question) are on-site at the school and are responsible for screening threats while Level 2 teams include threat assessment professionals who are tasked with conducting a more thorough analysis on those cases deemed more serious and credible (see, generally, Cornell, 2013). Particularly in cases of school shootings, which are infrequent yet likely to be very intense, the use of threat assessment teams has been shown to have considerable prevention potential (Meloy & Hoffmann, 2014).

Managing the Threat

Threat assessment is not a total solution for addressing leaking and other warning behaviors. As Nicoletti (2017) points out, threat assessment often refers to a cross-sectional, point-in-time review of someone's propensity to act. Threat management, on the other hand, seeks to monitor concerns over an extended period of time (Meloy et al., 2011). It also involves developing and implementing plans aimed at neutralizing or eliminating the threat (Meloy et al., 2014). Accordingly, threat management must be used in conjunction with threat assessment to have the greatest preventative power (Nicoletti, 2017; Simons & Meloy, 2017).

Fein and colleagues (2002) suggested that threat management, as it relates to school-based violence, has three key functions. The first function of the process is to control or contain the threat in order to prevent the possibility of an attack. Additional threat management protocols should focus on the protection and oversight of potential targets. The final key function emphasizes helping the student who made the threat successfully deal with their issues by providing support and guidance. Moreover, strategies and threat management plans should address not only short-term concerns but also long-term needs (Fein et al., 2002).

Calhoun and Weston (2003) note that depending on the needs of a student and the situation as a whole, threat management strategies can vary in intensity, from low to high. Monitoring individuals of concern is an example of low-intensity management, whereas disciplinary actions aimed at modifying behavior are indicative of a moderate intensity strategy. Comparatively, expulsion, arrest, or involuntary mental health commitment are examples of high-intensity management practices. Strategies also may combine intensities: status checks and voluntary counseling are considered low-to-moderate intensity, while violence risk assessment, temporary suspension, and mandated mental health evaluations are characteristic of moderate-to-high intensity (Calhoun & Weston, 2003).

Overall, Fein and colleagues (2002) note that "[a]n integrated systems approach can enhance the potential effectiveness of both short- and long-term strategies for managing threatening situations" (p. 73). As such, schools and their threat assessment and threat management teams should work together to create a plan that combines different strategies that meet the needs of the institution and maximize the capabilities and preventative effort of the team as a whole.

Lessons from Averted Rampages

There is an old adage that "good news travels fast; bad news travels faster." In the context of school and mass shootings, this could not be truer. More often than not, when we as a society read a headline or see a news story about one of these events, it is about one that has been completed, not one that has been prevented. While many lessons have been learned from Columbine and other completed attacks, numerous others have also been found in those rampages that did not come to fruition.

When it comes to school and mass shootings, there is a popular belief that the presence of metal detectors, security cameras, locked entryway doors, or school resource officers or other security personnel is sufficient to prevent the attack. The reality, however, is that these proposed solutions do little in the way of deterring these events or their perpetrators (Madfis, 2014b; see also Chapter 6 for further discussion on the securitization of schools). Rather, these protocols give people the impression that something is being done but fail to actually achieve their desired aims.

Instead, researchers (e.g., Daniels et al., 2007, 2010; Madfis, 2014a, 2014b) have found that people in the school and its community are the most likely reporters and thereby the greatest deterrents of mass shootings. As noted, nearly all perpetrators engage in some element of leakage or conveyance of the threat (Nicoletti, 2017; see also Vossekuil et al., 2004). While it has been found that it is most common for at least one person to know about an attack in advance, Vossekuil and colleagues (2004) found that in two-thirds of instances, more than one person knew.

In most instances of averted school shootings, other students are the ones to come forward and report the threat to either school officials or law enforce-ment (Daniels et al., 2007; Madfis, 2014a, 2014b; Vossekuil et al., 2004). This could be students whom the plotters tried to recruit, who had been specific-ally targeted or threatened, who had been told directly about the plan, or who had overheard it being discussed (Daniels et al., 2007; Madfis, 2014b). Madfis (2014b; 2018) found that the more distant students were from the plotter, the more likely they were to report a threat; if the perpetrator was a close friend or confidant, they were less likely to come forward. To a lesser extent, school administrators who were concerned about suspicious behavior or police officers who were notified in some way about the threat also helped to avert the rampage (Daniels et al., 2007).

Still, as Madfis (2014a, 2014b) pointed out, even when attacks are thwarted, it is not because everyone who knew about a plot comes forward (see also Meloy, 2014; O'Toole, 2000). In fact, the number of students who know and do not say anything often exceeds the number of those who do come forward (Madfis, 2014b). A common rationale for not reporting the leakage is that people did not think the plotter was serious (Meloy, 2014; Meloy & O'Toole, 2011). This sentiment also usually surfaces after the attack, when it is too late (Meloy, 2014).

Though it is unknown how many—if any—students specifically knew about Columbine before it happened and failed to say anything despite the clear leakage from the perpetrators, the 2005 shooting at Red Lake High School in Red Lake, Minnesota, provides a valuable point of reference (see, generally, Newman & Fox, 2009). After the school shooting that left seven people dead and five others wounded, it was estimated that upward of 40 people were aware of the plot and failed to come forward (Associated Press, 2006; Davey, 2005; Robertson, 2006). This failure to act actually led several of the shooter's friends to be indicted on conspiracy charges (Meloy & O'Toole, 2011).

So what determines whether a student comes forward or fails to report? The research shows that students are more likely to come forward when the school has a positive culture (Madfis, 2014b). Creating cultures that foster positive relationships between students and their school's faculty and staff, which makes the student feel more invested and connected, encourages them to come forward and report threats as they hear about them (Daniels et al., 2007, 2010; Pollack, Modzeleski, & Rooney, 2008). Conversely, when students anticipate a negative reaction to their reporting, such as being labeled as a "rat" or a "snitch," getting in trouble, or being interrogated themselves, they are less likely to come forward (Madfis, 2014a; 2018; Pollack et al., 2008). In fact, Madfis (2014a) suggests that punitive school policies such as zero tolerance and increased security and surveillance actually can discourage reporting practices by enforcing a "code of silence."

Drawing on these lessons, schools have worked to foster environments and policies that encourage reporting. Aside from working to improve campus climate, schools across the nation have implemented anonymous reporting platforms through various modes, including tip lines, email systems, and apps (Madfis, 2014b; McMillin, 2009; Payne & Elliott, 2011). The state of Colorado, based upon findings of the Columbine Review Commission (2001), led the efforts to create a hotline where people could safely and anonymously report tips (Webb, 2018). Their program, Safe2Tell, was established in 2004 and provided students with a 24-hour-a-day tool to alert the necessary individuals of any concerns over personal safety or known threats to others, initially through a tip line and later expanded to an app and web-based platform (Safe2Tell, n.d.b.).

Since the program's inception, over 30,000 reports have been made, with more than 9,000 coming during the 2016–2017 school year (Safe2Tell, n.d.a.), which was the most recent report at the time of this writing. Since 2014, a handful of other states, including Michigan, Oregon, and Wyoming, have launched similar programs, though many states remain without a standardized platform (Quinton, 2018). Though promising, this gap highlights the need to implement solutions that can produce results. As researchers (Larkin, 2009; Madfis, 2014b; Pollack et al., 2008) have noted, Columbine served as a "wake-up call" about the need to report leakage when it is discovered, but continued efforts to avert similar events must be a focus.

A Note of Caution

Simons and Meloy (2017) point out that it is impossible to say for certain if or when someone will commit an act of targeted violence. As this chapter has indicated, however, learning from events like Columbine provides an important foundation upon which to build prevention strategies. Given the particularly low base rate of events, it often is difficult to anticipate when and where a shooting will occur (Knoll & Meloy, 2014). Still, understanding how the actions and intentions of the perpetrators escalate along the pathway to violence provides opportunities to disrupt these events before they come to fruition (Nicoletti, 2017).

When it comes to threat assessment and management, there is no "one size fits all" approach or any simple solution, as the problem itself is exceedingly complex (Knoll & Meloy, 2014). As O'Toole (2000) pointed out, all threats and threateners are not equal, and most individuals are unlikely to make their warning a reality. Not all credible threats will become a Columbine either. Still, all threats should be taken seriously and evaluated accordingly (O'Toole, 2000). This is why threat assessment and threat management teams are so crucial to prevention efforts. It should be cautioned, however, that threat assessment and management are not methods of predicting violence (Simons & Meloy, 2017). The reality is that these events simply cannot be predicted (Knoll & Meloy, 2014)—but that does not mean that we should not try to prevent them. As Simons and Meloy (2017) so appropriately asserted, "prevention does not require prediction" in order to be successful (p. 628).

CHAPTER SIX

Securing Our Nation's Schools

An unintended consequence of the media coverage of Columbine and subsequent response was that many people believed that school shootings, as statistically rare as they were (and still are; see, generally, Schildkraut, Formica, & Malatras, 2018), were an epidemic (Altheide, 2002; Burns & Crawford, 1999; Muschert, 2007a; Newman & Fox, 2009; Schildkraut, Elsass, & Stafford, 2015; Springhall, 1999; see also Chapter 7). As with other types of crime phenomena, people who are fearful often overestimate their risk of victimization (Warr, 2000). Though often considered to be one and the same, the fear of crime and perceived risk of victimization are actually separate and distinct concepts (Ferraro & LaGrange, 1987), with the former causing the latter (Ferraro, 1995). Therefore, people who are more fearful subsequently take action to reduce their exposure to the problem and, by extension, their (either real or perceived) risk of victimization (Addington, 2009; Warr, 2000).

In the context of the fear over the perceived epidemic of school shootings sparked by Columbine, drastic changes in security-related policies and procedures in schools across the nation were implemented in an attempt to reduce students' opportunities for victimization (Borum, Cornell, Modzeleski, & Jimerson, 2010; Casella, 2003). Many of these practices, however, already had been in place at inner-city schools for some time (Addington, 2009; Kupchik, Brent, & Mowen, 2015). For years prior to the shooting, schools had implemented measures aimed at addressing property crimes like vandalism and graffiti (Lawrence, 2007); in the 1980s more specifically, that focus shifted toward preventing violence by integrating school security guards and metal detectors into safety plans (Crews & Counts, 1997; see also Addington, 2009). Thus, the demand for such protocols in the wake of Columbine represented a focus shift of what was already being used. Now, instead of school violence being primarily a problem for inner cities, the concern and subsequent demand for action represented an expansion of existing protocols to suburban and rural schools (Addington, 2009).

After Columbine, there was a sharp focus on increasing visible security measures in an attempt to prevent future incidents of school violence (Addington, 2009; Birkland & Lawrence, 2009; Crepeau-Hobson, Filaccio, & Gottfried, 2005; Kupchik et al., 2015), despite the fact that educational institutions continued to be (and still are today) one of the safest and most secure places for children (see, generally, Musu-Gillette et al., 2018). In this chapter, we explore these developments, from an increased security presence in the form of police and school resource officers (SROs) to surveillance cameras. Other policies, including (but not limited to) the use of locked or monitored school entries and metal detectors, also are considered in the context of target hardening. We then review other products that have flooded the consumer market, touting their ability to improve survivability in a school or mass shooting. The discussion then shifts to what we do know works—door locks and associated lockdown drills—and why it is necessary for schools to have each in place. Finally, we consider how the conversation about school safety and security has shifted since Columbine and in what direction it needs to move as we move forward from the 20th anniversary.

The "Two Cs"

Of those visible security measures that were implemented after Columbine, the "two Cs"—cops and cameras—were among the most popular (Addington, 2009; see also Birkland & Lawrence, 2009; Borum et al., 2010; Kupchik et al., 2015; Newman, Fox, Harding, Mehta, & Roth, 2004; Snell, Bailey, Carona, & Mebane, 2002). A number of studies (e.g., Crepeau-Hobson et al., 2005; see also Birkland & Lawrence, 2009; Lewis, 2003; Musu-Gillette et al., 2018; Snell et al., 2002) reported a significant increase in the presence of security personnel on school campuses around the nation, due largely in part to Columbine and the pressure from different stakeholders (e.g., parents, school administrators, and politicians) to do something. These included not only law enforcement but also private security and SROs (Addington, 2009). The U.S. Department of Education (2007), for example, reported that 45% of school administrators surveyed indicated they had either police or security officers present on campus during the 2003–2004 school year. Between 1999 (the school year immediately following Columbine) and 2005, Dinkes, Cataldi, Lin-Kelly, and Snyder (2007) found a 14% increase in the number of students who reported the presence of security personnel at their school, a figure that remained relatively stable through the 2015–2016 school year (Musu-Gillette et al., 2018; see also Figure 6.1).

Before leaving office in 2001, then-President Bill Clinton, who was the commander in chief when Columbine occurred, allocated more than $60

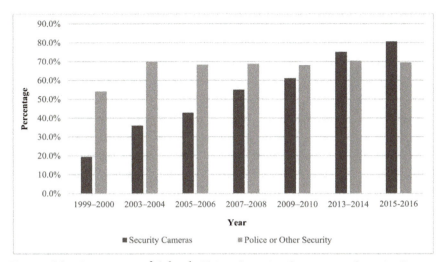

Figure 6.1   Percentage of Schools Using Security Cameras or Security Personnel. (Data imputed from Musu-Gillette et al., 2018 [Table 20.1—Security Cameras; Table 21.1—Security Officers]) NOTE: Data for security cameras derived from school administrators as part of the School Survey on Crime and Safety report. Data for school security officers based on School Crime Supplement of the National Crime Victimization Survey as reported by students ages 12–18 (Musu-Gillette et al., 2018).

million in federal funding to hire 452 school-based security officers as part of an initiative from the Office of Community Policing Services (COPS; Juvonen, 2001). By 2005, the COPS program had funded more than 6,100 SROs to the tune of $700 million (McDevitt & Panniello, 2005). Since then, additional funding has been offered to continue the trend of security personnel in schools. In 2013, shortly after the Sandy Hook Elementary School shooting, $45 million was awarded to create positions for 356 new SROs (U.S. Department of Justice, 2014); 166 new positions (valued at more than $22 million) were funded in 2014 (Office of Community Policing Services, n.d.a.). An additional 128 positions were created in 2015 through nearly $15 million in grants (Office of Community Policing Services, n.d.b.); 59 positions were created in 2016 at a value of nearly $74 million (Office of Community Policing Services, n.d.c.); and 16 positions, funded for nearly $20 million, were established in 2017 (Office of Community Policing Services, n.d.d.). Additional funding opportunities also have been presented through state-based initiatives, particularly in light of the 2018 shooting at Marjory Stoneman Douglas High School in Parkland, Florida (see, generally, Pennsylvania Department of Education, 2018; WRIC Newsroom, 2018).

Surveillance cameras were another form of visible surveillance that were heavily adopted after Columbine (Addington, 2009; Altheide, 2009; Kupchik et al., 2015; Lewis, 2003; Snell et al., 2002). Unlike school security personnel, which maintained a steady presence in the aftermath of the shooting, the use of surveillance cameras grew markedly in the years that followed. Musu-Gillette and colleagues (2018) reported that in the academic year following Columbine (1999–2000), just 19% of public schools used security cameras (see also Birkland & Lawrence, 2009; Dinkes et al., 2007). Over time, that proportion increased, reaching over 80% usage in schools by the 2015–2016 academic year (Musu-Gillette et al., 2018; see also Centers for Disease Control, 2017; Dinkes et al., 2007; Schwartz et al., 2016). Like school security personnel, the increase in cameras was due, at least in part, to a corresponding availability of federal funding to support the installation of such equipment (Addington, 2009).

Despite their considerable popularity, the reliance on security guards and surveillance cameras has been met with two important obstacles. The first is that even with the available federal funding, the implementation of either or both protocols represents a significant financial commitment from the school (Addington, 2009; Casella, 2003). Funding provided by the COPS program, for example, covers up to 75% of salaries and benefits for a school security employee for up to three years (Office of Community Policing Services, 2017). Furthermore, as a contingency of the grant, departments who receive COPS funding are required to retain all persons hired under the program for an additional 12 months after the 3-year period is up (Office of Community Policing Services, 2017). This means that schools are required to not only pay a minimum of 25% of a SRO's salary for three years, but they also incur the expense of the full pay for an additional year. Estimates put the cost of a school resource officer between $50,000 and $80,000 per year in salary alone, excluding fringe benefits (Hill, 2013). Similarly, grants to provide surveillance cameras for schools cover the equipment but not the necessary manpower to monitor them, additional costs for which the institutions administration must account (Casella, 2003). While this is not to say that these are not worthwhile expenses, all considerations (such as the return on investment and the acknowledgment that no two schools' needs are the same) must be weighed when deciding if this is the best practice for the institution.

Second, there is the fact that there was (and effectively still is) no evidence to support that either school security personnel or security cameras are effective in reducing school violence (Addington, 2009; Birkland & Lawrence, 2009; Gagnon & Leone, 2001; May, Fessel, & Means, 2004; Peterson, Larson, & Skiba, 2001; Schwartz et al., 2016). In fact, only one study that was published the year Columbine occurred assesses the impact of SROs on school crime. In her study, Johnson (1999) found that both major and minor crimes in the district, as measured by the number of corresponding suspensions, were lower after the SRO program was implemented. Her study, however, could not account for the already declining crime rate in schools before the SRO program began (May et al., 2004) and also did not address school shootings, which are one of the primary reasons that the use of protocols discussed in this section increased.

Even in nearly 20 years, no other study has analyzed the specific impact of SROs on school crime, which is all the more concerning given the significant expenditures made on this practice and the mass utilization of these individuals in districts across the nation. In lieu of such an assessment, other researchers have instead examined the perceptions of these programs, as well as surveillance cameras. In one report commissioned by the National Association of School Resource Officers (NASRO), 99% of the SROs surveyed believed their presence increased school safety, with a majority expressing that their presence on campuses also improved crime reporting (Trump, 2001); the latter proposition, however, has not been tested. In a separate study that examined public school administrators' perceptions of their SRO program, May and colleagues (2004) found that the majority reported that the possession (81%) and use (86%) of handguns on their campuses had stayed the same, rather than going down in occurrence, since the policy was implemented. Of the remaining 14 offenses analyzed, only fighting seemed to have a marked change after the SRO implementation—nearly 63% of administrators indicated that it decreased while 34% stated it stayed the same (May et al., 2004). Garcia (2003) found in a survey of school administrators that, despite a clear lack of evidence, security cameras were perceived to be the most effective and were the most widely used protocol in the districts surveyed (see also Schwartz et al., 2016). (It should be noted that in a separate study by Gill [2014], not only did security cameras not deter would-be offenders but they actually were found to escalate the perpetrator's actions.) Still, Gagnon and Leone (2001) reported that students are likely to report feeling less safe the more that physical surveillance (e.g., cameras and metal detectors, which we discuss in the next section) and security personnel (SROs) are present (see also Addington, 2009; Madfis, 2018; Peterson et al., 2001).

As noted, the sustainability of SRO programs and the influx of surveillance cameras in schools were largely influenced by the perceptions of safety following the Columbine shooting. Yet, as Kupchik (2010) astutely notes, both protocols were in place in the school on April 20, 1999 (see also Columbine Review Commission, 2001). As discussed in Chapter 4, SRO and Sheriff's Deputy Neil Gardner engaged with the shooters but failed to stop them or enter the school (due primarily to law enforcement protocols on the day of the attack). Further, the surveillance camera in the cafeteria did little more than perpetuate the shooters' fame (see, generally, Chapter 3) when stills of them in the midst of their attack were plastered across the media (*TIME*, 1999b; see also Gibbs & Roche, 1999). In sum, regardless of their perceived effectiveness, both had little bearing as a deterrent to Columbine (Kupchik, 2010) or other similar events.

More Target Hardening

For many, schools (among other locations) are viewed as "soft targets" (Greenberg, 2007; Hesterman, 2015). This means that they are "civilian-centric"—there is a large concentration of people in locations that are not typically fortified, ultimately leaving them vulnerable, unprotected, and not fully defended (Hesterman, 2015, p. 1). As a result, this type of location is often more attractive to perpetrators, such as school and mass shooters, because they are less likely to encounter any resistance as they carry out their attacks. Subsequently, in the aftermath of Columbine, many proposals called for the hardening of schools (targets) to make them less vulnerable to a would-be offender (Hesterman, 2015; see also Clarke, 1997; Hough, 1987; Pratt & Turanovic, 2016). The security personnel discussed in the prior section are one example of target hardening; schools across the nation also have employed additional methods in the wake of the shooting in an attempt to make their institutions safer.

Metal Detectors

Security devices such as metal detectors—both handheld wands and fixed walk-through devices—have been more visible in schools since the 1980s push to get tough on crime (Crews & Counts, 1997; see also Addington, 2009; Borum et al., 2010). Still, these efforts were concentrated in major urban areas (e.g., Chicago, Boston, and New York) where violence in schools was of particular concern. Indeed, these cities have experienced some (though not total) success in terms of a reduction of unwanted weapons in schools (Algar, 2016; see also Corcoran, 2015; Moore, Petrie, Braga, & McLaughlin, 2003; Winn, 2017), though there also have been instances where such devices have failed to work as intended, even letting through weapons that later were used in attacks (see, generally, National School Safety and Security Services, n.d.).

In 1994, approximately 10% of schools employed metal detectors in their institutions (Birkland & Lawrence, 2009). Since then, use of these devices has held or decreased slightly, depending on the report (see, generally, Dinkes et al., 2007; Musu-Gillette et al., 2018; Snell et al., 2002; U.S. Department of Education, 2007), though a slight increase was observed after Columbine (Lewis, 2003) and again after Sandy Hook (Winn, 2018). In schools with such devices, random checks of students are considerably more common than requiring them to pass through the detectors daily (Garcia, 2003; Musu-Gillette et al., 2018; Schwartz et al., 2016). Since the Parkland shooting, there have been renewed calls to install metal detectors in schools across the nation (see, generally, Travis, 2018), though it is unclear yet as to what impact the attack may have on the use of such devices.

Practically speaking, however, there are a number of drawbacks of these devices. First, the costs associated with metal detectors are a significant concern. Many schools cannot afford the initial investment for even one machine for the front entrance, let alone multiple entry points in a school (Winn, 2018). There also is the cost of the personnel to operate them (Green, 1999; Lohman, 2006). As Winn (2018) noted, each metal detecting station typically requires multiple people be in place—the screener of the initial check, someone to perform backup checks (e.g., with a wand) if a person fails the first screening, someone to check bags, and someone, typically an armed officer, to oversee everything (see also Schneider, 2001). Further, these scans cannot only take place at school start times; security checkpoints are recommended to run during the full school day to avoid the perception of weaknesses or laxed security protocols (Green, 1999; Winn, 2018).

In addition to cost, there also is the time component. The entire screening process is particularly slow to complete (Lohman, 2006). In schools with larger enrollments, this can lead to a delay in starting times or, in the case of some campuses in New York City, the need for creative scheduling in terms of staggered first periods to accommodate everyone (Green, 1999; Schneider, 2001). In a review of practices in New York City for the 2014–2015 school year, for example, WNYC (2015) found that 193 public high schools across the five boroughs had metal detectors in 68 buildings. Consequently, more than 91,000 high school students (not counting absenteeism) alone passed through these devices daily (WNYC, 2015). The return on investment, however, has been low. Assuming that every student was scanned in each day, the data show that in New York City schools, the searches returned just one dangerous item for every 23,034 students scanned (WNYC, 2015). While few other schools and districts would see this level of traffic, the fact that the practice is time consuming in general still must be considered, particularly in relation to the outcome it produces.

Moreover, the effectiveness of the protocol must be considered. As National School Safety and Security Services (n.d.) advises, "school metal detectors . . . [are] only as strong as the human elements behind the machines" (para. 27; see also Lohman, 2006). In the past, schools have been found to not be running these devices according to district and industry standards, have turned machines off and still passed students through, or have operated machines they knew to be broken; a lack of training also has been a concern (National School Safety and Security Services, n.d.; see also Daniels, Royster, & Vecchi, 2007). Conversely, schools have had greater success in detecting weapons with practices beyond metal detectors. In one school year, New York City schools reported that 57% of the weapons they confiscated were recovered without the use of such devices (Winn, 2017). The effectiveness—or lack thereof—of metal detector screenings for weapons even has been reviewed more broadly in the context of airports (Greenblatt, 2012; Halsey, 2015); fail rates neared 80% as recently as 2017 (Lardieri, 2017), with some individual airports as high as 95% (Blake, 2017).

Several cases also illustrate how metal detectors have been insufficient to stop school and mass shootings (see, generally, Nedzel, 2014). A standing detection unit was present at Red Lake High School in 2005 and was manned by an unarmed security guard (Connolly & Harris, 2005; "School gunman," 2005). The perpetrator shot and killed the guard and entered the school through the metal detector with three guns (Connolly & Harris, 2005). In 2013, a gunman shot his way past the security checkpoint—including metal detectors—at Los Angeles International Airport (Associated Press, 2013). One TSA officer was killed and two others wounded before the gunman was taken into custody following a shootout with police in the terminal (Associated Press, 2013).

Finally, while the visual presence of metal detectors may put people at ease because they can see that something, despite questions of effectiveness, is being done, it simultaneously has the potential to send the wrong message (Hankin, Hertz, & Simon, 2011; Schwartz et al., 2016; Winn, 2018). Researchers (e.g., Cornell, 2015; Gastic, 2011; Perumean-Chaney & Sutton, 2013) have found that the presence of metal detectors actually makes students feel *less* safe at school. Similarly, Mayer and Leone (1999) found that students whose schools employ these devices were more likely to perceive violence and disorder on their campus.

Critics also have argued that the use of metal detectors in schools is a largely discriminatory practice as they are more frequently installed in those institutions with more students of color (Touré, 2018; Winn, 2017, 2018). Reports for New York City schools, for example, show that approximately 48% of black and 38% of Latino/a high school students pass through metal detectors each year, as compared to just 14% of white students (WNYC, 2015). More students in the Bronx and Brooklyn, where populations are skewed more toward nonwhites, pass through metal detectors than in Manhattan or Queens (WNYC, 2015). Concerns also have been raised about the constitutionality of metal detector searches in schools and whether they infringe upon students' Fourth Amendment protections (see, generally, Berger, 2002; Nance, 2014). In sum, there are many considerations that must be weighed by administrators when determining whether or not to install metal detectors or other similar devices in their schools.

Entry Control

One of the more popular forms of target hardening comes in the form of controlled building access, primarily related to schools' main entryways. In the academic year after Columbine, three out of every four schools utilized such a protocol; nearly 20 years later, it is used in more than 94% of schools nationwide (Musu-Gillette et al., 2018; see also Dinkes et al., 2007; Schwartz et al., 2016). Entry control has two overarching goals: prevention and mitigation (Spicer, 2013). Through its various features, it can prevent unwanted individuals from entering the school; it also should mitigate that person's ability to access the building (Spicer, 2013).

The practice of entry control draws its inspiration from the theory of crime prevention through environmental design (CPTED), a concept introduced by Jeffrey (1971) whose practical applications are based on the work of Newman (1972, 1973) on defensible space. The overarching goal of CPTED is to prevent crime proactively through the design or modification of environments, thereby reducing the opportunities for such infractions to occur (Cozens, 2011). According to Newman (1973), defensible spaces, which are fostered through CPTED, have "real and symbolic barriers, strongly-defined areas of influence, and improved opportunities for surveillance; that combine to bring an environment under the control of its residents" (p. 3; see also Armitage, 2017; Cozens, 2011).

Among the main concepts of CPTED are territoriality, natural surveillance, and access control (Armitage, 2017; Cozens, 2011). *Territoriality* (a symbolic rather than physical barrier) reinforces a sense of ownership among users of the space. In return, these individuals have a greater investment in keeping the space safe because they view it as their own. *Natural surveillance*, which may occur either formally (active) or informally (passive), is important because it gives people the perception that they are being observed; as a result, they are less likely to engage in crime. Finally, *access control* is achieved by limiting the opportunities for an individual to converge with intended targets, often by restricting entry into buildings or specific rooms within them (Armitage, 2017; Cozens, 2011; Newman, 1972, 1973).

When designing safe and secure entrances, schools have relied on these three principles, either individually or collectively, to guide their efforts (Spicer, 2013; see also Green, 1999). Several techniques, such as single-entry points and visitor management systems, incorporate all three. Utilizing single entry points, often through the main set of doors at the front of the school (which is usually also closest to the administration office), allows for everyone who enters and exits the building to be monitored more easily. This enables the staff to more easily determine who is not supposed to be in the school (deploying a sense of territoriality) by employing natural surveillance through access control. Similarly, management systems that require visitors to present identification, sign in, receive guest badges, and be escorted through the school to their intended location (a form of access control in its own right) also highlights territoriality through monitoring efforts (Spicer, 2013).

Other practices implemented in schools also address several of the key concepts of CPTED (Spicer, 2013). Vestibule-type entries that allow visitors to enter one set of doors into a waiting area, where they connect with someone in the main office who grants them access into the building. An alternate form of double-entry protocols requires guests to be buzzed in from the outside, enter into the main office, check in, and proceed from there. These types of entry promote both territoriality (keeping out anyone who does not belong) and access control (regulating who does get to come in), as does the electronic entry technologies—which may be in the form of key cards, biometric scans, buzzer systems, entry pads, or even telephones or video intercoms that connect with the main office—that are incorporated in the process. Similarly, the structure of the door entry itself also incorporates both access control and territoriality. The vertical element that connects the two doors, called a center mullion, must be sturdy to help maintain the integrity of the entryway. Further, it is important these and all entry point doors remain locked (see, for example, Goodrum & Woodward, 2016, who report that the 2013 Arapahoe High School shooter gained entry through an unlocked door that was not the building's main access point); the handles or push bar devices should sit flush with the doors to prevent them from being bound together in a way that would delay law enforcement (Spicer, 2013; see also Virginia Tech Review Panel, 2007).

A final component of school entry points is a topic of greater debate. Many schools, Columbine included, utilize large windows and glass-paneled doors at their main entries. While they promote an open and welcoming environment and provide an opportunity for greater natural surveillance, they also create additional vulnerabilities for the school (Spicer, 2013), as exemplified by the shooting at Sandy Hook Elementary School in 2012. Though the school had multiple layers of security—a double-entry system with intermediate vestibule, electronic locking mechanism to automatically secure the doors at the start of the school day, a call box, and buzzer system with video camera—what it also had were plate glass windows that surrounded the entryway, which the perpetrator ultimately shot through and gained access to the building (Sedensky, 2013). Security experts recommend that entry windows be a minimum of 72 inches above ground level and, if below such height, are no more than 12 inches wide; security film also should be installed as an added reinforcement (Spicer, 2013). Doing so will help to limit access through territoriality.

The attack at Sandy Hook provides important insight into how school entry systems, even when designed with the best of intentions, can be defeated by a school or mass shooter. This is neither to say that access controls cannot mitigate the risk of an active shooter, nor that they do not have other benefits for the schools. Access control procedures, including checking in with the main office, can help with unwanted visitors, including sex offenders, known gang members, barred parents, and others who should not have access to the school (LaRowe & Raible, 2017). On the flip side of the coin, however, it is important to be mindful that if the goal of implementing these practices is to minimize school shootings, they likely will be ineffective for one key reason—the perpetrator will more often than not be a student at the school and therefore will be inside before the main entry locks and would not be flagged as someone who did not belong in the building. Thus, it is important to consider all scenarios—not just the most extreme—when deciding whether or not such a system is a good fit for a particular institution and which of the practices may yield the greatest results.

Arming the Educators

Perhaps one of the most controversial proposals to enter the discussion is to arm teachers. Proponents of such an idea, such as Wayne LaPierre, executive vice president and CEO of the National Rifle Association (NRA), argue that "the only thing that stops a bad guy with a gun is a good guy with a gun" ("Remarks," 2012; see also Nedzel, 2014), a rationale that has been used not only to support the arming of teachers but an increase in armed school security personnel as well (Kupchik et al., 2015). Those who stand in opposition of the policy assert that guns have no place in the academic setting (Strauss, 2012). Teachers overwhelmingly express that arming educators is a bad idea and, when presented with the choice, indicate that they would not carry if they were permitted to (e.g., Husser, Usry, Anderson, & Covington, 2018).

Regardless of where one's personal or political opinion on the matter lands as to whether or not arming teachers is a viable solution, there remain practical considerations to be accounted for when deciding whether or not to employ such a policy. Concern exists about firearms falling into the wrong hands, which could have the unintended consequence of increasing gun-related deaths in schools (Husser et al., 2018; see also Hansen, 2018). Similarly, the potential for accidental discharges increases with so many students and teachers in close proximity (Ciamacca, 2018), examples of which have emerged in recent school years. A month after the Parkland shooting, for instance, a gun discharged during a firearms safety course in a California high school, leaving three students injured (Ortiz, 2018); other examples soon followed in the news. Moreover, the impact that the presence of firearms has on the general learning environment is a concern (Husser et al., 2018), particularly as it may interfere with the fostering of relationships between students and their educators (Ciamacca, 2018). When polled, teachers also indicated that they believed that few, if any, of their colleagues could reliably stop a school shooting if they were armed (Husser et al., 2018).

Another consideration that should be accounted for is that no evidence exists that the presence of an armed individual would deter a school or mass shooter (Hansen, 2018). As was discussed in both Chapters 1 and 4, armed individuals—first the SRO and then responding law enforcement—were on scene at Columbine and that did not stop the attack. Similarly, 33 years earlier, armed civilians engaged with the shooter at the University of Texas but, while effective in distracting him, were unable to bring the attack to an end (Watkins, 2016). Furthermore, civilians have been more successful in bringing active-shooter situations to an end without the presence of a weapon. In 51 school shootings occurring between 2000 and 2016, 19 of the perpetrators were physically subdued by an unarmed civilian; not one attack was terminated by an armed civilian pulling and firing their gun (ALERRT, n.d.b.).

The potential for an individual to be able to accurately fire a gun in a stressful, high stakes situation like a school or mass shooting also must factor into the decision of whether to arm teachers. The ability to shoot a gun accurately is highly contingent on the body's nervous and mechanical systems (Vila & Morrison, 1994). In order to achieve the necessary steadiness and hand-eye coordination needed to accurately fire at the intended target, significant demands are placed on the person's nervous, muscular, and skeletal systems. These demands are only further heightened during an active-shooter incident, making it all the more difficult to achieve such needed accuracy (The Editors, 2018; Vila & Morrison, 1994).

Armed civilians aside for a moment, the examination of shooting accuracy by law enforcement officers paints an equally concerning picture. For more than 100 years, firearms training for police has increased in both quality and quantity; similarly, the quality of service weapons also has improved (Vila & Morrison, 1994). Nonetheless, the ability for officers to hit their targets in high-stakes combat-like situations has shown little improvement (Vila & Morrison, 1994). Morrison (2006) found that over more than two decades, despite training advancements, bullet hit rates lingered around one in five (or 20%). In a more recent study of the New York City Police Department (NYPD), Rostker and colleagues (2008) found that when a perpetrator was not shooting back at the officer, their accuracy rate was just 30%. When the suspect was returning fire, the average hit rate decreased to 18% (Rostker et al., 2008). A case involving the NYPD highlights this issue in practice. In 2012, a man shot and killed his former coworker outside the entrance to the Empire State Building (Ariosto, 2012). Two NYPD officers who were nearby engaged the suspect, ultimately killing him. In the process, however, they wounded nine bystanders who were nearby on the crowded street (Ariosto, 2012).

Proponents of arming teachers (and concealed carry more generally) often point to the 2007 shooting at a Colorado Springs, Colorado, church as an example of how a "good guy [or gal, in this case] with a gun" can stop a bad guy. When an armed perpetrator entered the church after shooting four members of a family in the parking lot, killing two, he continued firing, injuring two others (Johnson & Frosch, 2007). Churchgoer Jeanne Assam, a pistol permit holder, retrieved her weapon and fired on the shooter, wounding him (he subsequently committed suicide). What often escapes the discussion of this example, however, is that Assam was a former police officer with considerable training to fire her weapon in a tactical situation and not just an average civilian (The Denver Post, 2007).

Research also has found that even in active-shooter training simulations, police officers hit their intended target less than 20% of the time (Hansen, 2018). Even in the best of scenarios, educators who receive considerable firearms training are still likely to produce even lower accuracy rates (Hansen, 2018). Accordingly, while it is not our position to advocate either for or against the arming of teachers, it is important that all relevant pieces of information be considered and that those in decision-making capacities allow the data to speak for themselves. When attempting to create response strategies to be deployed in high-stress, high-stakes situations like school or mass shootings, the question that must be asked is whether any intended proposals have the potential to increase the lethality of the event rather than save lives.

School Security as a Big Business

Despite their statistical rarity, school shootings have sparked a fear that has translated into what security expert Kenneth Trump calls "a feeding frenzy" for consumer products (in Abramsky, 2016; Ma, 2018). In fact, the education sector of the security industry has been booming since high-profile shootings like Sandy Hook and Parkland—and continues to do so to this day. In 2014, an estimated $768 million had been spent on school security products (Abramsky, 2016); three years later, expenditures topped $2.7 billion, with steady continual growth projected (Dearing, 2018; Ma, 2018). Companies keep churning out products, and schools, in an effort to do something (even if it is not the most effective something), snap them up.

Among the most popular products are those that are touted as bulletproof. Some examples include backpacks, either made of bulletproof material (BulletBlocker, n.d.) or generic materials supplemented with ballistic panels (Hsu, 2018; see also Lansat, 2018); bulletproof whiteboards (Frankel, 2014); bulletproof clipboards (Lansat, 2018); bulletproof glass and window films (Rock, 2018); ballistic shelters in schools (Hsu, 2018); designer bulletproof clothing (Yurkevich, 2017); and even bulletproof underwear, designed to protect the groin region from shrapnel, have hit the market (Lendon, 2010). This, however, is merely scratching the surface; the list seems endless.

The associated costs are astronomical. Ballistic panels for bulletproof backpacks were for sale in one Florida school's bookstore for $120 each (Hess, 2017). The backpacks themselves range in price from $200 to $500 (Golgowski, 2018). The bulletproof whiteboards retail for anywhere between $399 and $999, depending on the size and level of protection (handgun versus assault rifle; Hardwire, n.d.). One classroom ballistic shelter at an Oklahoma elementary school, designed to hold 20 students, cost $20,000; bunkers can be designed to any size and shape modifications, with pricing varying accordingly (Garfield, 2018). "Blast boxers" sell for $86 per pair (Lendon, 2010), while one company's bulletproof tank tops retail for $1,500 and are their top seller with world leaders (Yurkevich, 2017).

Yet despite the costs, consumers have continued to eat it up. Amendment II, a bulletproof backpack company, reported that just one week after Sandy Hook, sales had spiked 500% (Russell, 2013). After Parkland, their competitor, BulletBlocker, reported a 400% increase in sales (Visram, 2018); annually, they have seen steady gains of between 35 and 40% (Stein & Cherkis, 2017). Another security company in Central Florida also reported a 150% increase in sales within a week of the Parkland shooting (Golgowski, 2013). Certain companies have sold out of their bulletproof backpack stock well in advance of upcoming academic years (Golgowski, 2018; Lansat, 2018). Other bulletproof products have shared in the success. In 2013, for example, the University of Maryland Eastern Shore purchased 200 personal-sized whiteboards for $60,000, with other schools making similar investments into the devices (Connor, 2013).

While these products may provide a visual representation that something is being done, the problem remains that not only are these lacking any evidence of their effectiveness, commonsense reviews show why they would not work during a shooting. The bulletproof whiteboards are just 18 inches by 20 inches (Hardwire, n.d.). Touted as being able to withstand a shotgun blast from a foot away and intended to be used as shields (Cloud, 2014), these whiteboards fail to provide full body coverage, meaning that there is more of a person exposed than is shielded behind the device. The same is true for backpacks, which are roughly the same dimensions, if not a few inches smaller (BulletBlocker, n.d.), as well as newer products such as ballistic seat cushions, ring binder inserts, desk calendars, and iPad cases (Lansat, 2018). Similarly, several streams of bulletproof products, such as the backpacks and seat cushions, are rated as soft body armor, meaning that although they should be able to stop bullets from a handgun, they are ineffective against assault-style rifles like those used at Sandy Hook and Parkland (Golgowski, 2018). Even the maker of bullet-resistant films noted that when applied over normal windows (those that have not been glazed with polycarbonate), they are in no way bullet*proof* (Schachter, 2018; Scott, 2018). Concerns also have been raised for such films; they have been found to be problematic because they can trap people inside a location during an emergency when they are unable to break the window (Hsu, 2018).

Other products beyond the bulletproof commodities also have entered the market. Panic buttons have found considerable success in school markets, particularly after the Virginia Tech shooting in 2007 (Rasmussen & Johnson,

2008). In fact, Garcia (2003) found that they are the preferred device to be used in K–12 schools. The idea behind the technology is that, when activated, they alert police to the location of the situation (Schneider, 2001), providing instant emergency response (Levkulich, 2014). Aside from the fact that the rapid nature of school and mass shootings largely renders the technology useless, as the event is over before police can respond (Petrosino, Fellow, & Brensilber, 1997), they have been found not to be useful in other mass shootings, namely the 2013 Los Angeles International Airport attack discussed earlier, because several of the devices were nonoperational ("Phone system," 2014). Still, despite the evidence, the school district in which Santa Fe High School is located voted to spend $650,000 installing the technology in the school following the May 18, 2018 shooting—also despite the fact that no single location ever has been the site of multiple mass shootings (Langford, 2018).

Recognizing the need to be able to secure doors quickly and effectively, a number of different devices have been introduced to fill the void (see, for example, Rawdon, 2014; Reinwald, 2014; Slinger, 2014). While seemingly effective, concerns have been raised over the need for specialized training to be able to deploy them efficiently in times of crisis (Welsh-Huggins, 2015) and potential conflicts with building and fire codes (Visram, 2018). Automatic lockdown systems that secure all doors with the push of a button also have been sought out by schools and districts (Forman, 2014; Peterson, 2014; Schneider, 2010). Such devices, however, are particularly expensive, require power to operate (thus would be inoperable during an outage, which could accompany serious emergencies), and present unforeseen yet inherent technical challenges (Schneider, 2010). Additionally, malfunctions in certain crises, such as school fires, could have deadly consequences (Schildkraut & Elsass, 2016). Still, the devices are sold at record rates; other products, including gunfire detection systems that immediately notify the police (even before 911 calls are placed) also have enjoyed success in the consumer market (Moreno, 2018; see also Noonan, 2018, who reports that the market shares for leading company of the technology, ShotSpotter, rose 170% in the first half of 2018), again despite the statistical unlikelihood of actually needing it.

As security experts have noted, there is a marked difference between feeling safe and actually being safe (Connor, 2013), and the products discussed here have led to serious questions being raised as to whether or not they can actually protect people in times of crisis (Golgowski, 2018; Stein & Cherkis, 2017). Undoubtedly, the financial rewards reaped from their introduction have been predicated solely on the fear that has been ingrained in parents and school administrators about the safety of children in education institutions. Security expert Gregory Thomas has cautioned, however, that "'feel-good' solutions like armored book bags and other bulletproof products don't hurt anything but the wallet" (in Connor, 2013). In his professional opinion, preventative efforts—as we discuss in the next section—are more effective than any of the consumer products discussed here and should be the focus of efforts to make schools and the people inside them safer (Connor, 2013).

Drilling the Fundamentals of Preparedness

At a 2017 symposium held at Columbine, Lieutenant Brian Murphy of the Oak Creek, Wisconsin, police department recounted his experiences responding to the August 5, 2012, shooting at a Sikh temple in his town. During his presentation, he reminded the audience that "what you do every day is what you will do under stress" (Murphy, 2017). As has been noted elsewhere in this chapter, during especially tense and stressful situations like active shooter events, individuals tend to lose fine motor skills, struggle with impaired vision (tunnel vision), and also may have trouble with decision making. In the absence of a recallable plan, panic can set in, which ultimately can lead to poor decision making and potentially catastrophic consequences (Johnson et al., 2016). Thus, having that plan in place and training it until it becomes a form of muscle memory is imperative for improving survivability during a school or mass shooting.

One of the earliest training models was offered by the ALERRT Center beginning in 2004. Avoid, deny, defend—or ADD for short—is an easy-to-remember method that individuals can use during an active-shooter event or other violent situation to help respond (ALERRT, n.d.c.). The first part of the concept, *avoid*, requires that individuals put as much distance as possible between themselves and the threat. Situational awareness is critical, as is having an exit plan. If it is not possible to get away from the threat, the next option is to *deny* them access to the individual. The goal remains the same—put distance between the threat and the individual—but this is accomplished through creating barriers. Individuals should get to a secure location, engage locking devices (discussed further in the next section), turn off all lights, and remain out of the line of sight as much as possible. Finally, in a last-resort situation, individuals should be prepared to *defend* themselves against the threat. In such a situation, survival is the ultimate goal, and any necessary means should be employed to achieve such an end. In all three steps, the knowledge of one's surroundings is a critical component in determining which action is the best to employ; thus, situational awareness becomes all the more important (ALERRT, n.d.c.).

A similar concept was introduced by the Houston Police Department several years later. "Run, Hide, Fight" shares many of the same concepts with ADD. When it is safe to do so, it suggests that individuals *run* and flee a scene (Harrington, 2018), similar to the avoid concept. If escape is not an option, individuals are encouraged to *hide* (similar to deny) or shelter in place. Individuals are encouraged to *fight* if the shooter finds them and there are no other options; like defend, it requires people to do whatever is necessary in the face of danger. A byproduct of a partnership with the Department of Homeland Security, Run, Hide, Fight has gained considerable attention since its inception (Harrington, 2018). Still, it is not without its critics. Some suggest that the protocol takes a more passive approach to active shooter situations and does not sufficiently account for the realities of such an attack (Wood, 2016). It further assumes that people will engage in these actions in a linear fashion, which can be problematic if the scene is not safe for a person to run (Wood, 2016).

Both strategies have been adopted at variable frequencies in schools across the nation. Other protocols, such as A.L.I.C.E. (which stands for alert, lockdown, inform, counter, and evacuate), also emerged after Columbine and have been adopted by schools (Buell, 2014; Johnson, 2014). Ultimately, schools have recognized the need to provide their students, faculty, and staff with the necessary information and training to survive an active shooter attack in their institution (Payne, 2014). All focus on improving survivability.

Another model that has been met with praise and is in use in more than 25,000 school districts around the nation is the Standard Response Protocol (SRP) from the I Love U Guys Foundation. The foundation was started by John-Michael and Ellen Keyes after their daughter Emily was killed in the 2006 Platte Canyon High School shooting. Unlike many other plans, SRP is action based, which means that it can be used for a number of different scenarios, including (but not limited to) active shooters (Keyes, 2018). It includes training directives for lockdowns (when a threat is within the building), lockouts (when the threat is outside and containment within the building is the safest option), evacuation, sheltering (for a specific type of hazard), and holding in place (keeping hallways clear if needed). The overarching goal of the SRP is to standardize the language, providing greater predictability for first responders and making it easier to train for students as young as pre-K. Moreover, it is easily deployable in times of crisis when rapid response is needed (Keyes, 2018).

Having an active shooter protocol in place is only half of the battle. In order to be able to recall it when needed, these plans must be practiced regularly to where the actions become second nature. Schools across the nation have taken this task to heart, regularly drilling students, faculty, and staff on the procedures (e.g., Almeida, 2015; Arnowitz, 2014; Hastings, 2018). Over time, these drills have become more realistic to prepare students for a real event rather than a training exercise that seemingly exists in a vacuum (see, for example, Arnowitz, 2014). Concerns have been raised over the psychological impact of such drills on children, both in the fear it creates immediately after the exercise and in the long-term ramifications of the induced trauma and anxiety (Hamblin, 2018). Still, the potential benefits of such drills are prioritized over such consequences. Days prior to the Sandy Hook shooting, the school had practiced its own active shooter plan (McCormack, 2012); had they not, it is possible that the death toll could have been even greater.

In reality, active shooter drills were not even a blip on the school safety radar until after Columbine (Hamblin, 2018). The youth who come up through schools across the nation today will never know of a world without active shooter drills. What these protocols emphasize is creating a culture of preparedness. It is important to note, however, that such a culture extends outward beyond the school; in reality, the entire community needs to be part of any plan enacted. As such, in addition to having protocols and practicing them, drills must include participation from other community stakeholders, including law enforcement, emergency management, school bus companies, and even the media, to ensure that in the event of an actual event, everyone knows their role and can execute them without hesitation. Doing so will save an untold number of lives.

Saving Lives with Time

In their study of active shooter cases, Blair and Schweit (2014) determined that the majority of events were over in five minutes or less (see also Blair, Nichols, Burns, & Curnutt, 2013). As discussed earlier, this often is due to the arrival of law enforcement and other first responders on scene, which can act as an impetus for the perpetrator to end their attack through either surrender or suicide. Therefore, a critical component of the lockdown protocol discussed in the previous section is creating a time barrier that separates the perpetrators from their intended targets until the attack ceases. Of all of the products and protocols available, there is one that has proven to be most effective in achieving this aim: door locks.

According to testimony presented to the Sandy Hook Advisory Commission (2015), there have been no school or mass shootings in which the perpetrator breached a locked door (see also Martaindale, Sandel, & Blair, 2017). Even at Columbine, where the shooters had virtually uninterrupted access to the school for nearly 50 minutes and an arsenal of bombs, they never attempted to gain access or made entry into a single locked room (Columbine Review Commission, 2001). As of the time of this writing, there have been just three school shootings in which individuals were killed behind locked doors. The first came on March 21, 2005, at Red Lake High School (Minnesota). The perpetrator attempted to enter a math classroom in the school by shooting out the locks, but they held; he instead broke through the window that ran adjacent to the door to gain entry to the room, where he killed five students and a teacher before committing suicide when law enforcement arrived on scene (Haga, 2012; Pioneer Press, 2015).

The second incident happened on September 27, 2006, at Platte Canyon High School in Bailey, Colorado. Student Emily Keyes was killed when SWAT attempted to breach the classroom where she had been held by the perpetrator—who had barricaded himself with his victims behind the locked door (Park County Office of Emergency Management, 2006; see also Alfano, 2006). The most recent incident was the 2018 shooting at Marjory Stoneman Douglas High School in Parkland, Florida, where the perpetrator fired his weapon through windows in the doors, killing people who had taken shelter behind the locked entrances (Spencer, 2018; Swenson & Schmidt, 2018). In each of these incidents, however, the deaths that occurred were not the failure of the locks themselves.

Yet there have been other shootings that have highlighted the need not only for door locks to be present but also for them to have certain functionality that enables them to be quickly deployed in times of crisis. At the time of the 2012 Sandy Hook Elementary School shooting, the doors to each of the classrooms were equipped with locks, but in order to secure them, an individual had to go outside into the hallway and use a key (Sedensky, 2013). No locking mechanism was present on the interior handle of the doors. As a result, many teachers had to make the decision as to whether they were willing to open the doors to their classrooms to secure the rooms. Most of them determined it was not safe to do so; the school's custodian, however, did go from room to room, locking each with a master key (see also Altimari & Wilson, 2013). Also hindering the process was the fact that the doors opened outward, meaning that they could not effectively be barricaded from the inside in lieu of locking them. The two classrooms where the students and their teachers were killed were both unlocked at the time of the shooting, and no sign of forced entry was present (Sedensky, 2013). This issue was highlighted again during the Parkland shooting, when a number of teachers indicated that they also were not able to secure their classrooms during the shooting (Mazzei, 2018; Spencer, 2018).

The number one recommendation to come out of the report of the Sandy Hook Advisory Commission (2015) was the need for door locks on all classrooms that could be secured from the interior of the room. Further, the report indicated that these locks needed to be able to be secured not only by teachers but also by substitutes, as one of the victims, Lauren Rousseau, was filling in for the regular educator on the day of the shooting (Sandy Hook Advisory Commission, 2015). Security experts also have echoed the need for door locks that are securable from inside the room (see, for example, School Safety Infrastructure Council, 2014; The National School Shield Task Force, 2013). Martaindale and colleagues (2017) recommended deadbolt locks that can be secured from the interior of the room without a key. This recommendation is based on two important considerations. First, deadbolts have been found to withstand attacks better than other types of locks (e.g., push button, thumb-turn). Second, in situations like a school or mass shooting, individuals frequently lose near vision and fine motor skills due to high levels of stress, which would make it nearly impossible to not only find the right key but also use it correctly in a matter of seconds (Martaindale et al., 2017; see also Grossman & Christensen, 2012; Ripley, 2008). Therefore, it is important not only to have locks that can be secured from the interior of the room but also those that can be deployed quickly and effectively in high-stress situations. When seconds count, these devices have been shown to put more time on the clock and save lives.

A Renewed Focus and a Layered Approach

School security is big business, with expenditures reaching nearly $3 billion in 2017 (Dearing, 2018). It is important, however, that those dollars be invested where they make the most sense and not where fear and apprehension dictates. Doing the latter has led school districts across the nation to invest money into new technologies that have been left unused or with protocols that are not backed by evidence (Schuppe, 2018). In an effort to "do something," many have fallen prey to a voracious consumer market that pushes untested products to these nervous school officials; in turn, districts ultimately have given in to the pressures to adopt them to meet the needs of a concerned public (Peterson et al., 2001; see also Snell et al., 2002, who found that school crime policy changes in the wake of highly publicized school crimes like Columbine are significantly influenced by both student perceptions of safety and parental complaints to get something done). As Peterson and colleagues (2001) summarized, "too often, well-meaning efforts are implemented independent of a secure-research supported rationale" (p. 348; see also Borum et al., 2010).

The need for evidence-supported solutions cannot be underscored enough. A problem, however, is that the majority of evidence presented relies on perceptions of security and not what actually has been proven to be safe through independent evaluations of product or strategy effectiveness (Addington, 2009). Part of this is the result of the rarity of events like school shootings that make it difficult to find and analyze data that can provide such insight into these policies (Birkland & Lawrence, 2009). Other contributing factors include the general misunderstandings about the nature of the threat of school shootings and unrealistic expectations of risk and its related mitigation (Borum et al., 2010). Still, when faced with a tough decision and a shiny marketing pamphlet, "people believe that particular policy interventions are effective even in the absence of evidence" (Birkland & Lawrence, 2009, p. 1417). As a result, what society has been left with is a false sense of security (Addington, 2009; Lawrence, 2007; Schwartz et al., 2016) and seemingly unrealistic expectations about safety in schools, particularly during a shooting event.

Collectively, researchers have found that most forms of target hardening offered in response to school and mass shootings have been shown to be "ineffective and prohibitively expensive" (Snell et al., 2002, p. 274). Such a statement is not intended to suggest that we as a society sit back and do nothing. Instead, it is important to do the things that have the best chances of working—and often, they cost the least to employ. These strategies include threat assessment and management, which, as discussed in the previous chapter, help to identify a potential issue before it reaches the level of a school shooting; and, in the event that such an attack happens, door locks that can buy precious time until law enforcement arrives on scene, along with active shooter protocols that inform students, faculty, and staff what actions they should be taking during the rampage.

In the aftermath of high-profile school shootings, the employment of techniques of CPTED also have been integrated into schools to help increase safety. When the new Hope Columbine Memorial Library was built, for example, the principles of CPTED were incorporated to increase light and visibility with large windows, shorter bookcases (no more than 48 inches high, so that students and staff can see over them), and an open floor plan (Lewis, 2003). The library also includes multiple surveillance points that provide staff with an unobstructed view of the entire room (Lewis, 2003). More recently, after the original Sandy Hook Elementary School was demolished following the shooting, a new campus was built that focused on subtly incorporating access control and natural surveillance in the design (Urist, 2014). Though it is among the most advanced in terms of security optimization, the majority of the features are not immediately noticed by the untrained eye, a purposeful design that prioritizes both comfort and safety and does not sacrifice one for the other (Urist, 2014).

Ultimately, as the new Sandy Hook school symbolizes, security does not have to be seen to be effective. Yet it is important to remember that in the context of dealing with humans, who are largely unpredictable, the ability to reduce the risk of a school shooting or any type of institutional violence to zero is impossible—there always is an inherent margin of error that leaves room for chance. While that does not mean stakeholders should not work to make schools safer, it does underscore the importance of making decisions that are cost effective, shown to work through research-based evaluation, and do not transform learning institutions into prisons, thereby instigating a whole host of other problems. The key to school safety is proactivity rather than reactivity: What can we do today to make our schools safer for tomorrow? Such a question should be the foundational starting point for any discussion pertaining to school safety and securitization.

CHAPTER SEVEN

An Outcry for Change

The shooting at Columbine High School has, as noted, become a watershed cultural moment in the United States' history (Larkin, 2007, 2009; Muschert, 2002). Aside from the changes to police responses, threat assessment, and school security, the events of April 20, 1999, also transformed the way that the public viewed these types of events. Now, 20 years later, these perceptions have extended beyond shootings in schools to similar tragedies that occur in other types of locations, including, but not limited to, workplaces, places of worship, restaurants and bars, movie theaters, military bases, and malls. For each, Columbine serves as a point of reference and comparison as, for many people, it is perceived to be the first of its kind (see, generally, Altheide, 2009; Larkin, 2007, 2009; Muschert, 2007b; Muschert & Larkin, 2007; Schildkraut, 2016).

One of the best indicators of the salience or importance of a social problem is how the public reacts to it. Accordingly, public opinion polls, such as those routinely conducted by Gallup, the Roper Center for Public Opinion Research, Pew Research Center, and many of the news organizations themselves, can provide important insight into how citizens perceive a certain topic or event as well as those issues closely related to it. It is not surprising, then, that given the perceived importance of Columbine, the public routinely was asked to weigh in on a variety of issues related to the shooting, including perceptions of school safety and security, fear of crime, and—among the most controversial—gun control after the shooting. Moreover, as the concern over events like Columbine has been sustained and subsequently reinforced over the past 20 years with each new shooting, examining such opinions can provide insight to how these other events have (or have not) driven concern over mass shootings in the United States.

Columbine and the Rise of Shootings as a Social Problem

As discussed in Chapter 3, the shooting at Columbine garnered an intense amount of media coverage. The demand for such coverage was fueled, at least in part, by an equal interest in the event by the public. One poll by the Pew Research Center (1999) indicated that 68% of respondents expressed that they had followed the news of the shooting very closely. Even broader, 92% reported that they followed the coverage either fairly or very closely (Pew Research Center for the People & the Press, 1999; see also Roper Center for Public Opinion Research, n.d.). The intense interest by the public led the shooting to be ranked as the top news story of the year and third of the entire decade behind the Rodney King trial verdict (1992) and the crash of TWA Flight 800 (1996) (Pew Research Center for the People & the Press, 1999). Other high-profile events of the 1990s, including the Oklahoma City (1995) and Olympic Park (1996) bombings, the O. J. Simpson murder trial (1994), deaths of Princess Diana (1997) and John F. Kennedy Jr. (1999), and two presidential elections (1992 and 1996), failed to exceed the public's interest in Columbine (Pew Research Center for the People & the Press, 1999).

Despite their highly sensational nature, however, not all mass shootings have generated the same intense interest from the public. When considering only those mass shootings that occurred in schools, no attack occurring either before or after Columbine has surpassed the event in interest. According to the Pew Research Center for the People & the Press (1998a, 1998b), 82% of individuals surveyed in the respective polls indicated that they followed the coverage of the March 24, 1998 shooting at Westside Middle School in Jonesboro, AR and the May 21, 1998 attack at Thurston High School in Springfield, OR either fairly or very closely. The shooting in Jonesboro slightly edged (49% to 46%) the rampage in Springfield in respect to those indicating very close following, though both still were a far cry from the 68% response generated by survey participants after Columbine.

In the years after the 1999 shooting, other, similar events occurring in schools across the nation also failed to capture the same level of interest. In data compiled by the Roper Center for Public Opinion Research (n.d.), the March 21, 2005, shooting at Red Lake High School in Red Lake, Minnesota, that claimed the lives of nine and left five others wounded attracted a close (either fairly or very) following among 71% of respondents. Additionally, the April 16, 2007, shooting at Virginia Tech in Blacksburg, Virginia, failed to eclipse the attention Columbine had received, despite a death toll of 32 that remained unsurpassed for just over nine years as the deadliest shooting in the nation. Despite its lethality, Virginia Tech garnered close attention from 82% of respondents polled, with just 45% indicating a very high interest (Pew Research Center for the People & the Press, 2007b). Even the December 14, 2012, shooting at Sandy Hook Elementary School in

Newtown, Connecticut, that claimed the lives of 20 first-grade students and 6 of their educators failed to generate interest beyond the level of Columbine. A Pew Research Center for the People & the Press (2012b) poll after the shooting found that 57% of respondents reported following the story very closely, with 83% in total expressing greater interest in the case (see also Saad, 2012, which found a comparable 87% interest).

Similarly, mass shootings outside of schools also failed to attract comparable interest. On January 8, 2011, for example, a gunman killed 6 and wounded 13 others outside of a supermarket in Tucson, Arizona. Among the injured was Congresswoman Gabrielle Giffords. Despite her high profile, respondents polled by the Pew Research Center for the People & the Press (2011) a week after the shooting indicated that 49% very and 77% in total (fairly or very) closely followed the coverage. Other particularly lethal and high-profile mass shootings also failed to gain significant widespread interest. The Pew Research Center for the People & the Press (2009) indicated that 78% of individuals polled indicated either fairly or very closely following the news coverage of the November 5, 2009, Fort Hood, Texas, military base attack, while 65% paid close attention to the September 16, 2013, shooting at the Washington, DC, Navy Yard (Pew Research Center for the People & the Press, 2013). A Kaiser Family Foundation poll found that 79% of respondents also reported fairly or very closely following the June 17, 2015, shooting at the Emanuel AME church in Charleston, South Carolina (Hamel, Firth, & Brodie, 2015). Even being close in physical proximity to Columbine was not sufficient to outpace the attention of the shooting by the July 20, 2012, attack at an Aurora, Colorado, movie theater. Despite sitting less than a half hour from the high school, leading many to draw constant comparison between the two events, and leaving 12 dead and 70 others injured, just 73% of respondents indicated that they either fairly or very closely followed the news about the Aurora shooting (Pew Research Center for the People & the Press, 2012a).

The extreme interest and attention paid to Columbine translated into specific attitudes about the shooting and the phenomenon as a whole. In a Gallup poll conducted the day after the shooting, 79% of individuals indicated that the attack served as an indicator for broader social problems in the nation (Saad, 1999, 2017a), a sentiment that was echoed later about the Sandy Hook Elementary School shooting in a Washington Post-ABC News poll (n.d.; see also Pew Research Center for the People & the Press, 2012b), albeit to a slightly lesser extent. Interestingly, 17% of respondents in the same poll called school and mass shootings isolated incidents, noting that they did not reflect anything about the country (Saad, 2017a), a finding that held nearly two years later after a shooting at a high school in Southern California (Moore, 2001a). Other shootings, including the aforementioned attacks in Tucson (2011) and Aurora (2012), also were perceived to be isolated incidents rather than indicators of social or cultural problems (Washington Post-ABC

News poll, n.d.; see also Pew Research Center for the People & the Press, 2012b; Roper Center for Public Opinion Research, n.d.). Interestingly, the shooting at Columbine also was found in one poll to be rated among the top 10 most significant historic events for millennials and Generation X respondents yet failed to garner similar support from individuals classified as the Silent Generation or baby boomers (Dean, Duggan, & Morin, 2016). The only other mass shooting to make these two lists was the June 12, 2016, attack at the Pulse nightclub in Orlando, Florida, which had occurred in the year the poll was conducted and likely was fresh on the minds of respondents (Dean et al., 2016).

So how do these perceptions compare to other issues the United States faces? According to Dugan (2012), the nation's economy regularly is named as the top problem by respondents, averaging 30% of votes. Despite the pervasive media and public attention that mass shootings receive, however, crime and violence are rarely ranked high on the list of national concerns. Specifically, when asked to identify the nation's top problem, crime and violence more broadly (not school or mass shootings in particular) were identified by 3% of respondents after Virginia Tech in 2007, 1% after the 2011 Tucson shooting, 1% after the 2012 attack in Aurora, and 2% after Sandy Hook in 2012 (Dugan, 2012; see also, generally, Gallup, 1999a). Several months prior to Columbine, 13% of respondents had indicated that crime was the most important concern for the country; one month after the shooting, this had increased to 24% (Dugan, 2012). For youth growing up in the "Columbine generation," crime has been ranked as the most important problem faced, particularly among respondents under 18: 53% of those polled indicated that gun violence was the most significant issue on their agenda (Page & Icsman, 2018). Still, the prioritizing of crime and violence on the public agenda remains low, barring the spike observed after Columbine.

How Likely *Are* School Shootings?

Despite the fact that the media attention makes shootings like Columbine appear commonplace (Burns & Crawford, 1999; Springhall, 1999), these attacks actually are statistically rare events (Schildkraut & Elsass, 2016). In the six school years (1992–93 through 1997–98) preceding Columbine, for example, there were 226 school-shooting associated deaths in the country (Donohue, Schiraldi, & Ziedenberg, 1998; Bernard, 1999). By comparison, within the more than 800,000 schools, over 50 million students were enrolled in kindergarten through 12th grade during the same period (Sanchez, 1998). While the loss of even one life to such senseless violence is one too many, this context is necessary to be able to inform legitimate policy. More broadly, students have million-to-one odds of being killed at school (Donohue et al., 1998). Comparatively, these same children have a greater statistical likelihood of being struck by lightning (Donohue et al., 1998; see also Bernard, 1999).

Despite these odds, which largely are excluded from media coverage of school shootings and thereby deny news audiences such important context (see Schildkraut, 2016), these institutions remain among the safest places for children to be (Goldstein, 2018). Public perception of the likelihood of these events—both among parents or other adults and students—is, however, at odds with the actuality of the problem. For example, in a Gallup poll conducted the day after the shooting, nearly one in three (30%) individuals surveyed indicated that a similar attack was very likely in their own community, a statistic that held a year later when the question was administered on a subsequent survey (Gillespie, 2000). This finding was consistent both within the sample of national adults and K–12 parents specifically (Gillespie, 2000). In the poll the day after Columbine, Gillespie (2000) reported that an additional 38% of respondents believed that it was somewhat likely a school shooting could happen in their own community. A year later, this figure dropped, albeit slightly—36% of national adults agreed a school shooting was somewhat likely in their community, while 33% of K–12 parents expressed similar sentiment (Gillespie, 2000; see also Carlson, 2001; Saad, 1999). In 2005, following the Red Lake shooting, 73% of respondents indicated that a school shooting was possible in their community, an *increase* over the response frequency found the day after Columbine (Kiefer, 2005). After Sandy Hook, just 52% agreed that a shooting was likely (either somewhat or very) in their community (Saad, 2012).

The belief that a school shooting is possible in one's own community was not solely linked to adults. In a Gallup Youth Survey conducted just weeks after Columbine and released just one day after the May 20, 1999, shooting at Heritage High School in Conyers, Georgia, 36% of respondents indicated that there were students in their school that could carry out a similar attack (Newport, 1999a), a figure that increased to nearly 50% when looking at just junior- and senior-aged students (Gallup, 1999b). Moreover, 30% of those students interviewed in the survey indicated that there were groups of students at their school that reminded them of Columbine's "Trench Coat Mafia" (Gallup, 1999b). Though the group later was absolved of any involvement in the shooting, the myth of their linkage persisted for quite some time, leading people to believe that similar students were capable of replicating such violence. Gallup (1999b) also indicated that in the weeks since Columbine, 37% of the students surveyed were aware of similar threats at their own school. He also found that one out of every three students knew of peers who had or regularly carried guns or knives at school (Gallup, 1999a).

The potential for shootings in one's own school continues to be a concern for students 20 years later. Such apprehension among the "Columbine generation" has been fueled, at least in part, by the February 14, 2018, shooting at Marjory Stoneman Douglas High School in Parkland, Florida, which claimed the lives of 17 students and teachers and left 17 others injured. Following the Parkland shooting, a group of Stoneman Douglas students formed the "March for Our Lives" campaign designed to bring awareness to the concerns of their generation related to gun violence in schools. In a poll conducted by USA Today a month after the shooting, one in four students (25%) indicated that it was somewhat or very likely that one of their classmates would bring a gun to school (Page & Icsman, 2018). The survey further indicated that 15% of respondents expressed that their school was likely to experience a shooting (Page & Icsman, 2018). Even following the May 18, 2018 shooting at Santa Fe High School in Santa Fe, Texas, one student interviewed remarked that "It's been happening everywhere. I've always felt it would eventually happen here too," aptly summarizing how students across the nation perceive the threat of mass violence in their schools (Beauchamp, 2018, para. 4).

A Fear for Safety and a Call for Action

As a larger of body of research indicates, though perceived risk of victimization and fear of crime are conceptually and empirically distinct (Ferraro & LaGrange, 1987), they still are interrelated in that the former is proposed to be a cause of the latter (Ferraro, 1995). Accordingly, it is no surprise that a heightened perceived risk of victimization to school shootings also would lead to greater levels of fear of crime. In the year prior to Columbine, for example, a Gallup poll found that 37% of parents feared for the physical safety of their child while at school (Saad, 2017a). The day after the shooting, that number spiked to 55% (Gillespie, 2000; Saad, 2017a), dropping down to 47% at the start of the next school year four months later (Saad, 2006) and 43% near the first anniversary of the attack (Gillespie, 2000). A separate poll conducted by the Pew Research Center for the People & the Press (2000) a year after the shooting found that only 40% of parents felt their child was safe at school.

Despite the spike in fear of the safety of their children following Columbine, this concern was not sustained. Within a year of the shooting, the level of reported fear had begun to wane, and it gradually has continued to do so even to this day (Jones, 2001; Reinhart, 2018). After other mass shootings in schools, fear over children's safety continued to run high. For instance, after the 2001 Santana High School shooting, 45% of parents express fear; after the October 2, 2006 attack at an Amish schoolhouse in Nickel Mines, Pennsylvania, concern peaked at 35% (Reinhart, 2018; see also Jones, 2006; Saad, 2006).

Following Sandy Hook, one of the few shootings that is considered to be comparable to Columbine in the reactions it elicited (see Schildkraut &

Muschert, 2014), just one out of every three parents (33%) indicated that they were fearful about their child's safety at school (Jones, 2017; Reinhart, 2018; Saad, 2012). Concern after each of these attacks, however, was short-lived, and the level of fear reported by parents continued to decline overall (Jones, 2017; McCarthy, 2015; Newport, 2006). Interestingly, even when there is a spike after a shooting, the level of fear is lower than the previous spike. Further, Jones (2017) indicated that the average concern over student safety in schools since 1977 is 29%. Given that just 24% of parents expressed such fear in August 2017 (the same proportion as when the survey was first administered in 1977; see Moore, 2001a) and have expressed similarly low rates in years past (Jones, 2017; Reinhart, 2018), it suggests that parents, and the public more broadly, truly are desensitized to the issue of mass violence in schools.

Fear over safety at school is, as alluded to earlier, not solely a parental concern. Students too have expressed their concern over feeling secure at school. Though Gallup has been asking parents about their fear over their child's safety at school since 1977, it was not until just after Columbine that they asked how the students themselves felt (Jones, 2017). Just after the shooting, approximately 18% of parents indicated that their children had expressed feelings of being unsafe at school (Jones, 2017; Saad, 2017a); conversely, a poll by Pew Research Center for the People & the Press (2000) found that one-third of respondents had received similar concern from their children, particularly among older youth (ages 12 to 17). Concern over safety at school for students in the Gallup polls peaked at 22% following the Santana High School shooting but, like parental attitudes, has continued to decline in subsequent years, peaking minimally with news of a new attack (Jones, 2006, 2017; see also McCarthy, 2015).

In one of the most recent polls, just 6% of parents indicated that their child had voiced such concerns—one-fourth the number of adults polled at the same time expressing such attitudes (Jones, 2017). Collectively, Jones (2017) notes that, over time, an average of 11% of parents indicate that their child has expressed concern over safety at school, nearly one-third the percentage of the adults themselves. Following the 2018 Parkland shooting, *USA Today* found that 19% of students polled indicated that they did not feel safe at school, the first time that such attitudes have been comparable to those after Columbine (Page & Icsman, 2018). Still, the trends show that it is much more likely for parents to be concerned for their child's safety than for the students themselves to exhibit such fear.

The academic research community also has examined what impact, if any, the Columbine shooting had on students' perceptions of safety. Using data from the Youth Risk Behavior Survey, Brener, Simon, Anderson, Barrios, and Small (2002) found that for students surveyed post-Columbine, 1 in 10 expressed feeling too unsafe to attend school. Following the shooting, students were more than two and a half times as likely to report missing school as a result of safety concerns (Brener et al., 2002). Addington (2003) took a different approach to assessing students' fear as a result of Columbine, instead utilizing the 1999 School Crime Supplement to the National Crime Victimization Survey. She found that students surveyed after the shooting were significantly more likely to report fear of victimization at school than before the attack (Addington, 2003). Despite increased fear at school, there was not a significant difference in the employment of avoidance behaviors by students (Addington, 2003). Interestingly, the effects of the Columbine shooting rippled beyond just high school-aged students. Stretesky and Hogan (2001) found that female college students who were being surveyed about dating violence at the time the shooting occurred expressed lower perceived safety (and, by extension, greater perceptions of risk) after Columbine. Their study, conducted in upstate New York, also allowed for consideration of the ripple effects of the shooting spatially (Stretesky & Hogan, 2001).

In the aftermath of Columbine, the fear of school safety and increased risk perceptions translated into conversations about what could be done among parents, students, and the institutions themselves. In a Gallup poll a week after the shooting, 78% of parents had discussed potential fears and concerns that their child had at school while 81% indicated they had talked about Columbine specifically (Gillespie, 1999; Saad, 2017a; see also Pew Research Center for the People & the Press, 2000). In those conversations, parents indicated that they cautioned their children to take safety precautions while at school (72%) and encouraged them not to get into confrontations with other students (81%) or make fun of those perceived as outcasts (80%), potentially over fears of escalating the situation to physical violence (Gillespie, 1999, 2000; see also Carlson, 2001; Saad, 2017a). Following the Parkland shooting, 67% of students polled indicated that their parents had similar conversations with them (Page & Icsman, 2018).

Despite such perceptions, only 23% of parents at the time indicated that they had contacted their child's school to discuss safety-related concerns (Gillespie, 1999; Saad, 2017a). A year later, the proportion of parents indicating that they had been in touch with their child's school to check on safety measures had increased to 57% (Gillespie, 2000). That same poll indicated that parents' reported activity in their child's school had increased (38%) over the year prior and that they were likely to supervise their children more closely (44%; Gillespie, 2000). The Pew Research Center for the People & the Press (2000) found that within a year of the shooting, 37% of parents polled indicated that their child's school had implemented security measures, such as metal detectors, security cameras, or an increase in police or security guards. Still, the general perceptions of parents and students alike, many of which persist today, indicate that there is more to be done to assuage concerns and fear over safety at school.

Who (or What) Is to Blame?

One of the most commonly asked questions to arise in the discourse after a mass shooting is "Why?"—and Columbine was no exception. In an attempt to understand how the event could have occurred, a number of potential causal factors were identified by the media, policy makers, and pundits alike with the goal of preventing future attacks. Not surprisingly, the public also weighed in with the own opinions as to who or what was to blame for the Columbine shooting.

One of the first places that blame was placed after Columbine was on the parents of the two shooters. After the breadth of the tragedy—and, by extension, the level of detail and planning that went into it—was revealed, many wondered how the parents could not have known what was going on under their own roofs. In one Gallup poll conducted the week of Columbine, 51% of respondents blamed poor parenting as one of the leading causes of the shooting (Saad, 1999, 2017a). Two weeks after the attack, a second Gallup poll indicated that 45% still believed the parents were at fault (Newport, 1999a). The home life more broadly was ranked as important by 96% of respondents at the two-year anniversary, with 57% ranking the factor as extremely significant (Newport, 2001). The outrage directed at the shooters' parents was so extreme that 25% of respondents in a poll taken one week after the attack believed that they should be prosecuted (Gillespie, 1999), and support for broader parental responsibility laws—that is, holding parents liable for crimes their children commit with firearms—varied between 20 and 70%, depending on the poll (e.g., Carlson, 2001; Gillespie, 2000; Saad, 1999).

While parents and other adults were quick to blame the parents, teenagers polled after the shooting were less inclined to agree. Specifically, just 4% of students polled after Columbine said that the parents or family were to blame (Newport, 1999a). Instead, teens were more likely (40%) to attribute the shooting to peer relations and associated social pressures (Newport, 1999a). Conversely, just 11% of parents suggested that social pressures were a cause of the attack (Newport, 1999a), while 43% of adults more broadly identified this as a root issue (Saad, 2017a). In a poll near the two-year anniversary, 85% of respondents indicated that bullying and teasing at school were an important cause of school shootings, with 29% ranking this as extremely influential (Newport, 2001). Such perceptions, however, may have been fueled by the discourse that the two shooters had been subjected to bullying, a myth that later largely was refuted (Chen, 2009; Cullen, 2009).

Gallup found right after the shooting that nearly half of respondents surveyed (49%) believed that violent media had potentially influenced the perpetrators (Saad, 1999, 2017a; see also, generally, YouGov Staff, 2012). This position was mostly supported by adults, particularly after it was revealed that the shooters listened to Goth rock music and watched violent movies like *Natural Born Killers*, which later became the moniker for the attack. While youth surveyed did not specifically identify violent media as a causal factor for the shooting, they did indicate that its consumption could contribute to violent criminal acts more broadly (Gallup, 1999a). A newer form of media—the Internet, which was in its early years at the time of the shooting—was perceived to be a contributing factor by 34% of individuals surveyed after the attack (Saad, 1999, 2017a).

While adult respondents were more likely to blame society or other adults (e.g., parents), the student respondents focused more on themselves and their peers as causes for the attack (Newport, 2001). Aside from proffered bullying and teasing, teenage respondents also suggested that warning signs of the shooters had been missed (Newport, 2001). Perhaps most astutely, however, teen respondents were the only group in all surveys reviewed for the present book that actually blamed the shooters themselves. Instead of criminalizing everything else, 16% of those youth participating in the survey suggested that the Columbine gunmen committed their act due to personal issues, including being "sick, angry, confused, jealous, or 'stupid'" (Newport, 2001). Such an attribution remains novel even to this day, as the discourse routinely focuses on blaming everything and everyone but the actual perpetrators.

The Gun Control–Gun Rights Debate

One of the most controversial issues—which, along with mental health and violent media, make up what Schildkraut and Muschert (2013) call "the usual suspects" in the debate about causal factors of mass shootings—is the weapons themselves. The availability of guns consistently has and continues to rank among the most prevalent reasons why these events occur (see, for example, Saad, 1999, 2017a; Newport, 2001). While legislative efforts (as discussed further in Chapter 8) often focus on this issue—either increasing regulation efforts or expanding the rights of gun owners—inevitably, little progress is made. A lack of movement on the issue may be due, at least in part, to the polarized public opinions on the matter.

After mass shootings, the guns issue has temporarily jumped in priority on the national agenda. Following Columbine, for example, 1 out of every 10 people (10%) polled listed guns and related control as the most important problem facing the nation (Norman, 2016). The concern, however, was short-lived, and by January of 2000 until the 2012 Sandy Hook shooting, the proportion of individuals listing guns as a significant issue of concern hovered around just 1% (Norman, 2016). Following other attacks—including Sandy Hook, the Charleston church shooting, and San Bernardino, CA on December 2, 2015—the proportion of people naming guns as the most important issue in the nation again spiked, reaching 7% in polls conducted after each event (Norman, 2016). Still, as it had after Columbine, the concern was brief and soon dropped back down to levels approaching zero (Norman, 2016). Interestingly, when the question about most important issues facing the nation was asked following the Parkland shooting, 13% of respondents named guns—a figure even higher than Columbine nearly 19 years earlier (Jones, 2018).

Despite the limited attention guns receive as a perceived national problem, particularly in the aftermath of school and mass shootings, the topic is one that routinely finds itself in public opinion polls. Specifically, two of the nation's leading polling groups—Gallup and the Pew Research Center for the People & the Press—routinely address the debate between gun control and gun rights but do so in different ways. Gallup has routinely polled individuals as to whether they believe the sale of firearms should be regulated more strictly, less strictly, or maintained as they were at the time of the poll. As Figure 7.1 indicates, support for stricter regulations of gun sales has regularly outpaced the belief that such transactions should be less strict or kept as they were. Noticeably, such support has shown temporary increases after school shootings, including Columbine, Sandy Hook, and Parkland (Jones, 2018). In a separate poll, YouGov Staff (2012) found that 48 and 43% of individuals polled after the Tucson and Aurora shootings, respectively, also supported strengthening gun sale regulations.

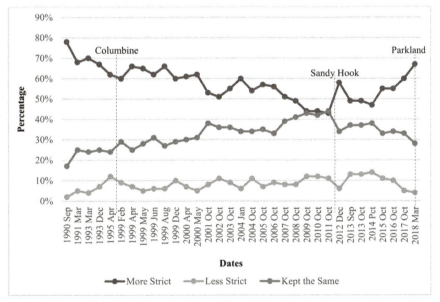

Figure 7.1   Gallup Poll Trends about Gun Sales Regulation over Time. (Data imputed from Jones, 2018)

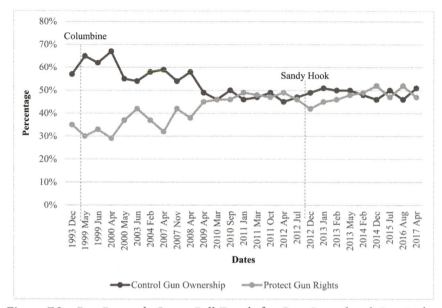

Figure 7.2   Pew Research Center Poll Trends for Gun Control and Gun Rights over Time. (Data imputed from Pew Research Center for the People & the Press, 2017)

The Pew Research Center for the People and the Press (2017) approaches the issue in a different light—asking respondents whether it is more important to control ownership or protect the rights of gun owners. The divide between opinions was marked before Columbine, as illustrated in Figure 7.2, with the gap actually widening in favor of more control in the year after the shooting (Pew Research Center for the People & the Press, 2017). Over time, however, a documentable shift has occurred, with more Americans indicating that protecting gun rights was a greater priority in the past decade. Additionally, few shootings—Sandy Hook being a noteworthy exception—have pushed favorability of restrictions ahead of the protection of rights (Pew Research Center for the People & the Press, 2017).

While both blanket support for more restrictions on ownership and a loosening of regulations on firearms continually fail to gain majority support, there have been measures behind which support has been garnered. For example, approximately 8 out of every 10 people polled support restricting firearms ownership for individuals with mental illness (Langer, 2015; YouGov Staff, 2012), which is consistent with laws in place that prohibit such possession (see, generally, Schildkraut & Hernandez, 2014). Universal background checks have been highly favored among nearly all individuals polled, particularly after extremely lethal events (Langer, 2015; Saad, 2017b; Steinhauser, 2012). Background checks for transactions between private parties and at gun shows also continue to generate considerable support—more than 80% in various polls (Langer, 2015; see also Newport, 1999b; Steinhauser, 2012). Despite the fact that the Columbine shooters acquired their weapons through such means, attempts to pass such regulations routinely failed in the aftermath of the shooting (as discussed further in Chapter 8; see also Schildkraut & Hernandez, 2014).

Other moderately supported proposals have included instituting a mandated waiting periods on handgun purchases (Saad, 2017b; YouGov Staff, 2012), creation of a national registry to track gun sales (Langer, 2015; Newport, 1999b; YouGov Staff, 2012), and obtaining a permit from law enforcement before a handgun can be purchased (YouGov Staff, 2012). Several polls have indicated that support exists for limiting the number of handguns a person can own (Steinhauser, 2012; YouGov Staff, 2012) or the number of rounds a magazine can hold (Madison, 2011; Newport, 1999b; YouGov Staff, 2012). Neither measure has been instituted, despite the Aurora theater gunman using a 100-round drum magazine (Ferner, 2014) and the 2017 Las Vegas shooter having 24 firearms in his hotel room, most of which were used in the attack (Las Vegas Metropolitan Police Department, 2018).

Given the polarity in opinions between control measures and gun rights, it is not surprising that attempts to regulate specific types of firearms have received less than favorable attitudes. One commonly proposed measure is to institute a federal assault weapons ban, despite that the majority of mass shootings are committed with handguns (Schildkraut & Elsass, 2016). Support for such a measure was highest in polls in August 1994 (Madison, 2011), around the time that the Violent Crime Control and Law Enforcement Act—better known as the Federal Assault Weapons Ban (AWB)—went into effect (Schildkraut & Hernandez, 2014; for more information on the AWB, see Chapter 8). Since then, support has declined steadily (Carlson, 2004; Madison, 2011; Langer, 2015; Steinhauser, 2012; YouGov Staff, 2012), reaching its lowest point in one poll—just 36% of individuals favoring such a restriction—in the aftermath of the 2016 Pulse nightclub shooting, though it rebounded slightly (to 48%) after the Las Vegas shooting the following year (Brenan, 2017). Such waning support may be due, at least in part, to the fact that the AWB was in place at the time of Columbine, yet one of the firearms used—the Intratec TEC-DC9—was expressly prohibited under the law (Schildkraut & Hernandez, 2014). Since the gun had been acquired through a private seller, the transaction went undetected (Schildkraut & Hernandez, 2014).

Support for banning handguns has been even lower among poll respondents. When asked whether handgun ownership should be limited to law enforcement and other similarly authorized persons, respondents in the initial poll in 1959 largely supported this measure, as indicated in Figure 7.3. As time progressed, however, support for a ban on handguns was found by

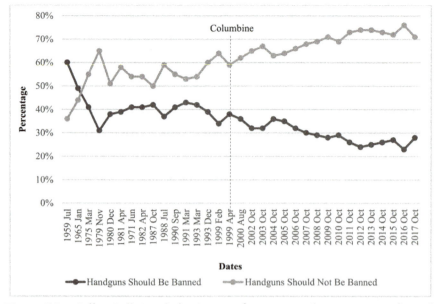

Figure 7.3   Gallup Poll Trends for Support for Banning the Possession of Handguns over Time. (Data imputed from Brenan, 2017)

Gallup to be waning, with respondents favoring ownership over restriction nearly three to one after the Las Vegas shooting (Brenan, 2017). Even though Columbine shifted responses, increasing support for such a ban marginally, the impact was short-lived (Brenan, 2017). Over time, other polls have yielded similar findings (Carlson, 2004; Madison, 2011; Pew Research Center for the People & the Press, 2007a, 2010; YouGov Staff, 2012). This trend also may be why marginal support has been garnered for restricting individuals' ability to carry their concealed handguns in public (YouGov Staff, 2012).

One broader question that stems from these polls is whether these added restrictions actually are necessary. One Pew Research Center for the People & the Press (2000) poll found, for instance, that 59% of respondents expressed that stricter enforcement of existing laws is needed over the creation of new laws (37%). In many instances following mass shootings, both in and out of schools, it is found that the perpetrators, in some way, were in violation of existing laws that simply had not been enforced, though some instances highlighted gaps in the laws themselves that permitted certain actions (e.g., firearms purchases) to occur (see, generally, Schildkraut & Hernandez, 2014). Still, as the Roper Center for Public Opinion Research (n.d.) aptly summarizes, "[a]lthough high-profile incidents can increase support (for stricter gun laws) briefly, the cumulative effect of the increasing number of mass shootings does not appear to be higher support for restrictions on guns" (para. 4).

Still, Can Shootings Be Prevented?

The question of whether school and mass shootings can be prevented is one that has been asked since (and potentially even before) the Columbine shooting. The responses, however, have not always been favorable. In a Gallup poll conducted the day after the attack, 53% of respondents expressed that similar attacks could be prevented if society and the government took the necessary precautions (Kiefer, 2005). At the same time, however, 43% indicated that regardless of what measures were put into place, these types of shootings still would happen (Kiefer, 2005).

The belief in the possibility of prevention of school and mass shootings has fluctuated over time. A year after Columbine, support had waned slightly from the post-Columbine poll, with 48% of respondents indicating that prevention was possible while 49% said such attacks would happen anyway (Gillespie, 2000). Following the shooting at Santana High School in Santee, California, on March 5, 2001, the proportion of individuals who expressed belief that school shootings could be prevented was at 49% (Moore, 2001a). On the other hand, 47% of respondents indicated they would happen regardless of preventative efforts (Moore, 2001a).

Over time, as illustrated in Figure 7.4, belief in prevention opportunities continued to wane, and after the 2005 Red Lake High School shooting, 60% of individuals polled believed that these types of attacks would happen

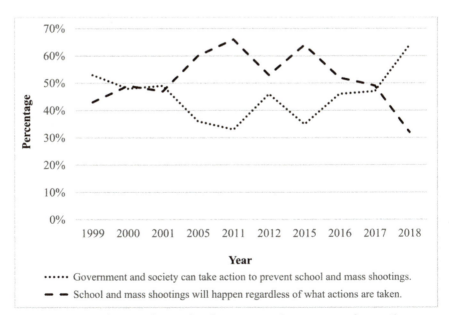

Figure 7.4   Distribution of Attitudes about Potential Prevention of Mass Shootings.

nonetheless (Kiefer, 2005). Conversely, only 36% expressed that prevention was possible (Kiefer, 2005). After the 2011 Tucson shooting, 66% of individuals surveyed believed that mass shootings would happen regardless of efforts taken for prevention (SSRS, 2018). Agreement to this statement dropped to 53% following Sandy Hook in 2012, rebounded to 64% after the 2015 Charleston church shooting, dropped back to 52% following the Pulse shooting in 2016, and remained close at 49% after the 2017 Las Vegas shooting (SSRS, 2018). Similarly, perceptions of the ability for government and society to take preventative actions were highest after Sandy Hook and Pulse (with 46% of respondents expressing agreement at both survey points), as well as Las Vegas (47%), but lower after Tucson (33%) and Charleston (35%; SSRS, 2018). Most recently, following the 2018 Parkland shooting, Americans were more likely to express agreement that the government could prevent such attacks (64%) than that they would happen regardless (32%) (SSRS, 2018; see also Ingraham, 2018).

How such attacks can be prevented also has been addressed through public opinion polls but largely mirrors the earlier discussion related to who or what the public perceives to be responsible for a shooting. In a Gallup poll conducted the day after Columbine, respondents were asked to rate the effectiveness of a panel of proposed solutions (Saad, 1999). A total of 62% expressed the greatest support (measured by response selections of "very effective") for stricter gun control measures for teenagers, while 60% ranked increased counseling services for students as equally effective (Saad, 1999). Other suggested remedies that were highly supported were metal detectors (53%), stricter regulation of violence in entertainment sources (52%), restricting access to information on the Internet (50%), and holding parents responsible (47%; Saad, 1999). To a lesser extent, school dress codes (36%) and random body searches of students (34%) were viewed to be highly effective at preventing future shootings (Saad, 1999).

In a separate poll released a month after Columbine, adults surveyed indicated that greater parental involvement and responsibility (32%), increased security at schools (16%), stricter gun control measures (12%), and more counselors in schools (6%) all could help to prevent future school shootings (Newport, 1999a). A poll by the Pew Research Center for the People & the Press (2000) similarly indicated that respondents overwhelmingly believed it was the responsibility of parents to ensure that their child did not engage in a school shooting (42%), whereas just 6% and 13%, respectively, believed that stricter gun regulations and a reduction of violence in popular entertainment could prevent a similar tragedy.

Following the 2001 shooting at Santana High School, adults again were asked which strategies could be used to prevent similar attacks. As with responses in the post-Columbine survey, respondents again prioritized parental involvement (31%), more school-based security (14%), and improved gun control laws (11%; Moore, 2001b; Newport, 2001). More broadly, efforts can be categorized as parental or family actions, which is where 40% of respondents indicate the greatest opportunity for prevention lies, followed by school-related actions (29%) and societal-level actions (18%), suggesting that micro-level responses are viewed as more effective than blanket national policies (Newport, 2001). Similar sentiments were echoed following the Virginia Tech shooting in 2007, despite the difference in location and age of the perpetrator (Saad, 2007).

Students, on the other hand, do not necessarily share the same ideas as their parents and other adults. In a poll following the Columbine shooting, students believed that future attacks were most likely to be prevented by increased security (24%), followed by more counseling and communication with their peers (18%), improved tolerance among students (18%), and, to a lesser extent (10%), improved awareness of potential dangers (Newport, 1999a). In a more recent poll following the Parkland shooting, approximately half of the students polled indicated that stricter gun control laws, including more comprehensive background checks, could prevent future mass shootings (Page & Icsman, 2018). These measures were more likely to be supported across respondents aged 18 to 24 (54%) as compared to those just 13 to 17 (47%; Page & Icsman, 2018; see also Gallup, 1999a). Similarly, these groups collectively were likely to express that assault weapons bans—a sentiment that was echoed just days after the Columbine shooting (Gallup, 1999a)—and keeping firearms out of the hands of individuals being treated for mental illness also could prevent mass shootings yet were less likely to support arming their teachers as a precautionary strategy (Page & Icsman, 2018).

So Why Does It All Matter?

Understanding public opinion, both immediately after and in the years since Columbine, is important for several reasons. First, the public has the ability to influence legislative change through their voting in (or out) of politicians who align with their ideals. These politicians also may be influenced by pressure from their constituents to introduce or back specific legislation aimed at addressing a particular issue. This can be problematic, however, as decisions made based on fear or emotion are rarely successful (Schildkraut & Hernandez, 2014). Further, public opinion can have a broader impact on other institutions, such as the economy. Cross and Pruitt (2013), for example, found that following the Aurora movie theater shooting, the parent company of the cineplex where the attack took place—Cinemark—experienced financial losses as people avoided these types of venues in the aftermath. In relation to firearms, manufacturing company Sturm, Ruger, & Company reported gains from an increase in sales after the Aurora shooting, though both it and Smith & Wesson experienced financial loss five months later after Sandy Hook (Cross & Pruitt, 2013). In sum, the public has a significant ability to affect legislation and other responses to these attacks in a variety of ways; thus, understanding the opinions that may be driving such action is particularly important for understanding the broader consequences of school and mass shootings.

CHAPTER EIGHT

The (Failed) Firestorm of Legislation

The events of April 20, 1999, highlighted many systems failures and missed opportunities that might have prevented the tragedy. Yet no matter how many issues surfaced, the conversation was dominated primarily by one: the guns. People wondered how the two perpetrators had gotten their guns and whether the event could have been avoided had they not been able to. (Keep in mind, however, that Columbine was never intended to be a shooting but instead a bombing; what happened that day was "Plan B" when the devices failed to detonate.) Perhaps most importantly, people wanted something done so that another Columbine would not happen in the state of Colorado or anywhere else in the United States.

During the legislative session in the year following the shooting, more than 800 bills related to firearms were introduced in states across the nation (Soraghan, 2000). The successful passage of these laws, however, was quite low—around 10%—even with the shadow of Columbine lingering (Soraghan, 2000). The firearms laws that were introduced and subsequently enacted after the shooting included provisions that made it illegal to possess a firearm on school grounds (Idaho), prohibited lawsuits against gun manufacturers (Idaho, Kentucky, Utah, Virginia), required trigger locks on guns sold after 2002 (Maryland), and required that schools be notified of their students' firearms violations (Washington), among others (Soraghan, 2000; see also H.B. 444 [Idaho], 2000; H.B. 663 [Idaho], 2000; H.B. 15 [Ky.], 2000; S.B. 211 [Md.], 2000; H.B. 199 [Utah], 2000; H.B. 905 [Va.], 2000; S.B. 6206 [Wash.], 2000). Additional efforts were made at the federal level, albeit with equally dismal success (Schildkraut & Hernandez, 2014).

In this chapter, we explore how the nation responded to—or, perhaps more accurately, attempted to respond to—Columbine legislatively. By and large, these efforts focused on the main issue identified as the cause of the shooting: the guns. Accordingly, we first review the history of firearms legislation predating the attack. Consideration then is given to how the shooters got their guns, as well as responses following the shooting that were aimed at addressing the gun show loophole that made it possible. We further explore the role of federal assault weapons bans that often are at the center of the debate following mass shootings. Finally, we consider how this and other shootings highlight missed opportunities for legislative efforts aimed at preventing future attacks.

A Brief Overview of Firearms Legislation in the United States Pre-Columbine

Perhaps the best-recognized right granted in the U.S. Constitution is the right to bear arms, found in the Second Amendment. Ratified on December 15, 1791, the amendment states that "a well regulated Militia, being necessary to the security of a free State, the right of the people to keep and bear Arms, shall not be infringed" (U.S. Const. amend. II). What exactly this wording means, however, has long been contested among the public, by politicians, and within the courts. In fact, several key U.S. Supreme Court challenges— including *Presser v. Illinois* (1886), *United States v. Miller* (1939), *District of Columbia v. Heller* (2008), and *McDonald v. Chicago* (2010)—have specifically sought to interpret the Second Amendment's meaning in relation to different firearms issues.

Typically, the Second Amendment was viewed as applicable strictly on the federal government and not the states (see, generally, *Miller v. Texas*, 1894). Still, it was not until the turn of the 20th century that new federal laws were being enacted in an attempt to offer more uniform national guidelines for gun regulation (Schildkraut & Hernandez, 2014). One of the first of these key provisions was the National Firearms Act (26 U.S.C. § 53), enacted in 1934 by President Franklin D. Roosevelt (see also Hardy, 1986; Singh, 1999). Proposed as a response to Prohibition-era violence, the act targeted weapons that were being used by gangsters, such as machine guns, rifles, short-barreled shotguns (those that were less than 18 inches in length), and silencers (Bureau of Alcohol, Tobacco, and Firearms, n.d.; Zimring, 2001). Under the National Firearms Act, all prospective gun buyers had to fill out paperwork at the time of purchase that then was subject to the U.S. Department of Treasury's final approval (Bureau of Alcohol, Tobacco, and Firearms, n.d.). Additionally, all gun sales were levied with a tax of $200 per weapon, a cost that has never been increased despite inflation (Bureau of Alcohol, Tobacco, and Firearms, n.d.). In fact, had inflation been factored in, the $200 tax levied in 1934 would be nearly $3,800 in 2018 (U.S. Department of Labor, n.d.).

Four years later, Roosevelt passed a second significant piece of legislation: the Federal Firearms Act (15 U.S.C. §§ 901–909). Enacted in 1938, the focus of the law was to regulate firearms through interstate commerce (Ascione, 1939; Zimring, 2001). Specifically, any dealers or manufacturers who would be selling or transferring weapons within and between states or who were importing guns were required to be licensed (Ascione, 1939). It further included provisions requiring dealers to keep records of all firearm sales; they also could not sell to a convicted criminal or any customer without the proper licensing (Ascione, 1939; Zimring, 2001). According to the original bill, one of the main goals of the act was to "eliminate the gun from the crooks' hands, while interfering as little as possible with the law-abiding citizen" (S. Rep. No. 82, 1937).

A renewed interest in revising national gun regulations came in the mid-to-late 1960s following the high-profile assassinations of President John F. Kennedy in 1963 (Singh, 1999; Zimring, 2001) and Robert Kennedy and Martin Luther King Jr. in 1968 (Hardy, 1986; Zimring, 2001). Subsequently, the Gun Control Act of 1968 (18 U.S.C. § 44) was enacted, which revised parts of the National Firearms Act of 1934 and repealed the Federal Firearms Act of 1938 (though many of its provisions were reincorporated into the new law). The act outlawed the sale of shotguns and rifles by mail order (Hardy, 1986), which is how Lee Harvey Oswald had secured the Mannlicher-Carcano rifle used to assassinate President Kennedy (Warren Commission Report, 1964). It further expanded the licensing and recordkeeping requirements for dealers, restricted the sale of handguns across state lines, and prohibited persons convicted of felonies, those who used drugs, or those who were found to be mentally incompetent from purchasing firearms (Schildkraut & Hernandez, 2014).

While the Gun Control Act of 1968 was quite rigid in its stipulations, several of these provisions were tempered with the passage of the Firearm Owners' Protection Act of 1986 (18 U.S.C. § 921). The requirements for dealer licenses were amended—individuals who regularly sold guns as their primary business were required to be licensed, whereas others who made occasional sales (e.g., a pawnbroker) or sold a gun from their personal collections were not (Firearm Owners' Protection Act, 1986; Hardy, 1986). The law further required that all multiple firearms sales had to be reported to the appropriate authorities, but, with the exception of armor-piercing bullets, records of ammunition sales no longer were mandated (Firearm Owners' Protection Act, 1986). Additionally, while owning or selling a machine guns remained illegal, the act loosened the prohibitions on felons owning firearms, now limiting it only to those individuals who had been convicted of "disabling crimes" (e.g., threatening or using force) as outlined by the U.S. Code (Hardy, 1986). Finally, the Firearm Owners' Protection Act (1986) reinstated the interstate sale and transportation of firearms that previously had been suspended (see also Hardy, 1986).

The following decade, and 1994 specifically, saw the passage of two critical pieces of legislation. The first of these was the Brady Handgun Violence Prevention Act (1993; amending 18 U.S.C. §§ 921–924), named for Ronald Reagan's press secretary, James Brady, who was injured in an assassination attempt on the president. The Brady Law, as it is more commonly known, mandated that the Federal Bureau of Investigation establish what became the National Instant Criminal Background Check System (NICS), which allowed for inquiries on the prospective buyers to be conducted instantly either electronically or by phone (18 U.S.C. §§ 921–924). Until such a system was established, the law also required a mandatory five-day waiting period on all unlicensed individuals seeking to purchase a firearm (18 U.S.C. §§ 921–924; Singh, 1999). Further, the Brady Law prohibited the sale of guns to anyone who had been committed to a mental institution or otherwise judged mentally ill (18 U.S.C. §§ 921–924). The second piece of legislation—the Federal Assault Weapons Ban—is discussed later in this chapter.

How They Got Their Guns

The journals that Shooter H left behind indicated that on November 22, 1998, the perpetrators were able to acquire three of the guns used in the attack—the two shotguns (one double-barreled and one pump action, both 12 gauge) and the 9-mm carbine rifle (see Jefferson County Sheriff's Office, 1999, p. 26,016). The only problem was that at the time the guns were purchased, both of the perpetrators were 17—Shooter H turned 18 just 11 days before the shooting, and Shooter K was still 17 at the time of the attack. Therefore, under both state and federal law, the two were ineligible to purchase any of the three weapons. The question that weighed on many people's mind then was, how did they get their guns?

The police investigation quickly turned up an answer: Robyn Anderson. The 18-year-old was a straight-A senior at Columbine High School and a friend of both of the gunmen (she attended the prom as Shooter K's date the weekend before the attack). As they were underage, they enlisted her help to purchase the weapons at a local gun show (Soraghan, 2000). Unaware of what they intended to do with the firearms, Anderson obliged using funds the two provided her (Columbine Review Commission, 2001). At the time, Colorado law permitted adults to transfer these types of long guns to juveniles without penalty (Columbine Review Commission, 2001).

Sometime prior to the purchase of the guns, Shooter H wrote in a class assignment that "[t]he biggest gaping hole [in the Brady Bill] is that the background checks are only required for licensed dealers . . . not private dealers. . . . Private dealers can sell shotguns and rifles to anyone who is 18 or older . . ." (Jefferson County Sheriff's Office, 1999, p. 26,538). (In an ironic coincidence,

Columbine victim Daniel Mauser, who researched the Brady background check law for the school's debate team that he was a member of, also had identified the same loophole just weeks before he was killed; see Soraghan, 2000). Additionally, federal law prohibited an individual from buying a firearm for someone who was ineligible to make the same purchase (known as a "straw purchase"; see Schildkraut & Hernandez, 2014); however, this rule applied only to licensed dealers and not private sellers (Columbine Review Commission, 2001).

In her testimony before the House Judiciary Committee, Anderson stated that the perpetrators had specifically sought out private sellers who would not run a background check as part of the purchase (Soraghan, 2000). This was done, in part, because she did not want to give her name in conjunction with the transactions, and she would have been required to do so on paperwork if a background check were performed (Soraghan, 2000). Although legislators pushed for her to be prosecuted, both federal and state prosecutors countered that she had not technically broken the law (Soraghan, 2000). In reality, they noted, she would have successfully passed the background check had she been given one (Soraghan, 2000).

The fourth gun used in the shooting—the Intratec TEC-DC9 used by Shooter K—was purchased privately for $500 (Columbine Review Commission, 2001). The perpetrators recruited one of their coworkers at Blackjack Pizza, Phil Duran, to help them find a gun to purchase. Duran connected them to Mark Manes, who sold them the gun. Despite not knowing, like Anderson, why they wanted the guns, both Duran and Manes were charged with and ultimately pled guilty to charges of illegally providing a handgun to a minor and possession of an illegal or dangerous weapon (as the pistol was prohibited under the Federal Assault Weapons Ban, discussed later in this chapter). Manes and Duran served six and four-and-a-half years in prison, respectively, the only two people ever charged with crimes related to the shooting (Columbine Review Commission, 2001).

The Gun Show Loophole

In light of the evidence that the shooters had, for all intents and purposes, found the loophole in the law, a heated debate about how it should be addressed ensued. Many people, including Robyn Anderson, said that the purchasing of those three weapons should have been more difficult and that laws should have been in place to regulate such transactions by way of background checks. Anderson further testified that had background checks been required for the purchases she made, she would not have made them. In Colorado, then-Governor Bill Owens introduced five gun regulations just a few months after Columbine. The package included a requirement for background checks on all sales at gun shows and increasing the minimum age of purchase at such events from 18 to 21. Both measures, as well as a safe storage requirement, were quickly defeated; the governor was successful in pushing through provisions to reinstate Colorado's background check system, include juvenile criminal records in background checks, and allow local prosecutors and police to enforce federal laws pertaining to straw purchases (Soraghan, 2000).

By the time Columbine happened, the debate over the gun show loophole already had been in full swing at the federal level. In fact, legislators had been trying since May of the year prior to the shooting to close the loophole. Congressman Rod Blagojevich of Illinois sponsored one of the earliest measures, House Bill 3833, which called for better regulation of the transfers of firearms at gun shows. Specifically, the bill required that the organizers of gun shows, through a surrogate role, comply with the rules of federally licensed dealers; sellers at the event then had to report the information of the prospective buyer, the firearm being sold, and the date and location of the transfer to them (H.R. 3833, 1998). Nearly as fast as it was introduced, the bill died. It was reintroduced in August 1998 as House Bill 442, Senate Bill 2527 in the following month, and House Bill 109 in January 1999. Each time the bill was introduced, it died.

With the help of New Jersey senator and notable gun control advocate Frank Lautenberg, Blagojevich repackaged the proposal as the Gun Show Accountability Act. Lautenberg introduced the act as Senate Bill 443 on February 23, 1999; Blagojevich proposed identical legislation as House Bill 902 on March 2, 1999. Similar to prior bills, the Gun Show Accountability Act sought to expand Brady background checks to gun shows, as well as require gun show operators to register and pay a fee to the Secretary of the Treasury, verify the identities of sellers and vendors at the event, and ensure that all sales were appropriately reported (H.R. 902, 1999; S. 443, 1999). Also similar to the prior bills, both pieces of legislation died soon after introduction (H.R. 902, 1999; S. 443, 1999). The Gun Show Accountability Act was reintroduced on May 20, 1999—a month after Columbine and the same day as the Heritage High School shooting in Conyers, Georgia—but failed to move beyond that stage (H.R. 1903, 1999).

Following Columbine, legislators again tried to close the loophole when the information about how the two perpetrators acquired their weapons from gun shows was made public. Three weeks to the day after the shooting, on May 11, New York Senator Chuck Schumer introduced the Youth Gun Crime Enforcement Act (YGCEA) of 1999 (S. 995, 1999). An identical bill was introduced in the House the following day by Michigan Congressman John Conyers (H.R. 1768, 1999). Like prior measures, the YGCEA attempted to extend Brady background checks to gun shows with many of the same provisions as the Gun Show Accountability Act (H.R. 1768, 1999; S. 995, 1999).

Unlike prior legislative attempts, however, the YGCEA also included provisions to prohibit transfers to juveniles, raise the age of handgun eligibility, prohibit possession of semiautomatic assault weapons by juveniles and enhanced penalties for those that did, require storage and safety devices for all firearms, and hold adults responsible for any deaths or injuries caused when juveniles had access to guns (H.R. 1768, 1999; S. 995, 1999). Both measures failed to pass, as did a separate bill introduced on June 10, 1999, by Florida Representative Bill McCollum that not only required mandatory background checks at gun shows but also prohibited fees being levied for such reviews (H.R. 2122, 1999).

Several other attempts to close the gun show loophole following Columbine also were made. On May 15, 2001, Arizona Senator John McCain introduced the Gun Show Loophole Closing and Gun Law Enforcement Act (S. 890, 2001). In addition to including previously introduced guidelines for implementing background checks at gun shows, the bill also provided federal funding for gun crime enforcement (S. 890, 2001). The bill's identical counterpart was introduced June 28, 2001, in the House of Representatives by Delaware's Michael Castle (H.R. 2377, 2001). Despite drawing bipartisan cosponsorship (which many of the other similar bills had not been able to do), both legislative efforts failed.

Also introduced in 2001 was the Gun Show Background Check Act (S. 767, 2001). Proposed by Rhode Island Senator John Reed, the bill required criminal background checks for guns purchased at gun shows, registration of the event's promoters, and the reporting of all sales to any unlicensed buyer (S. 767, 2001). After failing to move past introduction, the bill was reintroduced in subsequent years by Michigan Representative John Conyers (H.R. 260, 2003; H.R. 4034, 2002) and New Jersey Senator Frank Lautenberg (S. 22, 2013; S. 35, 2011; S. 843, 2009; S. 2577, 2008). Each additional attempt also died as quickly as it was introduced.

After his initial attempt in 2001, Senator McCain reintroduced his bill in 2003 as the Gun Show Loophole Closing Act (S. 1807, 2003). In addition to requiring criminal background checks to be conducted for all gun show transactions, the bill also mandated that improved recordkeeping was needed by those selling or transferring the firearms (S. 1807, 2003). As with his previous effort, the bill failed to make any headway in the Senate. It was reintroduced the following year in the House by Delaware's Michael Castle (H.R. 3832, 2004), where it promptly died. He subsequently reintroduced it in 2005 (H.R. 3540), 2007 (H.R. 96), and 2009 (H.R. 2324); New York Representatives Carolyn McCarthy (H.R. 141, 2013; H.R. 591, 2011) and Carolyn Maloney (H.R. 1612, 2017; H.R. 2380, 2015) also attempted to push the bill forward but were unsuccessful. In sum, despite numerous attempts to close the gun show loophole by members of both political parties, one of the most debated perceived causal factors for the Columbine shooting remains unaddressed 20 years later.

The Federal Assault Weapons Ban

A common misconception about school and other mass shootings is that they are all carried out with assault rifles (Schildkraut & Elsass, 2016). Although more than half are carried out with handguns (Fox & DeLateur, 2014; Schildkraut, Formica, & Malatras, 2018), assault-style weapons are often the focus of legislative efforts after such events. This can be traced back to two potential reasons. First, "assault weapons" typically are considered in the context of military-grade guns (typically rifles) that use a semiautomatic firing mechanism (Kleck, 2009). That mechanism, however, is not solely limited to rifles; instead, numerous different makes and models of handguns employ similar technology (Schildkraut & Elsass, 2016). Second, assault-style rifles have been used in other highly lethal shootings, including Aurora (2012)—13 killed; Sandy Hook (2012)—26 killed; San Bernardino (2015)—14 killed; Orlando (2016)—49 killed; Las Vegas (2017)—58 killed; Sutherland Springs (2017)—26 killed; and Parkland (2018)—17 killed. Thus, the belief exists that if these types of weapons were banned, highly lethal mass shootings would not occur. (It should be noted, however, that another particularly lethal school shooting—Virginia Tech (2007), in which 32 people were killed and more than 20 others injured—was carried out with two semiautomatic handguns.)

What often escapes this discussion, aside from the point about Virginia Tech, is that there *was* an assault weapons ban in place at the time that Columbine happened. The Violent Crime Control and Law Enforcement Act of 1994, which amended 18 U.S.C. §§ 921–922, included a section specifically addressing assault weapons (H.R. 3355, 1994). Most commonly known as the Federal Assault Weapons Ban (AWB), it declared that it was "unlawful for a person to manufacture, transfer, or possess a semiautomatic assault weapon" (18 U.S.C. §§ 921–922). In addition to prohibiting large-capacity magazines (those holding more than 10 rounds) for civilian-used firearms, the bill also banned the production of 19 specific firearms (18 U.S.C. §§ 921–922; see also Singh, 1999). Included in that list was the Intratec TEC-DC9 used in the Columbine shooting. Moreover, the AWB made it illegal for a juvenile to possess a handgun or its ammunition and for another person to sell or deliver a handgun to a juvenile (18 U.S.C. §§ 921–922), which provided the grounds for prosecution of Phil Duran and Mark Manes for their role in the shooting.

Passed at a time when crime rates were on the rise, the AWB received considerable pushback nearly as soon as it was enacted. On January 11, 1995, less than three months after the AWB went into effect, Maryland Representative Roscoe Bartlett introduced legislation to repeal the act (H. R. 464, 1995). He filed a second piece of legislation aimed at withdrawing the restrictions on both semiautomatic assault weapons and large capacity magazines just 15 days later (H.R. 698, 1995). Both bills failed to make any headway, as did a piece introduced by Alaska Representative Don Young in 1998 (H.R. 4137, 1998). Entitled the Second Amendment Restoration and Protection Act of 1998, the bill not only sought to repeal the assault weapons ban, it also attempted to nullify the Brady Handgun Violence Prevention Act discussed earlier in this chapter (H.R. 4137, 1998).

The AWB had an important feature that presented a challenge for gun control advocates: a sunset clause that had been written in to the original law that made the ban good only for 10 years (Singh, 1999). Several efforts were made to overcome the sunset clause. Prior to the ban's expiration, California Senator Dianne Feinstein (S. 2109, 2004; S. 2498, 2004) and Delaware Representative Michael Castle (H.R. 3831, 2004) introduced legislation to extend the sunset clause for an additional 10 years. Others approaches to address the sunset provision also were tried. Feinstein (S. 1034, 2003), along with New Jersey's Frank Lautenberg (S. 1431, 2003) and New York's Carolyn McCarthy (H.R. 2038, 2003), each introduced legislation to eliminate the sunset provision completely. With the failure of Congress to renew the ban, it expired on September 13, 2004.

Although the ban had lapsed, legislators continued to try to regulate assault-style weapons. Bills were introduced by Feinstein (S. 620, 2005), Lautenberg (S. 645, 2005), and McCarthy (H.R. 1312, 2005; H.R. 1022, 2007; H.R. 5100, 2004), as well as Florida Representative Alcee Hastings (H.R. 5099, 2004) and Illinois Representative Mark Kirk (H.R. 6257, 2008), to reinstate the now-lapsed ban; each failed to move forward past introduction. Others—including Feinstein (S. 150, 2013; S. 2095, 2017), McCarthy (H.R. 437, 2013), David Cicilline of Rhode Island (H.R. 4269, 2015; H.R. 5087, 2018), and Florida's Frederica Wilson (H.R. 5077, 2018)—each have introduced new variations of the original assault weapons ban. With the exception of the more recent bills (H.R. 5077, 2018; H.R. 5087, 2018; S. 2095, 2017) that have less than a one in four chance of passing (as of the time of this writing), all other attempts to create a new ban also failed.

Further attempts were made to address the issue of assault weapons but circumvent the issues that appear to plague a full-on ban. In their respective parts of Congress, McCarthy (H.R. 138, 2013) and Lautenberg (S. 33, 2013) each introduced legislation to ban high capacity magazines that hold more than 10 rounds. Henry Waxman (H.R. 2910, 2013) and Michael Honda (H.R. 376, 2015), both representatives from California, each introduced legislation designed to make "do-it-yourself assault weapons" kits (which, in their simplest form, are kits that contain all the parts of these types of guns but require the consumer to assemble them at home) illegal; Jackie Speier, also from California, introduced a bill to ban assault weapons that were imported into the U.S. (H.R. 4748, 2016). Despite such efforts, all pieces of legislation died. More recently, Sheila Jackson Lee of Texas proposed a seven-day waiting period on the transfer or sale of semiautomatic weapons, as well as silencers, armor-piercing ammunition, and large-capacity magazines; though the bill has yet to fail, it had less than a 2% chance of passage at the time of this writing.

By and large, state legislatures have been equally unsuccessful at enacting legislation related to assault weapons. To date, just six states have a prohibition on *all* semiautomatic weapons, as does Washington, D.C. (Giffords Law Center to Prevent Gun Violence, n.d.a.). Hawaii also has a ban in place, but theirs applies only to semiautomatic pistols; rifles and shotguns with this feature are not excluded under the law (Giffords Law Center to Prevent Gun Violence, 2017b). Minnesota and Virginia have state-mandated regulations for assault weapons in place but have not fully banned the weapons (Giffords Law Center to Prevent Gun Violence, n.d.a.).

The first state to enact an assault weapons ban was California. Following the 1989 shooting at Cleveland Elementary School in Stockton, California, in which 5 students were killed and 32 others were injured, the State Assembly passed the Roberti-Roos Assault Weapons Control Act (Cal. Penal Code §§ 16350, 16790, 16890, 30500-31115; see also Ingram, 1989). The act bans nearly 60 individually named firearms (Ingram, 1989) and further identifies specific characteristics that characterize assault weapons (Cal. Penal Code § 30515). An additional Senate bill passed the month before Columbine added three new provisions to the act, including banning large-capacity magazines over 10 rounds (under Cal. Penal Code §§ 16350, 16890, 30515), enhanced penalties for crimes committed with assault weapons, and establishing a one-year period for existing owners of such weapons to register them with the Department of Justice (Cal. S.B. 23, 1999). The bill went into effect on January 1, 2000.

The constitutionality of the ban was challenged in the case of *Kasler v. Lockyer* (2000). The California Supreme Court held that the law did not violate equal protection, the separation of powers doctrine, or any due process concerns and subsequently was not unconstitutional (*Kasler v. Lockyer*, 2000). Appeals to both the California State Supreme Court and the U.S. Supreme Court subsequently were denied. Additional restrictions later were added with the passage of the .50 Caliber BMG Regulation Act of 2004, including the banning of additional specified firearms amending § 494).

In May 1990, following California's lead, the state of New Jersey enacted its own assault weapons ban that outlawed more than 50 specific firearms or their copies (N.J. Stat. Ann. § 2C:39-1(w)(1), (2); see also Giffords Law Center to Prevent Gun Violence, 2017e). Those weapons that were legally purchased and registered with the state prior to May 1, 1990, among other procedural requirements, were allowed to be retained by their owners (N.J. Stat. Ann. § 2C:58-12b). In 2018, bills were introduced in both the State Assembly (N.J. A. 3697, 2018) and Senate (N.J. S.B. 548, 2018) to further strengthen the existing ban; the fate of the legislation was yet to be determined at the time of this writing.

The state of Massachusetts enacted its assault weapons ban in 1998, approximately one year before the Columbine shooting happened, yet during the time that the federal law was in place. Under the state's legislation, individuals were prohibited from owning an assault weapon or large-capacity magazine that was not lawfully possessed before the federal ban went into effect (Mass. Gen. Laws ch. 140, § 131M; see also Giffords Law Center to Prevent Gun Violence, 2017d). Firearms dealers also were similarly prohibited from selling, transferring, or otherwise delivering such weapons not lawfully possessed by the deadline (Mass. Gen. Laws ch. 140, § 123). In 2018, a U.S. District Court judge upheld the ban during a challenge to its constitutionality, saying that assault weapons for civilian use fell beyond the scope of the Second Amendment's right to bear arms (Raymond, 2018).

Connecticut was actually the third state to pass an assault weapons ban, which they did in 1993 (Conn. Gen. Stat. § 53-202c(a), (c); see also Giffords Law Center to Prevent Gun Violence, 2017a; Rose, 2013). Additional restrictions were passed in 2001, including the prohibition against armor-piercing bullets; the following year, however, certain types of weapons became exempt related to possession the following year (Rose, 2013). After the 2012 shooting at Sandy Hook Elementary School in Newtown, Connecticut, the state passed legislation that imposed substantial further restrictions on assault weapons, including banning the firearm that was used in the attack as well as large-capacity magazines (Rose, 2013).

Both Maryland (Giffords Law Center to Prevent Gun Violence, 2017c) and New York (Giffords Law Center to Prevent Gun Violence, 2017f) also had enacted their own assault weapons ban prior to the expiration of the federal law in 2004. Both introduced additional legislation after Sandy Hook. Maryland's 2013 legislation banned the purchase of new assault weapons, limited the capacity of magazines to 10 rounds, and required new handgun owners to undergo training and fingerprinting (Gabriel, 2013). Four years later, a challenge of the constitutionality of the ban was brought before the U.S. Supreme Court, but they declined to hear the case (Chung, 2017).

New York also passed one of the most comprehensive gun control packages in the nation after the shooting. Known as the Secure Ammunition and Firearms Enforcement (SAFE) Act, the legislation expanded the state's legal definition of assault weapons to change qualification tests (from two features to one), limited magazines to seven rounds, required background checks by ammunition dealers, and created a universal background check provision, among other measures (N.Y. Penal Law §§ 265.00(22)(f–h), 265.02(7), 265.10; see also Kaplan, 2013). Since its enactment, challenges to the constitutionality of the SAFE Act have appeared in the courts (Associated Press, 2014a), and its repeal has been the focus of opposing legislative efforts

(Hamilton, 2017; Reisman, 2018), but the ban and its associated provisions remains largely intact. In sum, despite political and public concern over the role of assault weapons in school and mass shootings, Columbine included, no action at the federal level and little among the states has been successful in abolishing the source of those fears.

The Point That Is Being Missed

Legislative efforts in the aftermath of the Columbine tragedy, particularly as it related to guns—the most highly criminalized cause of these events, even beyond the perpetrators themselves (Schildkraut & Muschert, 2013)—were largely unsuccessful. In many respects, this too became a pattern for other mass shootings. With the exception of the several states discussed earlier that enacted assault weapons bans after Sandy Hook, the majority of shootings, even those that are highly lethal, fail to propel legislative efforts forward from bill to actual law. Even when strides have been made, such as with the passage of the NICS Improvement Amendments Act (H.R. 2640, 2007) after the 2007 Virginia Tech shooting, their enforcement was lax at best. This act, for example, allocated $1.3 billion in federal funding to improve state and federal coordination and reporting of records to the background check system—the very records that could have disqualified the Virginia Tech shooter from purchasing his guns but did not because they were missing (Brady Campaign Press Release, 2011; Schildkraut & Hernandez, 2014; Witkin, 2012). Following the November 5, 2017, shooting at a church in Sutherland Springs, Texas, more than 10 years later, the very same issue again presented itself when it was discovered that the Air Force also had failed to report valuable information to the background check system that would have disqualified the perpetrator from *legally* acquiring his guns (Johnson, 2017).

This is not to say that there have been no legislative efforts in the last 20 years related to firearms. In fact, two new firearms laws have been enacted. The first, the Tiahrt Amendments, named for the U.S. Representative from Kansas who sponsored the piece, were provisions attached to a 2003 Department of Justice appropriations bill that "effectively shields [firearms] retailers from lawsuits, academic study, and public scrutiny" (Grimaldi & Horwitz, 2010, para. 1; see also Giffords Law Center to Prevent Gun Violence, n.d.b.). Specifically, the amendment prohibits gun dealers from submitting inventories to the Bureau of Alcohol, Tobacco, and Firearms (ATF), restricts disclosing firearms trace data to anyone outside of law enforcement (and only in connection with a specific criminal investigation or prosecution), and requires that the FBI destroy the records of all authorized gun purchasers within 24 hours of approval (Giffords Law Center to Prevent Gun Violence, n.d.b.). Several attempts, spearheaded by California representative Barbara

Lee, have been made to repeal the Tiahrt Amendments, albeit unsuccessfully (see H.R. 661, 2013; H.R. 1449, 2015; H.R. 5271, 2018).

The second law was the Protection of Lawful Commerce in Arms Act [PLCAA] (S. 397, 2005). After seven failed attempts, the law was finally enacted in 2005 under President George W. Bush. The PLCAA prevents firearms manufacturers and dealers from being held responsible if their products are used in the commission of a crime (S. 397, 2005). Regardless, families after the Sandy Hook (Hussey & Rojas, 2018) and Parkland (Vann, 2018) shootings, among others, have sued the manufacturers of guns used in the respective attacks. Like the Tiahrt Amendments, legislation was introduced to repeal the PLCAA (S. 2469, 2016), though it too later died in session. Not only did neither of these laws address many of the issues raised in the aftermath of Columbine and other similar events, but they also largely failed to do anything to prevent the next one.

Further, there is a significant point that is being missed. In a number of these events—and school shootings more particularly—existing laws and the new ones being proposed would fail to stop the shooters before they commit their acts. In the case of Columbine, both Robyn Anderson and Phil Duran would have passed background checks had they been subjected to them; therefore, even if the gun show loophole had not existed, they still would have been able to purchase the guns (Soraghan, 2000). As the two shooters then also acquired their weapons outside the constraints of a background check (effectively being handed the guns by Anderson and a private sale through Duran and Mark Manes), they also—had they even been old enough to lawfully purchase the weapons—would not have been flagged. Perpetrators of other events, including those in Sandy Hook and, more recently, Santa Fe, Texas (2018), have taken guns available in their households—guns that were purchased legally by parents or other family members who followed the existing laws, submitted to a background check, and met the mandated requirements to own the weapons.

We should be clear that our position is not to advocate for one side or the other (gun control versus gun rights). Instead, it is our aim that these considerations spark broader thinking about this highly contentious topic. While, as we have shown in this chapter, considerable legislative efforts (and resources) have been dedicated to the issue of guns, they often represent little more than "feel-good legislation" that gives the public the illusion that something is being done when, in reality, little progress is made. Instead, in order to make meaningful change on whichever end of the political spectrum one finds oneself, it is important to understand the situation in its context—and that context includes thoroughly understanding the complex relationship between mass shooters and firearms laws in the United States.

CHAPTER NINE

The Larger Community Footprint

When word of a shooting breaks, all eyes immediately focus on the families of those killed and the injured, and rightfully so. Yet, at the same time, this seeming tunnel vision has created an inaccurate understanding of just how impactful these events really are. As renowned trauma psychologist John Nicoletti (2017) asserts, the social and psychological footprints of these events are much larger, rippling from an epicenter that consumes the injured and the dead. This includes the people who are directly affected by the event but may not bear the physical scars of the shooting. Their wounds are invisible, yet they still require attention. As such, we contend that there needs to be a reconceptualization of the idea of the "survivor" as it pertains to school and mass shootings.

As this book is focused on the lessons learned from Columbine, understanding the breadth of those affected, the injuries they sustained, and the resources they needed and either have or have not received is crucial to addressing the needs of communities as they work through recovery in the aftermath of one of these tragedies. All too often, we find that individuals directly affected by the shooting simply because they were present do not get the resources they need because they are not considered survivors. In the same vein, the shortsightedness of excluding them also means that those resources often are not available for them in the first place. Thus, as with other chapters in this book, learning what went wrong for so many after Columbine can help improve responses and recovery strategies for future survivors of mass tragedies.

In this chapter, we further explore April 20, 1999, through the experiences of 16 survivors who were affected that day. They each come from different perspectives—family members of those murdered, a parent who had children at the school, students and teachers who were inside, and others from the community. Each shared their story with this book's authors as part of a larger project about the needs of mass shooting survivors related to recovery over four months beginning in October 2017, shortly after the attack in Las Vegas, Nevada. With the exception of two people—Heather Martin and Zachary Cartaya, both seniors at Columbine on the day of the shooting who consented to having their names on record—pseudonyms have been assigned to the individuals to protect their identity as they share their story. Still, these are their stories in their own words, invaluable lessons from the most unexpected of teachers.

Someone Has a Gun

For so many people, April 20, 1999, began like any other day with, in retrospect, a welcome sense of normalcy. Zach was in choir class, alongside Heather, Brian, and Monica, all seniors. Freshman Maddie was in math class, while senior Kristina was in science. Louis, a teacher, was holding class in the auditorium, just off the commons area that included the cafeteria. There, starting their lunch period, were Kelsey, a freshman, Karissa, a junior, and Andrea, a senior, scattered among the other students.

In an instant, everything changed. Kelsey and Andrea were at different tables in the cafeteria when the gunshots erupted just outside the building. Initially thinking it was a senior prank like so many others but soon realizing the gravity of the situation, they quickly took cover underneath the tables when teacher Dave Sanders first came in and told them to get down. A short time later, when Dave returned and ordered the students to flee, both girls did. Andrea described her next steps:

> [I] ran out and we were getting shot at as we're running out. Then I don't know how I got home. . . . It's a blur, but I know I did go to someone's house and hid under a table of theirs. I remember hearing all the bombs, and the guns, gunfire, and being just extremely scared.

Karissa, who had been in the lunch line, was able to get out of the school quickly by following other students through the kitchen area, into the auditorium, and out an upper-level entrance. She got a ride home from another student and spent the rest of the day like so many others—glued to her television screen, waiting for answers. In her math class, Maddie watched through the room's exterior window as terrified students ran across Pierce Street, a typically busy road that runs adjacent to the school, without looking where they were going; then the fire alarms went off. As she started to leave her classroom, other kids were yelling, "They have guns, they have bombs, get out of here." She took off and made it to the safety of the park across the street, where she met up with a friend and fled to a nearby neighborhood, finding shelter in the homes of residents who had opened their doors (and telephones) to the terrified students. Kristina, seeing people run past the window of her science classroom in the hallway, followed her teacher to the back of the classroom, where they, along with 12 other students, hid in a storage closet for three and a half hours.

The choir class that was in session when the shooting broke out had around 120 students and was located just across the hall from the science wing. One of the students who had stepped out of the room came running back in and yelled, "There are kids downstairs with guns!" When the chaos set in, about half of the students—including Monica—were able to flee the room with their teacher, who guided them to the auditorium nearby, the same room where Louis was holding his class. The other 60 students, including Heather, Brandon, and Zach, remained in the room, as they could not safely evacuate. A small office of approximately 12 feet by 30 feet adjoined the chorus room, and the students immediately started piling in to get out of harm's way. Realizing his sister was still out in the school, Zach and a classmate, whose brother also attended Columbine, left to go find them:

> Then we go down to the hallway and [the shooters] were right there, firing up. We never saw them specifically, but the fireball from their gun we definitely saw. And that was where we saw Mr. [Dave] Sanders get hit and we all froze. There was about five or six of us, I believe. We all froze. . . . And then a science teacher came running up. . . . There was this wood paneling on the corners of every single wall and I remember that paneling just exploding behind her. She [the teacher] screamed, "Get in and get down." And we did.

Brandon, who recalls how the floor had been vibrating because so many people were trying to escape, also had attempted to flee the choir room. As he ran into the hallway, he also saw the barrel of a shotgun as it fired and immediately turned back to the classroom. Once inside, Brandon, Zach, and their classmates barricaded the door to the room with furniture and filing cabinets to make sure that the gunmen could not get in and that no other students could get out. Over the next three hours, the 60 students, on their own without an adult, listened to the sounds of gunfire as it moved throughout the school, first from the perpetrators shooting in the cafeteria and library and then from responding law enforcement, as well as the deafening ring of the fire alarm. They rotated around so that students, as they became overheated from being packed into such close quarters, could put their heads up into the ceiling tiles to get air. They tried to get through to 911, but the lines were jammed; they instead reached out and were able to connect with the FBI and relay information. Not knowing what was going on beyond the door that was protecting them, Brandon noted that "because we had been told there were guns, we knew it was a life and death situation and we stayed put."

In the auditorium where Louis was holding class, a student who had left to use the restroom and quickly came back also alerted them of someone with a gun. Confused by what he was being told, Louis went to investigate:

> *I walked out into the commons area. It was almost a surrealistic scene because people were on the floor. It was smoky and hazy. I believe it's when Officer Gardner had his shootout in the parking lot with the boys, that's when all hell broke loose. In fact, Dave Sanders was just about seven, eight feet away from me at the stairs telling kids to go up the stairs and then I was telling the kids to go to the auditorium.*

He quickly returned to the room and directed his students to the upper level of the auditorium that connected with the north hallway. Moving around to the back door that connected to the commons area, Louis also was able to coax approximately 60 other students and two custodians, who had taken shelter in the bathrooms, into the auditorium.

Once inside and on the upper level, people began to flee the auditorium when they believed it to be safe, only to quickly return when they realized the gunmen were roaming the halls. Louis and the chorus teacher, who had now found refuge in the auditorium with his students, locked the auditorium doors and tried to keep everyone calm. At one point, Louis stuck his head out of the set of doors closest to the cafeteria to survey the scene: "I think it's when [the gunmen] were on the steps shooting at the propane tanks because the sound almost deafened me when I opened the doors and heard the shots and blast." Returning to the room, he and the others waited for about 20 more minutes, when they were rescued by a custodian who saw a window of opportunity and took it.

Monica, who had been able to flee to the safety of the auditorium, had also been one of the students to attempt to evacuate through the north hall. After hiding for about a half hour, she stepped out of the auditorium:

> *I looked to my left and I looked to my right, and I could see the doors. When I looked back to my left, there is a man dressed in black, white shirt, black suspenders.* [The person she describes is Shooter H, whom she knew from coaching soccer together.] *He had—I assumed they were bombs, like little pellet things down his vest or his suspenders. He had guns and he said, "On your marks, get set, go." I ran zigzag through the halls. . . . [B]ullets passed my body. He did hit a shrapnel bomb that was around the door. It exploded and I had shrapnel on my leg.*

Still running, Monica was able to get out of the school and to a nearby park, dragging an injured student alongside her. At the park, they were able to get medical attention from first responders who were triaging the situation; they also were able to secure transportation in one of the students' vans. Contemplating going back to try and save others, students in the park decided it was not safe upon seeing gunfire come out of the school's doors. Instead, Monica made her way to a nearby church, lay on the floor, and cried, trying to make sense of how someone she knew would want to hurt her.

When Kelsey fled the cafeteria, she ran up the stairs she had seen Dave Sanders ascend back up after warning them of the danger. At the top of the stairs, she had a choice—go left toward the library or right into the science wing. She turned right and soon took shelter in one of the classrooms. The teacher had her and the other students line up against the wall, out of sight from the shooters if they looked through the window next to the door. A short time later, Dave Sanders, who had just been shot, came into the room and collapsed. For the next several hours, Kelsey watched as two students administered first aid, and everyone pitched in trying to save him.

Room by room, SWAT teams were freeing those students who remained in the school—Heather, Brian, and Zach in the choir office; Kelsey and Kristina in separate science rooms. Unaware of who or where the shooters were, the police took no chances, which, as a result, led to the students coming face-to-face with assault weapons that had been trained on them. Specific orders were given—hands up and don't touch a thing; other directives, such as don't look down, were not. Kristina remembered the experience:

> The SWAT team came in and got us out about three and a half hours after we were first stuck in there and led us outside. It was still very much a crime scene and they let us know that areas were hot, meaning just move as fast as possible. We ran through the building and ran outside across the street. And at that point, I kind of realized, "Wow." The street in front of the school was closed down. I don't know what's going on, but it's pretty major.

The students from the choir office were led out through the auditorium, into the cafeteria that now had inches of standing water from the activated sprinkler system, and out of the school, past the bodies of students Rachel Scott and Daniel Rohrbough that lay where they had fallen, open for everyone to see. As they passed, Zach recalled: "I gave Danny [Rohrbough] a ride to school that morning. I knew exactly who he was and what had happened to him." Once a safe distance away from the school, the students boarded buses and were transported to nearby Leawood Elementary School for reunification.

"There's Something Really Bad Going on Over at Columbine"

As the gunfire erupted at Columbine, others in the community also were in the midst of their daily routines. David, the father of one of the victims killed in the library, was away on business. His wife, Stephanie, was at work, as was Chantel, who also lost a family member in the shooting. Abigail, a sixth-grade student, was currently in class at Columbine Hills Elementary, located less than five minutes south of the high school off Pierce Street and Canyon Avenue. Kerry, an employee at a neighboring elementary school, had gone home for lunch that day. Two of her four sons were students at Columbine.

Unknowingly, at the moment the shooting started, Kerry, whose house was very close to the high school, heard the first two rounds as they were fired but shrugged it off as thinking she slammed the garage door too hard, knocking pictures off the wall upstairs. She went inside, started some laundry, unloaded the dishwasher, ate her lunch, and then headed back to work. As she reached the end of her neighborhood, she noticed people standing on the corner, watching a flurry of activity up Pierce Street in front of the high school. She recalled:

> When I turned to go back [towards work], I got a sicker and sicker and sicker feeling in my stomach. When I got to school, the nurse was walking out of the building and I said to her, "There's something really bad going on over at Columbine." She said to me, "Yes there's shooting over there." I said, "My kids are over there."

Kerry's younger son, after fleeing Columbine, actually went over to the elementary school looking for her. Before he left, he told the people in the office to get the children off of the playground because there was a shooting. He contacted his mother later by phone from a friend's house. What seemed like an eternity later, her older son also was able to connect with her by phone.

By that time, news of the shooting was spreading fast across local media. Abigail's school went into a lockdown; her teacher turned on the news:

> He made a joke like, "Nothing happens in Littleton. I'm sure it's just a car chase." He turned on the TV, and obviously, it was the aerial view of the high school, and then he looked at us and was like, "Oh, my gosh. My kids are there."

The school's principal came to reprieve her teacher so that he could go search for his children. A short time later, Abigail's mom came to pick her and her younger sister up from school. Abigail's mother had heard reports that it was the elementary school the girls were in that was under attack and was quite frantic when picking them up. Once home, Abigail and her family went to a neighbor's house, where their son had not yet been found. They watched the news, seeing reports of victim counts change and suddenly realizing that there definitely were fatalities.

Stephanie learned of the shooting from a coworker, who came to her desk after hearing about the event on the radio. Knowing that her daughter was there, Stephanie left work and headed toward the school, ultimately finding herself at Leawood, waiting to be reunited with her child. Her husband, David, had called over to a satellite office in between meetings. He recalled finding out about the shooting from the receptionist who answered:

> *The lady who answered the phone says something like she heard about the shootings at the high school in Colorado. I said, "I hadn't heard about it because I had been in meetings all day. What happened?" She said, "Well, it was in Littleton," and I said, "Well, what school?" They told me it was Columbine. I said, "Well, all my kids go to Columbine." She got really quiet and I said, "I didn't know anything about it." She said, "Do you still want to talk to the person?" I said, "No, I better call back home and find out what's going on."*

He reached out to Stephanie, who already had left her office. Sometime later, he was able to reach her on a cell phone that she had borrowed from a coworker. There was no news yet on their child.

Chantel's boss had a television in his office and was watching the coverage unfold. As he commented about "the stupid kids at Columbine," Chantel reminded him that she had connections to the school. The tone immediately changed:

> *Everybody just turned white and they pushed me out of the room and shut the door. It was very strange. Then they pulled me into this other office, and they said there has been a shooting at Columbine High School. It's interesting because this was right after the Kentucky, I think Heath High School shooting. I said—I feel really bad about this now. I said, "What else is new? There's 2,000 people in that school, he's [her family member] fine." It was like this immediate denial. I went back to my desk and I started working.*

Realizing that she did not understand the gravity of the situation, Chantel's coworkers drove her to her family home. As they approached, she recalled what she described as "strange":

> *It was so surreal because you could see the helicopters swirling and you could see the people were parked in the middle of street. It was almost like this apocalyptic moment because people were standing in the median of the street and people just would park their cars.*

Waiting for Answers

The scene at Leawood Elementary School was nearly as chaotic as the one at Columbine. As Columbine was one of the first events of its kind, there was no real template for how to handle the reunification process, and, as a result, there was no organization. A lot of misinformation was shared. Parents did not know where to go when they arrived at the school but soon were shuffled into the auditorium. As buses arrived from Columbine, the students were paraded across the auditorium's stage so that waiting parents could easily see them. Before they were released into the custody of their families, the students were debriefed by police, often without their parents or a victim's advocate present. Soon, Louis had made his way over to the school and was helping to greet students, providing many with a calm and familiar face. Zach, Brandon, and Kristina each were picked up by members of their families shortly thereafter.

Kerry had also been reunited with her two sons at Leawood and took them back with her to the school she worked at until her husband picked them up. There, she helped parents of the school's students find their children so they could be taken home. By 5:00 p.m., the school was clear and she was able to go home and come together with her family. After going to her friend's house, Maddie made her way back to her own home; Andrea and Karissa also were able to make it home safely. Kelsey, who had been in the science room with Dave Sanders, was reunited with her father at the library in Clement Park after being taken there by police officers who cleared their classroom. Monica, who had fled to a church at a neighboring high school, was picked up by her sister and brother-in-law after going to her boyfriend's house.

Now in the security and comfort (as it were) of their own homes, many started searching for answers and information. The easiest way to do that was the through television. By now, the wall-to-wall coverage was in full effect. With the students and others in the building still not really understanding what they had been through, the news media provided something—anything—that they could use to try and make sense of it. As Karissa explained, "all that watching, all that footage, over and over again was horrific. I didn't know what else to do. There were no other resources for information." Brandon similarly remembered that "there was so much misinformation coming out, and yet we couldn't not watch it, because we had no idea." He recalled how his girlfriend, who also was a Columbine student but had taken lunch off campus that day, found out that one of her best friends had been killed through the media as the names of the victims were released.

Answering machines were clogged with voice mails trying to find out the status of people. Caller ID devices blinked uncontrollably from the massive influx of calls, eventually maxing out when the volume became too great. Students spent hours calling one another, reaching out to make sure their friends were okay and, most importantly, alive. Back and forth across Jefferson County, phones rang, followed by sighs of relief to find out their friends were okay. Yet even in the moments of reprieve, making those calls also took a toll. As Maddie remembered:

You answer the first couple of voice mails. It was a couple of girls that I grew up with, it's their parents calling and asking if my parents have seen me and if I knew where their child was. Calling them back and making sure that every one of those calls were taken care of was really, really hard for somebody who is 14 years old, to tell them you didn't see their child.

There also was a change in the dynamics between the students and their families. Some were insulated by family and friends, creating somewhat of a cocoon of emotional support to isolate the students from what they just had experienced. Kerry, whose two sons had been in the school, remembered that she "could not just see them, I had to touch them, I had to physically touch their bodies" so that she knew they were okay. For others, the experience created a wedge between family members. Monica recalled how her mother responded, both in the immediate and since: "[She] drank a bottle of Jack and said, 'We're never going to talk about this.' She has no idea what happened to me that day. She's never asked questions. She's never acknowledged the day."

One thing that was very important to the students was being with one another—people who had a shared experience and who could, while nothing made sense, still understand what the others were feeling. As Kelsey explained:

My mom tried. My dad tried too, he was right there. I know there was—at least in my heart, there was a real emotional separation between me and people who weren't there, and also a real bond between me and people who were there who got it, who I didn't have to explain things to.

Maddie shared a similar experience:

I wouldn't let [my parents] hug me. . . . I was trying to be at these vigils and these ceremonies and everything as much as I possibly could because the hugs from somebody else who you knew made it and was alive meant more than a hug from my parents for some reason.

That evening, a local church, Light of the World, opened its doors, and many students flocked there, finding comfort in one another.

Meanwhile, back at Leawood Elementary School, there were families still waiting for answers. Stephanie had been sitting there for several hours, having made her way over as soon as she was notified of the shooting, trying to make sense of how something so violent could have happened in her community. Her husband, David, boarded the first flight he could find to make his way back to Colorado from California. Sometime around 6:30 p.m., after checking for their missing loved one at one of the local hospitals that was taking in victims, Chantel and her family made their way to the elementary school. She recalled what she saw when they arrived: "There are all these news vans set up outside. People standing in line to plead—find their kids. There were all these lists on the windows of people that had not been found yet." Soon, they were asked by the sheriff at the scene to provide details like what their family member was wearing and the name of their dentist to secure records—all part of what was written off as "standard procedure."

Over the next several hours, the remaining students were reunited with their families and made their way home. By around 9:00 p.m., the only people who remained at Leawood were, unbeknown to them at the time, members of the families of the 13 people who were killed. They soon were sent home with victims' advocates, not knowing the fate of their loved ones. Yet as Stephanie remembered, "it was not confirmed, but I'll tell you, when they don't come home, you had a pretty good idea." David, who arrived home from his business trip around midnight, recalled something he had heard earlier in the day as he kept in touch with his wife:

Sometime on Tuesday afternoon, the county sheriff came on television and said everybody had been accounted for, so at that time we knew. He basically announced to everybody because if your child wasn't at home, they were accounted for, so that was pretty upsetting.

Nevertheless, home with the victim's advocate and surrounded by family, they still were clinging to the idea that their daughter might be found alive.

There was no sleep that evening for the 13 families, including David, Stephanie, and Chantel. They all recalled holding out hope that their loved one was hiding in a closet and just had not been found yet, but that, as David considers now, was one of those "things that you look back now and say, 'Well, that didn't really make any sense,' but that's what you were thinking at that time." He and Stephanie stayed tuned in to the TV that evening, hoping to find out anything about their child in the absence of official information. Chantel and her family did several press interviews trying to have someone come forward with information about their loved one. People milled in and out of each family's house.

Then came the official notification: their loved ones were killed in the shooting. Notifying the families took several days because, as David pointed out, "nobody was prepared to go through recovering all these bodies from a high school at one time and doing the official notifications." It was late on Wednesday afternoon when the families were told. The families met individually with the sheriff and a victim's advocate. Chantel recalled the moment when a family meeting was called, and she found out that her loved one was officially gone:

The sheriff showed up and he showed my mom—I know this is probably policy or procedure but he showed my mom a picture of him. His driver's license was in his damn pocket and his face was not destroyed so why did they have to show her a picture of him dead, I don't know but anyway. They needed her to identify him and so she threw up and she passed out and I went outside and it was almost as if my brain broke. I could literally feel it break. I couldn't think; it was weird. I went out and I laid on the front lawn and I remember looking up at the sky, at the clouds and thinking how does flour and sugar actually mix? How does that become one to make cookies? How? I remember people around me, standing above me, looking down at me, talking but I couldn't understand. It sounded like they were in a tunnel. . . . I finally heard somebody say, "I think we need to call an ambulance" and I by no means was going to go to a hospital because of me. I was like, "No, no. I am okay." I remember nothing of the next two hours after that. It's gone.

Grieving in a Fishbowl

The media, having descended on the Columbine community, were relentless about getting the information to share what they already knew was going to be one of the biggest stories of their careers. They had shown up at Leawood Elementary School trying to catch the first glimpses of surviving students, and soon they appeared in neighborhoods, at the homes of students and (unbeknown to them) family members of the people killed. They also called—within an hour of arriving home, Kristina remembers her phone was ringing off the hook with calls from the media. When Louis finally returned home, he had a message on his answering machine from *The Boston Globe*; some time later, other reporters showed up on his doorstep after finding out he knew one of the shooters. Upon checking her family's voicemail, Maddie found a message from a French newspaper, asking for an interview and offering to pay her €2,000 (nearly $4,000 in U.S. currency at the time) for a copy of her yearbook. (She did not sell her yearbook, but other students did, and soon it was plastered across national and international media outlets.)

The next morning, students were paraded in front of news cameras: *The Today Show. Good Morning America.* Interviews with Dan Rather, Katie Couric, Phil Donahue, and other media heavy hitters. Later in the day, it was *Oprah Winfrey* and *Inside Edition*. The shows sent limos over to the houses, transporting them to Clement Park's media city one by one, like an assembly line of tragic stories; yet when the story did not fit what the show was looking for (as many outlets came in with a predetermined narrative), students were asked to change it. There seemed to be no boundaries for what the press would do to get the story.

Thinking back to one interview opportunity, Andrea, who played sports under Dave Sanders' coaching, remembered:

A couple of my teammates went and did it, but I couldn't do it. I physically was sick to my stomach. I couldn't do it. They [the media] were pretty rude. They were not sensitive. It was a media shitstorm. It was everywhere. They would jump

out of bushes to get an interview with you. It was ridiculous. They were not sensi-
tive to what we had gone through. They were in your face.

Kelsey, who had been in the science room with Dave, also recalled the invasive nature of the media:

One of my good friends lost her brother in the shooting in the library. At least one
of the stories that she told me was that there were reporters who jumped her fence
and took pictures of her family through their back door. Stuff like that. And just
said they were very invasive. Very, very invasive. We did the first initial inter-
views, I think, within the first 48–72 hours. Just with The [Denver] Post *and*
stuff. I think TIME *came later, but I don't really remember. Basically, I just*
remember there being huge, invasive, unkind feeling that our community—at
least to some we felt that we had been very much treated unkindly and taken
advantage of, and just—I don't know. Just the sensationalization and just sound
bites, and stuff—I don't know. There was just so much about how the media
reported things that did more damage than did anything good.

Others, like Brandon, purposefully took media interviews in an attempt to
correct the misinformation they saw being spread, but, in many instances,
the damage already had been done.

As invasive as it was for those who had survived the shooting, it was even
more intense for the people who had lost loved ones in it. Upon receiving
notification of the identities of the victims, the press had descended upon
their families' homes, blocking streets and doing whatever it took to get the
interview. Chantel recalled:

We didn't cover the address when we did the first interview so [the media] all
knew where we lived. We were just shuttled from hotel to hotel to hotel to do inter-
views and then brought back home. . . . It was just so chaotic. [The] Associated
Press stole family pictures off the walls that were later found in the media.

David also remembers the media attention, though as he and Stephanie and
their family took a more private approach, they were less hounded by the
press than those families that had chosen to be more visible and out front.
Able to be more selective regarding whom he decided to speak with, he still
recalled that "we quickly learned there were some media that we could talk
to and trust and some that we couldn't." Nevertheless, some precautions
were taken to protect the families overall, such as setting up the parameters
that the media could not directly photograph them. A small concession, it
likely made the grieving process somewhat easier.

Another problem with the media city sitting in Clement Park is that the
grounds also had become home to a makeshift memorial for the victims.

Flowers, teddy bears, candles, and signs stretched for as far as the eye could see—the size of a football field as described by some who had witnessed it. When members of the Columbine community wanted to pay their respects to the 13 victims or have a moment of reflection about what they had experienced, they did it with a national spotlight and a countless number of camera lenses pointed on them. The victims' funerals were televised. The students' graduation that year was covered by the press and ended up having an attendance of around 10,000 people. (Monica, who graduated that year, remembered her commencement ceremony as "a media circus. It was ridiculous. We didn't have any normalcy at all." Others shared similar feelings.) Visits from President Clinton and Vice President Gore only increased the media's hunger for coverage. There was no privacy, only media scrutiny. The Columbine community was truly grieving in a fishbowl—a sentiment echoed by many.

Columbine was not only a media hotspot; it soon became a tourist destination, a historical marker that people traveled to see. Monica recalled that a couple of months after the shooting,

> *I was outside doing yard work. The street I lived on was a cul-de-sac. This van, I remember just kept driving up and down. I think "you can't go anywhere, we're a cul-de-sac" and they stopped and they're from Arkansas and the parents got out and said, "Did you go to Columbine?" That was the first—And I was like, "Well, yeah." They said, "Can you show my kids where those kids died?" And at that point, I said—it just shocked me that this was now like a hotspot. You want to see the monuments, the national monuments, you want to see the White House, and let's go see Columbine. That's when it hit me that this was bigger than I thought it was.*

Beyond the pilgrimages to see the school, the community also was plagued with threats and communiques from people who worshipped the perpetrators (for additional discussion, see Chapter 10).

Not everyone, however, was able to grieve their losses and openly process what they had been through. Some, like Karissa, had to contend with the fact that they had been friends with the shooters. Describing the pair as people who were part of her clique, Karissa had hung out with the perpetrators, finding herself at the same parties, seeing them before and after school, and sharing rides to different places—the normal stuff friends do. When the media found out about her connection, she also was hounded by a barrage of reporters hoping to tell the story of the gunmen from the people that knew them. One news outlet stole pictures she had of one of the shooters at the recent prom on a roll of film—they had promised to get her photos developed in exchange for an interview and, at her young age, she had trusted them. She struggled inwardly with immense confusion; she tried to "reconcile that

I lost friends too, but I could not talk about the grief I had over the friends that I lost because they were horrible murderers." In the end, that very interview that she had given also ended up costing her even more: "all my other friends completely dumped me as a friend when they found out I did the interview and lashed out against me." Karissa, like others, became isolated and guilty by association.

Tragedy Strikes Again . . . and Again . . . and Again

While the Columbine community tried to return to "normal," there were several obstacles that stood in their way and stunted the healing process. The first came six months after the shooting. On October 19, 1999, a senior at Columbine was arrested for threatening to "finish the job" that had been started months earlier (The Denver Post, 2000). He appeared in court three days later ("Columbine survivor's mother," 1999). That same day, October 22, 1999, Carla Hochhalter, the mother of student Anne Marie, who was paralyzed in the attack, entered the Alpha Pawn Shop in nearby Englewood, Colorado (Olinger, Robinson, & Simpson, 1999). She told the clerk that she was interested in looking at handguns and, after looking at several options, selected a revolver from a case and said that she wanted to buy it. As the clerk turned to begin writing up the sales paperwork, Carla loaded the gun with bullets she had brought to the store with her. She first fired at the wall before turning the gun on herself. She was pronounced dead minutes after arriving at Swedish Medical Center—the same hospital Anne Marie had been brought to after the shooting. Carla, who was especially close with her daughter, had long struggled with depression that was further exacerbated by the shooting (Olinger et al., 1999).

The Columbine community was rocked once again on December 15, 1999. Junior Erin Walton received an email from Michael Campbell, an 18-year-old from Florida, who threatened to finish what had started in April and warning her to stay home from school the following day (Nicholson, 2000). As a result, the final two days of the semester, including exams, were canceled as the FBI traced the threat (The Denver Post, 2000). Campbell was arrested two days after making the threat and pled guilty to communicating a threat across state lines (Nicholson, 2000). He subsequently served 16 weeks in a correctional facility for the felony conviction and was released (Nicholson, 2000).

The spring brought even more shock and tragedy to the community. In the early morning hours of February 14, 2000, an employee of the local Subway sandwich shop drove by and noticed that the lights were still on nearly three hours after closing (Janofsky, 2000; KUSA Staff, 2000). Suspicious, he checked inside and found that 15-year-old Nick Kunselman and his girlfriend, 16-year-old Stephanie Hart-Grizzell, both Columbine sophomores, had been shot and killed. The inseparable pair often were found together when Stephanie would come to pick up Nick, who closed the restaurant some evenings, and keep him company (Janofsky, 2000; KUSA Staff, 2017). They shared a passion for music and art; many believed them to be more in love than was possible for kids their age (KUSA Staff, 2017). Five days after the murders, the couple was buried together (Associated Press, 2000; KUSA Staff, 2017). Their murders remain unsolved to this day, though the case has stayed open with hopes that the killer will be brought to justice (KUSA Staff, 2017).

Just after the first anniversary of the shooting, the community was again rocked by tragedy. Greg Barnes, a 17-year-old junior who was a star basketball player, committed suicide on May 4, 2000 (Olinger & Devlin, 2000; Weller, 2000). Despite a bright future ahead as a shooting guard named to the All-Colorado team and being heavily recruited by top collegiate programs, Barnes succumbed to the demons that he had carried with him since April 20 (Olinger & Devlin, 2000). He was close friends with Matthew Kechter, who was killed in the shooting (Olinger & Devlin, 2000). He also had watched Dave Sanders being shot twice through the window of his science classroom and was in the room where Dave had bled to death (Weller, 2000). Many remarked that Greg had shown no signs of depression or suicidality, causing his death to be all the more shocking to those who knew him and the community at large.

The Long Road

The shooting itself happened late in the academic year, and, as a result, students were not able to finish out at Columbine. In order to accommodate them, the students were moved to nearby Chatfield High School, which happened to be Columbine's rivals. The school day was split—the Chatfield students attended in the morning, the Columbine students in the afternoon. Though everyone tried to keep the experience as normal as possible for the students, there were certain circumstances that made the situation difficult. Karissa recalled how counseling had been offered through the intercom system:

> *We'd be sitting in these classrooms and we would have to get into these small groups with people in our class. The person on the intercom would come on and say, "Talk about how you're feeling today." Then they'd give us five minutes and then they come on back on and say, "Talk about a new struggle that you're having." I remember that so clearly of being the worst thing that could have possibly been done.*

While at Chatfield, there was a clear outpouring of support from the community and beyond: Blankets. Teddy bears. Letters. Books. The local Walmart donated backpacks and other school supplies. One action, however, over-shadowed all of that for students like Maddie:

You walk in the school and you go into your class and there's an empty desk there. It's from a classmate who passed away. Change up the seating arrangements when your kids walk in the door. Be there to greet them every class and that didn't happen. It didn't—A couple of classes never changed seating arrangements. You don't know what somebody else is thinking. I don't know if the teacher was trying to be sentimental, to let the student know that his other students were thinking about them. There's always going to be a spot for them in our hearts. I never said anything about it but it really bothered me.

The time at Chatfield was also marked by attempts to create new safety proto-cols, such as locked-down campuses. True to their mascot's name (the Reb-els), the Columbine students were defiant of the rules. Many violated the security policies, often ditching school and pushing the limits to see what they could get away with. They were angry and frustrated and made it clear to the administration and others around.

For the seniors, their time at Chatfield was hard—they graduated just 32 days after the shooting. As Zach remembered, "I never entered Columbine again as a student." Soon they were off to college—some stayed close to home; others went away to school. Often, they would conceal that they had gone to Columbine to avoid awkward looks or a barrage of questions, instead giving a different school name. They didn't want to be known for being asso-ciated with Columbine.

While in school, some thrived; others crashed. Some turned to drugs (like Heather, who also subsequently developed an eating disorder) or alcohol to try and dull the pain. Most, however, felt lost and alone. The younger stu-dents had been able to go back into the school, rejoin their community, and continue on the recovery journey together, though they had to do so with the glaring media spotlight on them much of the time. The seniors, now college students, were not provided with any of those safeguards, and the effects were detrimental to say the least. As Monica remembered, "I think my class felt like we were just shoved out into the world and said, 'Good luck.' It wasn't fair, in my mind." Andrea added, "We weren't really part of the heal-ing process. We were adults now and stuck in the real world after going through this trauma."

The aftereffects of the shooting were severe: insomnia, anxiety, depres-sion, post-traumatic stress disorder (PTSD), all compounded by the anger, confusion, resentment, and fear that plagued those who were exposed to the shooting. Counseling was a big part of the recovery effort but, despite shared experiences, was not utilized uniformly among the survivors. Some parents, like Zach's, encouraged it: "They saw that a different person walked out of the school that day. The person who left for school that morning never really came home. A different person came home that night, and they saw that." Other families chose not to address the issues or not seek out resources, believing that they could take care of the issues within the family unit. Anger from the students also got in the way of seeking help, as did the lack of understanding about available resources or the extent of the challenges that they now were facing. For some, that realization did not come until many years after the shooting; for others, even 20 years later, they still have yet to come to terms with what they experienced that fateful day.

Another of the biggest impediments to mental health care was resources—namely money. Services were provided to the Columbine community through the state for three years, but availability was based on need and exposure on the day of the shooting. Some survivors, like Zach, were able to seek counseling through their own insurance that allowed them to build long-term relationships with their medical providers. Those who relied on the state-sponsored resources found themselves in trouble when the deadline passed. With the rising cost of therapy sessions (some as much as $150 per hour), the students and their families could not afford to continue paying and were left without any professional help.

Even when the resources were available, they were only to be used by the people who had been in the school on April 20, 1999. This created another problem: What about the larger ripple effect? What about the parents of the students, like Kerry, who were in the school and had to wonder about whether or not it was their child who had been killed? What about the siblings, grandparents, and others who were affected in some way? Such concerns also were raised for the families of the 13 killed that day. While resources often were provided for the biological parents, they were not as readily available for stepparents, children, siblings, grandparents, and others affected. As a result, many of the families who lost loved ones relied on donated money, their own finances, and insurance to spread out the resources to make sure that everyone was taken care of.

One resource that the families had that was unique to their experience was each other. While many were affected by the events of April 20, only a small group shared in the ultimate loss. David recalled that aside from his and Stephanie's large family and the counseling he sought almost immediately after the shooting, one of the best resources they had were the other families:

We had 12 other families who had lost somebody and we became close with them. Although it was this horrendous tragedy, that familiarity was extremely important in terms of getting through all this and seeing how they dealt with it. Walking into this group of people and knowing you didn't have to explain how you felt. They were there and they knew and you could just start talking. They knew it was okay to laugh sometimes. Where you always feel like when you're out in public and people knew who you were that if you start laughing and joking about something, they would somehow think badly of you that you're somehow finding some happiness. However, with those other families, there were no worries about that. They knew what was going on.

Together, they also worked to honor the legacies of their loved ones. When the school district wanted to refurbish the library where the majority of their family members were killed, they banded together and raised the money needed to raze the old library and build a new structure in a different part of the school. Though the memory of those taken from them on April 20, 1999, are forever with them, the families—including David, Stephanie, and Chantel—continue to push forward, turning their tragedy into much-needed action, even 20 years later.

A Principal, a Protector, a Pillar

Columbine High School principal Frank DeAngelis was in his office in a meeting with another teacher when his secretary came in and told him that there had been reports of gunfire. Initially thinking, like so many others, that the shooting was a prank, he exited his office into the main hallway, where he saw the two perpetrators coming in his direction. The teacher he was with fled down a hallway, but Frank ran toward the gunfire when he noticed several girls coming out of the locker room and into the shooters' path. As he pulled them toward safety, he found that their intended shelter was locked. Miraculously, on a ring of many keys, he immediately found the right key on the first try and was able to get them out of harm's way. The shooters then heard Dave Sanders coming up from the cafeteria. It was at that point that they abandoned their pursuit of Frank, turning their attention and their guns toward Dave.

Seeing SWAT arriving at the school, Frank was able to get the girls out of the building to safety. When he tried to go back in to save more students, however, the officers would not let him. Taken to a command center in a nearby park, Frank worked with law enforcement by drawing maps of the layout of the school's ventilation system, answering questions, and doing anything he could to help. He later went to the reunification center at Leawood Elementary School to help answer questions and soon found himself working with the grief counselors to help update families who still were waiting on their children.

In the early hours of the following morning, Frank met with the district superintendent and school board to determine their next steps. Concern existed over the potential for lawsuits, and the district wanted to protect itself. He was assigned a lawyer to ensure consistency in his statements and was discouraged from talking with the families of the deceased. Later, he defied the directive he had been given—relationships were (and still are) important to Frank, and he wanted to let know the families he was there for them despite backlash he faced from the community as somehow being responsible for the event. On the first weekend after the shooting, Frank went to visit a majority of the families. On Mother's Day, the first the families would have without their children, he took flowers to all of the mothers. His compassion, authenticity, and support in the face of tragedy and persistence to "do what was right" by the families regardless of the threat of litigation is one of the main reasons why they remain in contact to this day.

Then came the media. As the principal of the school, Frank almost instantly became the face of Columbine in the aftermath. On April 23, just three days after the attack, he gave 17 different interviews to various news organizations. In the days, weeks, months, and years after, the cameras never stopped rolling on Frank—in the aftermath of other events, he usually is called upon for interviews to offer perspective on his experience at Columbine and the years since. He also has been an invaluable resource for leaders in other communities struck by similar tragedies, who often reach out to him in the immediate aftermath, looking for answers, even to this day.

Frank had a goal: he knew he needed to rebuild the Columbine community and that his role as principal would allow him to do just that. A starting point was making sure his "kids," as he called the students of Columbine, were kept together. When the district was trying to figure out how to the students would complete the school year, there was discussion about splitting the school by grades and sending each grade to a different location. Frank, however, would not have it—he told them, "No, we need to be together." It was that determination that paved the way for the students to go to Chatfield High School together to finish out their school year. He also tirelessly advocated for his students not to go back to school for two weeks after the shooting to allow them time to grieve and attend the funerals of their classmates and teacher without the added pressure of coursework and grades hanging over their heads. Most importantly, he made sure that the following school year, classes resumed at Columbine. He wanted his community back where it belonged.

Frank's dedication was not only to his students but also his faculty and staff. Many struggled with whether or not they, like the students, could come back. It also was difficult, if not impossible, to tell his team that they needed to seek counseling, something that Frank had sought almost immediately after the shooting stopped. Rather than telling them what to do, he instead led by example. In sharing his experience, it was, as he points out, "almost granting them permission to do so [seek counseling]." Though some of his administrative team and faculty left after the shooting, others stayed with their leader, who had proven to be an invaluable source of support and guidance.

The aftermath of the shooting was not without its setbacks for Frank. His need to take care of everyone else (meaning the Columbine community) had its costs—namely, relationships with his family. His first marriage ended in divorce, and he experienced a strained relationship with his daughter, who also was a sophomore in high school (in a different county) at the time of the attack. After the first anniversary of the shooting, his health began to suffer. Through his counseling and his faith—something Frank always credits with providing him the strength to continue on a path that he was not prepared to take—he has made strides in both. He later married his high school sweetheart and continues to work to improve relationships that were damaged during the recovery effort. Ever the positive person, Frank refuses to dwell on the past, instead using these lessons as "what not to do" when he talks to others, encouraging them not only to seek professional help but also to include family members in the process.

Through counseling, Frank also learned about reclaiming ownership and the need to direct his memories of April 20, 1999, into a more positive approach:

> *I kept talking to my counselor and he said "Frank you need to replay that video in your mind, that when you walk out of your office, instead of envisioning those gunmen coming towards you, instead of envisioning those kids lying in a pool of blood, envision them living their lives." So I would envision Lauren Townsend playing volleyball. I would envision Isaiah Shoels high-fiving me. I would envision Danny Mauser and Kelly Fleming going to church on Sundays. . . . So now as I walk[ed] out of my office, that picture of that horrific day, it's not that I forgot what happened, but if I was going to continue, it was almost like a celebration of their life. . . . For me, I had to change what was happening in my mind about that day and that has helped me to continue to go back in that building.*

And go back into that building he did. One particular statement made by his priest at a prayer vigil several days after the shooting had stuck with him: "You should have died that day, but you were spared for a reason. God has a plan for you and you will not have to travel the journey alone; God will be with you." The priest further clarified the plan he believed lay before Frank: "You've got to rebuild that community." It was a message that Frank took to heart:

> *I could not ask the students and the parents who were in that building that day to come into our school if I wasn't there. I made that promise a day after the shooting when I met with students, and staff, and community members. I said, "I will promise you, I will be here for three years until every one of you graduate, the class of 2002." As 2002 was approaching, that school year, 2001–2002, I said, "I didn't fulfill that promise to rebuild this community. There's still work to be done."*

That's when I decided to stay until every kid who was in elementary school [in the area at the time of the shooting] graduated.

Though the shooting happened in 1999, it was not until 2014 that Frank retired as Columbine's principal. He remains in contact with many of his "kids," still getting together to find out how they are doing and how he can be of support to them. He also speaks both nationally and internationally about the lessons he learned from April 20, 1999, particularly as it relates to recovery, and has remained an integral part of the Jefferson County School District, for whom he serves as a consultant on safety and emergency management. His leadership efforts have not gone without recognition—he was selected as Colorado High School Principal of the Year and was a finalist for National Principal of the Year. In addition, he received the Jefferson County Lifetime Achievement Award and the Gandhi, King, Ikeda Community Builders Award. Still, forever a principal, he remains a pillar of strength not only for his community but also for the members of the club that nobody wants to be a part of—mass shooting survivors.

The Rebels Project

One of the many lessons learned in the aftermath of April 20 was the need for support. Long after the financial resources ran out, it was the social support—the intense connections of tragedy—that remained to help the survivors continue on the path of recovery. Even to this day, many still struggle with the aftereffects of their individual experiences on the day of the shooting. The shared experience, however, provides a platform on which to work through those struggles with other people who understand.

Following the July 20, 2012, shooting at the Aurora, Colorado, movie theater 30 minutes east of Columbine, Heather Martin realized she had to do something. A senior at Columbine when the shooting had happened, she had struggled ever since to cope with her experience, often feeling unsupported because others could not relate to what she had been through. With each new mass shooting—Aurora being her tipping point—she realized that there were other survivors out there who likely were feeling the same way she did.

With Jennifer Hammer, Heather formed the Rebels Project (www.therebelsproject.org) just three days after the Aurora shooting. The group was named after the Columbine High School mascot—the Rebels, after the independent militias from the Revolutionary War. In that sense, the name is fitting. The Rebels Project is independently organized, just like the militias. They also provide a rapid response in times of need, just like the Revolutionary War rebels.

Soon after their formation, the Rebels Project teamed up with another newly formed Columbine-based organization. Phoenix 999 (www.phoenix999.org)

was established by Martin, Zach Cartaya, and Stephen Houck as a way to provide financial and educational resources to those who had been affected by mass violence. The group also works to help place survivors with resources related to PTSD, including subsidizing treatment for those in need. A nationally recognized 501(c)(3) organization, Phoenix 999 is a testament to rising from the ashes, in this case of trauma, with the 999 representing 1999, the year the founders graduated from Columbine. Since 2016, the two organizations have merged to create a cohesive organization aimed at addressing the multiple layers of survivor needs.

The Rebels Project (2017) operates with a clear mission statement: the group seeks "[t]o provide safe, empowering platforms for survivors to connect, share experiences, foster relationships, and cultivate healing." To achieve this goal, the organization focuses on fostering relationships among survivors, not only from Columbine but also from other mass shootings across the nation. The group, which originally began with just over 100 members mostly from Columbine, has grown to more than 800 with the connection to survivors of other mass shootings, including (but not limited to) Heath High School (1997), Virginia Tech (2007), Aurora (2012), Sandy Hook (2012), Washington D.C. Navy Yard (2013), Pulse Nightclub (2016), Las Vegas (2017), and Parkland (2018).

A key to the success of the Rebels Project is that its members use their experiences to help others. They work to validate experiences and emotions and encourage by inspiring survivors with their own stories. With the growth of the survivor community, they also help to build and foster support systems and share resources. Though the Rebels Project's leadership team has changed some since its inception—Heather, the CEO, now runs the organization with Zach Cartaya (CFO), Amy Over (Director of Fundraising; Columbine survivor), Sherrie Lawson (Director of Development; Washington Navy Yard survivor), Missy Mendo (Assistant Director of Fundraising; Columbine survivor), and Chelsea Sobolik (Director of Digital Media; Aurora survivor)—the group has stuck to its values. In addition to hosting an online support group through social media and raising funds to assist survivors to access needed resources, the group also organizes monthly support meetings that are attended by nearly 300 survivors (physical and virtual attendance combined), hosts annual gatherings, and has a pen pal program, each designed to help keep individuals connected with others in their survivor network.

Forging a New Path

Twenty years later, the students of Columbine on the day of the shooting are now grown. They have married, started their own families, and are well into their various careers—some are even teachers, determined to give back to other students. Many of the faculty, like Frank, have since retired, moving on to the next chapter of their lives that remains to be written. For all, they are "a Columbine Rebel for life," as is inscribed on the Wall of Healing at the Columbine Memorial. As the inscription continues, "No one can ever take that away from you."

For much of society, as we discuss in Chapter 2, Columbine was a cultural shockwave, a legacy that persists even 20 years later. Yet for those who lived that day, it was just that—one day. As Louis noted, "It was one bad day out of over 40 years of being a school community. It just happens to be a very famous bad day." Monica also remembered:

> *I had a great experience. . . . I sang in the choir, I played soccer, I went to all the dances. I just had fun, it was a fun experience. It just was unfortunate that it ended the way it did. I wish it was different but this is—I think after going through what I've gotten through, I'm here for a reason.*

As an event, the shooting did not define Columbine. Instead, it highlighted the strength, tenacity, and perseverance of individuals and a community as a whole in the face of evil, and it did not let it win. Even many of those individuals who tried to denounce or escape their experience often come back to the communities nestled in the Rocky Mountain foothills because "it's home."

The lessons learned from those affected by the events of April 20, 1999, highlight the fact that recovery is an ongoing process that does not work on any given timetable, and communities must plan and prepare for that. Some were able to make strides quicker; others are only beginning to come to terms with what they experienced that day. As Zach has remarked as he looks back on his journey since that day, "You're never going to go back to what you were. It's making things normal and then a new normal, but you're never going to have it back." Survivors of the attack have had to learn how to cope with their new normal, learning what triggers (such as cars backfiring, corks popping, and fireworks) take them back to the shooting, and how they can respond in a way that brings them calm and peace.

Even 20 years later, there are bad days. The month of April is hard for most. Some get out of town and find solace away from the school and its surroundings. Others, like David and Stephanie, venture into the community to reflect on the events of a day that reshaped their future—one without their daughter in it. Each year on the anniversary, they visit each of the grave sites and leave a flower for the kids and Dave. It is a small gesture, but one that brings a smile to their hearts and lets those taken on April 20 know that they are never forgotten.

CHAPTER TEN

The Infamy of the Shooters

Sadly, 20 years after the shooting, few people remember the names of any of the victims killed on April 20, 1999, and even fewer know all 13. What they can tell you, however, is the names of the two perpetrators. Once their identities were released by police, the Columbine perpetrators rose to an instant infamy and celebrity status, household names that are known by many and unfamiliar to few. Not only has the event cemented itself as a cultural event, but the two have, in their own right, inspired a generation of a different kind.

In this chapter, we explore the collateral effects of the notoriety of the Columbine gunmen. To do so, we first consider where and how the narrative about these two individuals originated and how the pair effectively scripted their event for others to follow. Next, we explore other school and mass shooters who went on to adapt the Columbine gunmen's script as their own, leaving a trail of devastation behind. Not all supporters of the pair, however, resort to violence to show their dedication. In that vein, the "Columbiners"—a group of followers loyal to the shooters for a variety of reasons—are examined. Finally, we consider how, in the end, the shooters' ultimate goal of infamy has been achieved in the last 20 years and what we can do moving forward to take them back from household names to unknowns, an act that could undoubtedly save numerous lives.

(In)Famous

The Columbine perpetrators knew what they were doing and what their end goal was: "We're going to kickstart a revolution" (Shooter H in Gibbs & Roche, 1999, para. 8). They planned out not only how they were going to carry out the attack but also how they would script their own identities (Newman, Fox, Harding, Mehta, & Roth, 2004; see also Carvalho, 2010;

Larkin, 2009; Muschert & Ragnedda, 2010; Tonso, 2009). In the weeks leading up to the shooting, the two filmed a series of videos—known as the Basement Tapes—that detailed not only what they were going to do on what they called "Judgment Day" or "NBK" (named after the Oliver Stone film *Natural Born Killers*) but also how it would create a legacy. They anticipated that the videos would be aired worldwide, which would enable them not only to make a statement but also to amass a cult following (Gibbs & Roche, 1999).

The pair had the foresight to recognize how impactful their story would be, and they carefully documented it through the videos. They considered who would be best to deliver the script: Quentin Tarantino or Steven Spielberg. "Directors," they noted, "will be fighting over this story" (Shooter K in Gibbs & Roche, 1999, para. 12). The plot was carefully orchestrated, just like a movie.

For the two perpetrators, celebrity status was only part of the allure, though its attainment certainly was a vital cornerstone of their anticipated revenge (Muschert & Ragnedda, 2010). They also viewed themselves as martyrs for other downtrodden and outcast youth. By sacrificing themselves for what they perceived to be the greater cause, the pair would live forever through the memories (and nightmares) of those left in their wake, ghosts who would haunt the survivors of their wrath. As stated by one FBI agent interviewed in the *TIME* magazine piece about the tapes, "They wanted to be famous, and they are. They're infamous" (Mark Holstlaw in Gibbs & Roche, 1999, para. 11).

The performative or cultural script left behind by the two perpetrators provides for an understanding of the shooting as an act of expressive violence (Carvalho, 2010; Larkin, 2009; Muschert & Ragnedda, 2010; Newman et al., 2004; Tonso, 2009). As Newman and colleagues (2004) noted, events like Columbine are effectively "prescriptions for behavior" that use violence to resolve some type of dilemma (p. 230). They further suggest that "the script provides an image of what the shooters want to become and a template that links the method to the goal" (Newman et al., 2004, p. 230). That template subsequently has been used by other school and mass shooters—even without the release of the Basement Tapes—as we discuss further in the next section.

How Two Teens Inspired Others to Kill

The copycat effect of the Columbine shooting and, more specifically, its perpetrators remains as strong today as it was after the attack 20 years ago. As planned, the two gunmen have "a cult following unlike anything [that's] ever [been] seen before" (in Follman, 2015b). The campaign they laid out through the clues they left behind and the attack itself have continued to reappear in the plans of would-be and actual mass shooters (Follman, 2015b).

In many respects, they have kick-started the revolution that they had hoped for. They are celebrated and revered by others who see themselves in the shooters (Fernandez, Turkewitz, & Bidgood, 2018).

Several studies have assessed just how pervasive the copycat effect stemming from Columbine is. Follman and Andrews (2015) found that over a 15-year period after the shooting, there were 74 copycat cases across states (see also Follman, 2015b). Of these, 21 were attacks that came to fruition, leaving 89 people dead and 126 others wounded (Follman, 2015b; Follman & Andrews, 2015). The remaining 53 were plots or threats that were stopped by law enforcement before they were able to be carried out (Follman, 2015b; Follman & Andrews, 2015). In at least 14 of the cases, the plotters intended to carry out their attack on the anniversary of Columbine, though none of the completed attacks occurred on April 20 (Follman, 2015b; Follman & Andrews, 2015).

Perhaps even more telling than the number of copycat cases is the extent to which the plotters referenced Columbine and its shooters more specifically. In 13 of the cases in the study, the individuals in question directly stated that their intent was to exceed the body count of the April 20, 1999, shooting (Follman, 2015b; Follman & Andrews, 2015). In 10 of the cases, the plotters identified the Columbine perpetrators as martyrs, heroes, idols, or gods (Follman, 2015b; Follman & Andrews, 2015), including the 2007 Virginia Tech shooter, who idolized the pair and considered them his "brothers" (Associated Press, 2007; Nicholson, 2007). At least three of the individuals traveled to Columbine as part of their planning and preparation, two of whom subsequently carried out attacks when they returned back home (Follman, 2015b; Follman & Andrews, 2015). The third—a 16-year-old from Utah—was arrested when he returned home from Denver for plotting with a friend to bomb their high school, but not before he had posed as a student journalist writing for the school newspaper in order to meet with Principal Frank DeAngelis (Follman, 2015b; Follman & Andrews, 2015).

In a separate study examining how mass shooters drew inspiration from one another, Langman (2017) found that of 55 perpetrators analyzed, 32 of them specifically viewed the Columbine killers as role models. These included individuals who carried out their acts both in and out of schools. Some of the perpetrators have imitated the clothing of the Columbine gunmen: the 2014 Columbia, Maryland, mall shooter's outfit was similarly styled (Clary, 2014), while the Orange High School gunman in North Carolina (2006) wore a black trench coat like theirs that he had actually bought while on a sightseeing trip to Columbine (Karas, 2009), as did the Santa Fe (Texas) High School (2018) perpetrator (Fernandez et al., 2018). Some, like the 2005 Kingston, New York, mall (Holl, 2006) and 2012 Sandy Hook Elementary School (Sedensky, 2013) perpetrators kept a collection of information and memorabilia about the shooting. Others openly listed the pair as role models, including the perpetrators at Perry Hall High School in Maryland in 2012 (Hellgren, 2012) and a Kennesaw, Georgia, FedEx facility in 2014 ("Documents reveal," 2014). Perhaps most interesting is that several analyses have found that plotters who were not even born when Columbine happened still are referencing its perpetrators as sources of inspiration for their own attacks (Follman, 2015a; Thomas, Levine, Cloherty, & Date, 2014).

The inspirational reach of the Columbine gunmen was not solely limited to other American mass shooters. In fact, perpetrators of similar attacks in other countries also cited the pair as sources of inspiration (Follman, 2015b; Langman, 2017; Larkin, 2009). Perpetrators in Germany (Bingham, 2009; "Columbine killer," 2006; Lemonick, 2002), Canada (Couvrette, 2006), and Finland (Rayner, 2008; Schoetz & Goldman, 2007) also praised the Columbine shooters and emulated components of their attacks (see also Fox, Levin, & Fridel, 2019).

In one of the most extreme examples of copycatting the Columbine killers, the perpetrator of the 2007 shooting at Jokela High School in Tuusula, Finland, demonstrated the clear influence of the 1999 attackers and Shooter H in particular (Langman, 2017). In the manifesto he left behind, the Jokela gunman utilized language nearly identical to the Columbine perpetrator and even titled his media package the "Manifesto of a Natural Selector," a nod to the phrase on Shooter H's shirt on the day of the attack. He also left behind a series of videos, some which mimicked the productions made by both the Columbine and Virginia Tech shooters, others which were montages blending the gunmen's favorite songs with surveillance footage of the cafeteria on April 20, 1999 (see, generally, Kiilakoski & Oksanen, 2011a, 2011b; Ministry of Justice, 2009; Oksanen, Nurmi, Vuori, & Räsänen, 2013; Paton, 2012; Sumiala & Tikka, 2011a, 2011b). In sum, the performative script written by the Columbine killers has since provided a foundation adopted by other school and mass shooters across the globe and across the last 20 years.

The "Columbiners"

Many of the individuals who have mimicked the actions of the two gunmen are part of a larger following known as the "Columbiners" (see, generally, Monroe, 2012), a cornerstone of the online *fandemonium* of mass shooters that emerged more than 10 years after the shooting (CBC, 2015). Some of the Columbiners aim to copy the shooting or advocate for violence more generally (Beaumont, 2015; CBC, 2015). People who feel persecuted or bullied find comfort in the shared experiences of others, an untold number of whom romanticize Columbine and its perpetrators as their heroes (CBC, 2015; Hari, 2004; Lindberg, Oksanen, Sailas, & Kaltiala-Heino, 2012). They see themselves as a "society" rather than a fan club (CBC, 2015, para. 17; see also Ames, 2007; Oksanen, Hawdon, & Räsänen, 2014; Paton, 2012).

Aside from violent ideation, there are other draws of the Columbiners that have helped to increase its membership. Some people are fascinated by the criminology and science behind the perpetrators and the attack (Beaumont, 2015). They have a "morbid fascination with true crime" (CBC, 2015, para. 26). Others can relate to the two gunmen—they share similar feelings, even beyond the homicidal tendencies (Beaumont, 2015), some applauding them for standing up for themselves and their beliefs (Hari, 2004) yet, in some cases, condemning the methods through which they chose to express it (Paton, 2012). Certain members are depressed or suicidal and reach out within the group, looking for other people to talk to (Beaumont, 2015).

Still, there is a subset of members who often are among the most active members—those who express romantic feelings or sexual attraction to the shooters (CBC, 2015; Monroe, 2012). They take the last names of the perpetrators: some online, some in real life through legal name changes (CBC, 2015). Some have sent letters to the shooters' parents, professing their love (Associated Press, 2016). Others, like the copycat plotters, travel to the school (some to "see where their husbands [the killers] died")—"[t]hey want to see where it happened, want to feel it, want to walk the halls. They try to take souvenirs" (John McDonald in Follman, 2015b, para. 40). Many exhibit traits of *hybristophilia*—sexual attraction to murderers (Buxton, 2014; Monroe, 2012). The celebrity status and associated adoration that has been bestowed upon the Columbine shooters rivals that of Justin Bieber by his "Beliebers," Taylor Swift's "Swifties," and One Direction's "Directioners" (CBC, 2015; Monroe, 2012).

The Columbiners exist primarily online—the Internet, of course, knows no boundaries, which makes it a perfect place for such "fandemonium" (see, generally, Fast, 2008; Larkin, 2009; Muschert & Larkin, 2007; Paton, 2012). The virtually unconstrained limits of the online world allow them to constantly share information about the shooting or its perpetrators (Oksanen et al., 2014). In some cases, they re-share information that already is made and available; in others, they may create new pieces, such as mash-ups or montages that combine clips from the shooters' original posts, news programs, documentaries, and even the surveillance footage from the cafeteria (Sumiala & Tikka, 2011a; Paton, 2012). Often, they are limited only by the constraints of their imaginations (and, perhaps, their technical abilities).

Another draw of the online world is its broad reach, allowing these digital shrines to easily be shared with a click of a mouse button (Kiilakoski & Oksanen, 2011b; Sumiala & Tikka, 2011a). Facebook, for example, allows users to share content, easily reposting the messages to other members (Osborne & Dredze, 2014). (It should be noted, however, that Facebook did take down content related to the shooting for violating the platform's standards after being contacted by survivor Anne Marie Hochhalter in the wake of the 2018 Parkland shooting [see Wright, 2018].) Twitter, a microblogging platform, allows users to share or "retweet" content of interest, regardless of whether or not they are directly connected with the original source (Kwak, Lee, Park, & Moon, 2010). As a result, a single message can reach an average of 1,000 (or more) users through the retweeting process (Kwak et al., 2010). Tumblr also is highly popular with the Columbiners, with thousands of entries about the shooting and the killers (Schildkraut & Elsass, 2016; Wright, 2018). Taken together, the Columbiners and their online networks have helped to perpetuate the infamy of the shooters 20 years after the attack.

A Need to Refocus and Revisit No Notoriety

Five years after Columbine, members of a FBI-hosted summit on the shooting publicly shared their conclusions about the motivation behind the shooting:

> It wasn't just "fame" they were after . . . they were gunning for devastating infamy on the historical scale of an Attila the Hun [one of the most barbaric rulers and military leaders to attack the Roman empire; see A&E, 2017]. Their vision was to create a nightmare so devastating and apocalyptic that the entire world would shudder at their power. (Cullen, 2004)

The notoriety the two perpetrators received has two particularly detrimental (and lethal) consequences. First, it effectively has rewarded the two Columbine gunmen for carrying out their plans, giving them exactly what they wanted—and anticipated. At the same time, it signals to other like-minded individuals that if they also carry out a targeted act of violence like Columbine, they could be immortalized in the same way as the shooters—and some, like the Virginia Tech and Sandy Hook perpetrators, have been. Thus, removing the rewards and incentives for shooters must be a priority.

At the heart of this issue is the media attention that was discussed earlier in Chapter 3. The amount of coverage these types of events receive, combined with the manner in which the event is presented, has the ability to inspire copycat attackers (see, generally, Garcia-Bernardo, Qi, Schultz, Cohen, Johnson, & Dodds, 2017; Kissner, 2016; Lankford & Tomek, 2017; Towers, Gomez-Lievano, Khan, Mubayi, & Castillo-Chavez, 2015). As the majority of perpetrators do not directly observe events like Columbine, the media serve as a model for these individuals about how to commit their own shootings (Meindl & Ivy, 2017; Weatherby, Luzzo, & Zahm, 2016). As Meindl and Ivy (2017) summarized:

> Social status is conferred when the mass shooter obtains a significant level of notoriety from news reports. Images displaying shooters aiming guns at the camera project an air of danger and toughness. Similarities between

the shooter and others are brought to the surface through detailed accounts of the life of the shooter, with which others may identify. Fulfilled manifestos and repeated reports of body counts heap rewards on the violent act and display competence. Detailed play-by-play accounts of the event provide feedback on the performance of the shooter. All of these instances serve to create a model with sufficient detail to promote imitated mass shootings for some individuals. (p. 369)

Unquestionably, no school or mass shooter to date has achieved the social status of the Columbine killers, which is the primary reason that they continue to be a source of inspiration for so many.

Twenty years later, it is time to refocus and put the attention back where it belongs: on the 13 lives cut short that day. Not only is it vital to adopt policies like No Notoriety that call for a limiting of the use of shooters' names and photos (NoNotoriety.com, n.d.; see also Chapter 3 for a further discussion of the protocol as well as DontNameThem.org, n.d.) for future attacks that may take place, but such a stance also must be adhered to when discussing the Columbine attack and its two perpetrators. Though they always may have their followers in groups like the Columbiners, it still is possible to refocus the spotlight and rewrite the script on April 20, 1999.

CHAPTER ELEVEN

Profiling School and Mass Shooters

Ever since the Columbine tragedy, people have been trying to determine who the next school or mass shooter would be. As a result, there has been a standard profile of who would be such a perpetrator. In an article published after the 2017 shooting in Las Vegas, Nevada, Doyle (2017) suggested that "as a general rule, if you check three out of four boxes on the 'angry/white/man/ gun' list, you do, indeed, fit the stereotypical profile of a mass shooter" (para. 5). This characterization, however, is not new—it is a description that was offered almost as soon as the Columbine shooting ended. After April 20, 1999, other attributes, such as youth who wore trench coats or dressed in Gothic-style clothing, also (incorrectly) became a cause for concern (Frymer, 2009; Ogle, Eckman, & Leslie, 2003).

The reality, however, is that "there is no one-size-fits-all profile of who carries out mass shootings in the United States" (Victor, 2018, para. 1; see also Deruy, 2015; Ferguson, Coulson, & Barnett, 2011; Neuman, Assaf, Cohen, & Knoll, 2015; O'Toole, 2000; Vossekuil, Fein, Reddy, Borum, & Modzeleski, 2004), particularly given the low base rate of events from which to draw information (Knoll & Meloy, 2014; see also Chapter 5). Further, the fact that approximately half of school and mass shooters commit suicide makes understanding the root causes of such attacks all the more difficult (Ferguson et al., 2011; Schildkraut & Elsass, 2016). School and mass shooters and the events themselves do share some commonalities but also exhibit marked differences. Attempting to draw up a checklist of seemingly arbitrary characteristics (e.g., sex, race, clothing choices) to identify the next school or mass shooter can have significant unintended consequences, including labeling otherwise nonviolent individuals as potentially dangerous or—even worse—deadly (O'Toole, 2000; see also Pappas, 2012). Many people across the nation share numerous traits with school and mass shooters yet never will go on to commit similar acts (O'Toole, 2000; see also Ferguson et al., 2011; Victor, 2018).

In this chapter, we explore alternatives to profiling. We first explore two typologies that enable researchers to classify school and mass shooters or their acts based on categorical similarities. Langman's (2009; 2015) typology focuses on the perpetrators themselves while Muschert's (2007a) classification scheme emphasizes the need to instead contextualize the event more broadly. While these typologies do not enable predictions of who will commit one of these acts, it allows for a more focused study on those events that already have occurred. Additionally, we consider what is known about school and mass shooters and their attacks in terms of the context of the issue, which is a necessary starting point for attempting to implement any policies or protocols aimed at reducing their occurrence.

Langman's Typology of School Shooters

While many people have attempted to profile school and mass shooters based on seemingly arbitrary characteristics (e.g., physical appearance, clothing), scholars instead have sought to describe these perpetrators in terms of their behavioral cues and personality traits. Several consistent characteristics have been found across a number of studies. Specifically, researchers (e.g., Leary, Kowalski, Smith, & Phillips, 2003; McGee & DeBernardo, 1999; Meloy, Hempel, Mohandie, Shiva, & Gray, 2001; Newman, Fox, Harding, Mehta, & Roth, 2004; O'Toole, 2000; Verlinden, Hersen, & Thomas, 2000; Vossekuil, Fein, Reddy, Borum, & Modzeleski, 2004; see also Ferguson et al., 2011) have found that school shooters typically exhibit signs of depression, a preoccupation with or fantasizing about violence, and a precipitating loss or triggering event before their attacks. Nearly all found that the shooters were loners or experienced social isolation (Leary et al., 2003; McGee & DeBernardo, 1999; O'Toole, 2000; Verlinden et al., 2000; Vossekuil et al., 2004; see also Consalvo, 2003; Frymer, 2009; Hong, Cho, Allen-Meares, & Espelage, 2011), though Meloy and colleagues (2001) reported that the majority of perpetrators in their study were part of the respective school's "mainstream culture" (see also Newman et al., 2004). Meloy and colleagues (2001) also determined that nearly 4 out of every 10 perpetrators had an arrest record; conversely, both McGee and DeBernardo (1999) and Vossekuil and colleagues (2004) found that prior involvement with law enforcement was rare. Other commonalities among school shooters include narcissism or low self-esteem (McGee & DeBernardo, 1999; O'Toole, 2000; see also Bondü & Scheithauer, 2015; Neuman et al., 2015); poor coping or anger management skills (Leary et al., 2003; O'Toole, 2000; Verlinden et al., 2000); come from strained or dysfunctional family environments (Leary et al., 2003; McGee & DeBernardo, 1999; O'Toole, 2000); and express feelings of persecution or experiences with bullying (Leary et al., 2003; Meloy et al., 2001; Newman et al., 2004; O'Toole, 2000; Vossekuil et al., 2004; see also Neuman et al., 2015).

Building off these previous studies and identified traits, psychologist Peter Langman (2009; 2015) created a typology that has been used to categorize school shooters based on their commonalities. In doing so, he identified three specific classifications: the traumatized, the psychotic, and the psychopathic (Langman, 2009, 2015). According to Langman (2009, 2015), school shooters who fell under the label of traumatized were more likely to come from broken homes in which at least one of their parents had either a criminal history or a substance abuse problem. Further, traumatized shooters were likely to have suffered either physical or sexual abuse at some point prior to their attack (Langman, 2009, 2015).

Both psychotic and psychopathic shooters come from homes that are intact with no histories of substance abuse, criminal action, or any other form of dysfunction in the family (Langman, 2009). They differ, however, in respects to the individual personality traits of the shooter. Psychopathic perpetrators, according to Langman (2009, 2015), are egocentric, sadistic, and narcissistic, displaying a lack of conscience, an absence of empathy, and a sense of grandiosity. Psychotic shooters, however, exhibit traits of schizophrenia (such as paranoia or hallucinations), are prone to depression, and often struggle in social situations (Langman, 2009, 2015).

In applying this framework to the Columbine shooting, Langman (2009, 2015) suggests that Shooter H is emblematic of the psychopathic typification. Shooter H exhibited narcissistic behavior, both outwardly and through his journal writings (see, generally, Jefferson County Sheriff's Office, 1999). Despite that he often appeared to be vulnerable in his writings, he made up for it by outwardly expressing beliefs that he was superior to others, a practice that Langman (2015) terms compensatory narcissism. The shooting at Columbine, both in planning and in its actual happening, was about exhibiting power and domination over others, playing god by determining who lived and who died, something that he long had fantasized about (Langman, 2015).

Shooter K, however, is more emblematic of the psychotic shooter according to Langman (2009, 2015). One of the most distinct attributes of Shooter K was his difficulty in social functioning. He was particularly shy and insecure, which Langman (2009, 2015) suggests is part of the reason he adopted such a violent persona, particularly as he was so heavily influenced by Shooter H and adapted his personality so as to not lose the friendship he valued most. He had struggled since his early childhood with feelings of inadequacy and isolation from his peers, which created social anxiety throughout his life. At the same time, he was envious of his classmates and longed for a romantic relationship, a desire that went unfulfilled. These social failures, both individually and collectively, left Shooter K struggling with depression and suicidality through the end of his life (Langman, 2009, 2015).

Langman's typology (2009, 2015) also has been useful in understanding other school shooters both before and after Columbine, including (but not limited to) those at Westside Middle School in Jonesboro, Arkansas (1998); Thurston High School in Springfield, Oregon (1998); Virginia Tech (2007); Northern Illinois University (2008); and Sandy Hook Elementary School (2012). As noted, this typology is not offered as a way to predict who will become a school or mass shooter. Instead, it is used to categorize perpetrators based on common threads in their personalities and psyches. Understanding these commonalities is critical to prevention efforts, including the development of threat assessment protocols (as discussed in Chapter 5).

Muschert's Typology of School Shootings

Whereas Langman (2009, 2015) sought to classify school shooters based on common traits, Muschert (2007a) instead focused on how best to categorize events themselves. One of the main contributing factors to an inaccurate understand of the breadth of the school shooting problem (also discussed further in the next section) is the role the location plays in determining whether or not it actually should be tallied as such. Should a gang shooting that takes place at or near a school be counted as a school shooting? Similarly, how would one categorize an attack where an adult comes onto school grounds and shoots at students, such as the attack that happened at Deer Creek Middle School in Littleton, Colorado, on February 23, 2010?

To answer these questions, Muschert (2007a) proposed five different categories of incidents. The first of these categories is *rampage shootings*, which refers to events like Columbine. The perpetrator is a current or former student of the school who attacks others at the institution for symbolic purposes, such as revenge. Muschert (2007a) also suggested that attacks perpetrated by current or former employees whose motivation is similar could fall into this category; later studies (e.g., Schildkraut & Elsass, 2016), however, suggest that these events are better classified as workplace shootings as the school functions as the perpetrator's place of employment.

Attacks on school communities also can be perpetrated by outsiders. This type of school shooting is identified by Muschert (2007a) simply as a *mass murder*. While the motivation of the perpetrator is the same as the rampage school shooter (e.g., symbolic significance), the difference is that he or she is not directly part of the school community either as a current or former student or employee. The earlier referenced shooting at Deer Creek Middle School would fall into this category, as would the January 17, 1989, incident at Cleveland Elementary School in Stockton, California (Associated Press, 1989) or the October 2, 2006, attack at the Amish schoolhouse in West Nickel Mines, Pennsylvania (Kocieniewski & Gately, 2006). Similar attacks also have occurred in other countries, as evidenced by the March 13, 1996, shooting at Dunblane Primary School in Scotland (Clouston & Boseley, 2013).

A third form of school shootings may come in the form of *terrorist attacks* (Muschert, 2007a). In these events, the schools again are chosen for their symbolic importance. Perpetrated either by groups or individuals, these attacks may be ideologically or politically motivated in some way. One such example is the school siege in Beslan, Russia, that occurred between September 1, 2004 and September 3, 2004. Over the course of the three-day period, militants held more than 1,100 people hostage at an elementary school in an effort to garner attention for the Chechen independence movement; more than 330 people were killed when the attack finally reached its conclusion (Khomami, 2017). Such attacks, however, are not typical in the United States.

Targeted shootings are a fourth category of attacks proposed by Muschert (2007a). These types of attacks share a commonality with rampage shootings in that the perpetrators can be either current or former students or employees. How these two types of attacks differ is in respect to motivation. Unlike rampage shootings, those events that are classified as targeted center around the perpetrator exacting revenge either for a real or perceived injustice. The January 5, 2011, shooting at Millard South High School in Omaha, Nebraska, provides an example of this type of attack. Following a suspension from school for a criminal trespass charge, the 17-year-old student returned to the campus armed with a pistol. After making his way to the school's administrative office, he shot and killed the assistant principal who had suspended him; the principal also was wounded (Welch, 2011).

The final category within Muschert's (2007a) typology is the *government shooting*. Rather than a current or former member of the school community or even an outsider, the perpetrator in these events are government agents, such as the military or the police. Their actions often are in response to some type of crowd behavior, such as a protest or a riot. Perhaps the most notable example of this type of event is the May 4, 1970, shooting at Kent State University in Kent, Ohio. In response to students protesting the United States' bombing of Cambodia as part of the Vietnam War, members of the Ohio National Guard opened fire into the unarmed crowd. Four people were killed, and nine others were injured in the shooting (Adams, 2016).

Though Muschert's (2007a) typology differs from efforts by Langman (2009, 2015) and others, his model proves to be useful in laying a foundation for potential prevention efforts. By typifying the event rather than the perpetrator, it allows for consideration of these events in the context of motivation irrespective of the shooters themselves. Doing so can be useful for moving responses forward, given the earlier finding that there is no specific profile of school shooters. Similarly, this classification system also can add much-needed context to the understanding of the problem of school and mass shootings in the United States, which we discuss further in the next section.

What We Do Know about School and Mass Shooters

In order to address the problem of school and other mass shootings, it is important to do so in context. Yet, in the absence of a national database of events or universally agreed-upon definition, this is particularly difficult to do (see, generally, Langman, 2009; Schildkraut & Elsass, 2016). Certain organizations offer definitions that are overly broad, thereby leading to an increased number of events that are included in their database and, by extension, an inflated understanding of just how big the problem is (or is not), a problem known as a "false positive" (Deacon, 2007; Soothill & Grover, 1997). Conversely, other organizations' definitions are more narrow in scope, leading to events that may otherwise qualify as a school or mass shooting to be omitted from consideration; this is considered to be an issue of "false negatives" (McGee & DeBernardo, 1999; see also Deacon, 2007; Soothill & Grover, 1997).

In an attempt to overcome these issues, Schildkraut and Elsass (2016) examined these and other definitions and categorizations of mass shootings to determine where such deficiencies in understanding the context of these events existed. By doing so, they were able to craft an alternative definition aimed at addressing both the false positive and false negative issue that plagued other descriptions. This definition, which serves as the basis for the following analysis discussed, identifies mass shootings as:

> an incident of targeted violence carried out by one or more shooters at one or more public or populated locations. Multiple victims (both injuries and fatalities) are associated with the attack, and both the victims and location(s) are chosen either at random or for their symbolic value. The event occurs within a single 24-hour period, though most attacks typically last only a few minutes. The motivation of the shooting must not correlate with gang violence or targeted militant or terroristic activity. (p. 28)

Using this definition, Schildkraut and Elsass (2016) were able to track mass shootings in the United States as far back as the 1800s.

Examining mass shootings that occurred between 1966 and 2016, Schild-kraut, Formica, and Malatras (2018) determined that 340 events occurred, resulting in the deaths of 1,141 individuals; a further 1,385 people were injured in the attacks (see also Schildkraut & Elsass, 2016). The number of events has been steadily increasing, albeit marginally in comparison to other crimes; there are fewer than 20 shootings per year, on average. The likelihood of victimization remains quite low—individuals have less than a 0.00004% chance of being killed or injured in such an attack. While mass shootings occurred at a variety of locations, they were most likely to happen at workplaces (29.7% of attacks) and schools (27.6%), which are areas that the perpetrators most commonly have easy access to. Further, despite the common conjecture that all mass shooters use assault rifles (see, for example, Dickinson, 2018; Ingraham, 2016), the reality is that these perpetrators are nearly three times as likely to use a handgun or pistol (Schildkraut et al., 2018).

Over the course of the 50 years of shootings analyzed, there were 352 perpetrators, as eight attacks involved multiple offenders (Schildkraut et al., 2018). The majority of shooters were male, though not exclusively (of the 352 perpetrators, 14 were female). They ranged in age from 11 to 88 years old, with an average age of just over 33 years. Further, despite the perception that all mass shooters are white, as indicated by the quote at the onset of this chapter, the reality is that racial and ethnic variation has been found among the shooters. Of those shooters where race and ethnicity could be identified, more than one in four was black, and nearly 10% were of Hispanic descent (Schildkraut et al., 2018).

Similar patterns exist when looking solely at school shooters. Of the 94 shootings, the majority (nearly 77%) occurred at primary and secondary schools, with the remainder taking place on college and university campuses. Collectively, school shootings accounted for 250 fatalities and 431 injuries sustained. Like all mass shooters combined, the majority of the 101 school-based perpetrators were male. The average age of all school shooters was approximately 20 years, with a mean age of just under 18 years for K–12 shooters and about 28 years for college attacks. Of the 56 primary and secondary school shooters for whom race and ethnicity was known, a vast majority (over 71%) were white. Conversely, postsecondary school shooters (of whom there were 25 with identifiable races or ethnicities) were more likely to be black (nearly 58%) as compared to white (26%). In sum, there is neither a clear nor a discernable pattern across either school or mass shooters that would make profiling such individuals an advantageous endeavor.

Context Matters

All too often, responses to events like Columbine (such as those discussed in Chapter 8) represent little more than emotionally charged responses to demands for action (also reviewed in Chapter 7). Without sufficient context, not only do these policies and protocols largely fail to come to fruition, but those that do also are unsuccessful at meeting their intended objectives due to the lack of a foundation based on evidence (see, generally, Schildkraut, 2014; Schildkraut & Hernandez, 2014). In order to adequately respond to the phenomenon of school and mass shootings, we first have to understand the problem in its real—not media-generated—context. Such context also involves an understanding and acknowledgment that school and mass shooters cannot be profiled and that attempting to do so can have significant and detrimental consequences for so many who may fit the physical description but lack the motivation to carry out such an attack.

CHAPTER TWELVE

A Piece of Popular Culture History

When people looked to understand why Columbine happened, one of the first things blamed (along with guns and mental health) was violent entertainment media. After all, the perpetrators had named their attack after the popular 1994 Oliver Stone film *Natural Born Killers* (Cullen, 2009; Frymer, 2009; Larkin, 2007; Newman, Fox, Harding, Mehta, & Roth, 2004), though other highly popular films, including *The Basketball Diaries* (1995) and *The Matrix* (1999), also have been suggested as influencing the pair (Birkland & Lawrence, 2009; Springhall, 1999; see also *Sanders v. Acclaim Entertainment, Inc.*, 2002). The two had played violent video games like Doom, and reports suggested that they drew inspiration from the game for their attack (Cullen, 2009; Larkin, 2007; see also Columbine Review Commission, 2001; Schildkraut & Elsass, 2016). They listened to German "Goth rock" bands like Rammstein and KMFDM (Powers, 1999; Schildkraut & Muschert, 2013). In the eyes of many, any one of these outlets—and collectively, all of them together—must have been the cause for the shooting.

As a result, "violent movies and video games . . . have been converted into objects of fear" (De Venanzi, 2012, p. 262). Campaigns to regulate violent media in the wake of the shooting came on quickly but were largely unsuccessful (see, generally, Schildkraut & Elsass, 2016). The family of Dave Sanders, the teacher killed in the attack, also attempted to spark change through litigation, filing a wrongful death suit in 2002 against a number of media companies, including Nintendo, Sega, Atari, New Line Cinema, Time Warner, and Sony Computer Entertainment (*Sanders v. Acclaim Entertainment, Inc.*, 2002). Among the allegations raised in the suit was that "but for the actions of the Video Game Defendants and the Movie Defendants, in conjunction with the acts of the other defendants herein, the multiple killings at Columbine High School would not have occurred" (*Sanders v. Acclaim Entertainment, Inc.,* 2002, p. 1268). The case, however, was dismissed before oral arguments were offered. Similar efforts by families from other school shootings (see, for example, *James v. Meow Media,* 2002, which argued similar responsibility for the 1997 Heath High School shooting) were equally unsuccessful.

Despite the fact that little progress has been made in remedying perceptions that violent media is somehow responsible for shootings like Columbine, a key piece of the discussion seems to be missing. Specifically, what often is not discussed is how these same media producers go on to create *more* movies and similar commodities that actually are based on the attacks themselves. In other words, absent from the discussion is how Hollywood has actually turned these tragedies into sources of further profit. In this chapter, we explore how Columbine and similar attacks have been immortalized through movies, television shows, music, and even Broadway-style theatrics to leave a lasting mark on popular culture (see, generally, France, 2009). Broader consideration of the implications of such commodification also is offered.

Columbine on the Silver Screen

One of the ways that Columbine has been immortalized is on the silver screen through movies. Two such movies were Ben Coccio's *Zero Day* and Gus Van Sant's *Elephant,* both released in 2003. *Zero Day* follows the story of two students, Andre and Calvin, who plan out an attack on their high school. Both the plot and the production mirror that of Columbine, including the pair making video diaries of their plans and the audience seeing parts of the shooting through the vantage point of the school's security cameras (Coccio, 2003; Fuchs, 2005). *Elephant* offers a different take on the shooting, following the normal ebbs and flows of a high school as the day of the shooting unfolds and students cross paths with the two perpetrators, only to be killed later in the film (Ebert, 2003; France, 2009). The movie uses long tracking shots (Ebert, 2003) and routine ambient noises (such as birds chirping) interwoven with music from Beethoven in lieu of actual dialogue, which is largely absent in the film (Edelstein, 2003). While both *Zero Day* and *Elephant,* which won multiple awards and accolades, directly depict the events before and during the Columbine shooting, other films, including *Duck! The Carbine High Massacre* (1999), *Bang Bang You're Dead* (2002), *The Only Way* (2004), and *Reunion* (2009), all are said to draw inspiration from but not directly replicate the attack.

One of the most controversial yet critically acclaimed films to come out of Columbine, however, was one that was not necessarily produced for entertainment purposes but instead to explore the root causes of the shooting and other episodes of gun violence (Bort, 2017; Curiel, 2002). Released in 2002 at the Cannes Film Festival, *Bowling for Columbine* is a documentary written, produced, directed, and narrated by filmmaker Michael Moore that explores the epidemic of gun violence in the United States, both in response to Columbine and more broadly, including comparisons to other nations (Bradshaw, 2002; Kellner, 2008a). The film centers on discussions with numerous stakeholders in the gun debate, including then–NRA president Charlton Heston, musician Marilyn Manson (discussed in more detail later in this chapter), and others with vested interests in the discussion (Bort, 2017; Bradshaw, 2002; Kellner, 2008a).

One of the most poignant scenes in the documentary is when Moore visits the Kmart headquarters in Troy, Michigan, with Columbine survivors Mark Taylor and Richard Castaldo, asking for a refund on the bullets that remain lodged in their bodies after the shooting (Reid, 2002). After the group goes to one of the chain's nearby stores and purchases all of their ammunition before returning to the headquarters, Kmart's spokesperson announces that they will change their policy and end the sale of handgun ammunition (Reid, 2002). In addition to what Moore viewed as a victory with this changing practice, *Bowling for Columbine* went on to receive strongly favorable reviews (see, for example, Pierce, 2002; Scott, 2002), break box office records worldwide (Welk, 2018), and become a necessary spark to ignite a conversation about gun violence in the United States (Bradshaw, 2002).

School Shootings on the Small Screen

Though Columbine never has been directly depicted in television shows, the attack has served as a catalyst for a number of different plot lines that incorporate teenage characters embarking on mass school rampages (France, 2009). An early episode of the WB hit show *Buffy the Vampire Slayer* (1997: Season 2, Episode 3) hinted at school-based violence, but it was not until the following season that the show tackled the issue of school shootings specifically. Two episodes—"Earshot" (1999: Season 3, Episode 18) and the second part of the season finale entitled "Graduation Day" (1999: Season 3, Episode 22)—both featured elements of school shootings in their story lines. "Earshot," originally scheduled to air three days after the Columbine shooting, was delayed until September, while "Graduation Day: Part 2" was delayed nearly two months from its late-May release (Bonin, 1999; Cheng, 2018; Ryan, 1999).

Other WB teen dramas also have tackled the school shootings issue. The show *7th Heaven* featured two episodes involving gun violence in schools— one the year before Columbine (1998: Season, 3, Episode 7—"Johnny Get Your Gun") and one two years after (2001: Season 6, Episode 2—"Teased").

Cult classic *One Tree Hill* highlighted such an attack in an episode titled "With Tired Eyes, Tired Minds, Tired Souls, We Slept" (2006: Season 3, Episode 16), in which ostracized student Jimmy Edwards brings a gun to school to exact revenge on his tormentors, eventually turning the gun on himself after being in lockdown with many of the show's main characters (Brucculieri & Delbyck, 2016). The FOX hit show *Glee* examined gun violence in a school from a different angle in their episode "Shooting Star" (2013: Season 4, Episode 18), in which a student fearful of the future brought a gun to school to kill herself and her friend in a perceived act of mercy, though no one was injured when the weapon did fire (Brucculieri & Delbyck, 2016; see also Cheng, 2018). Additional facets of school shootings have been incorporated into other shows, including Season 1 of *American Horror Story* and the Season 1 finale of *Degrassi: Next Class* (Brucculieri & Delbyck, 2016).

Though these episodes initially were linked to teen-focused shows, the main concepts quickly were expanded into prime-time crime dramas with both school and mass shootings. *Law and Order* (2001: Season 11, Episode 22) incorporated a school shooting into the plot of its episode entitled "School Daze." Its equally popular spinoff series, *Law and Order: SVU*, also tackled a school shooting in the episode "Manic" (2003: Season 5, Episode 2). Other crime dramas, including *CSI* (2001: Season 2, Episode 4), *NCIS* (2006: Season 3, Episode 18), and *Criminal Minds* (2011: Season 7, Episode 4) each have broached the topic with similar content. More recently, hit shows like NBC's *Chicago PD* (2015: Season 2, Episode 22), *Chicago Fire* (2016: Season 4, Episode 13), and *Chicago Med* (2018: Season 3, Episode 18) each have addressed how first responders deal with mass shootings.

Murder, Mayhem, and Music

Beyond the visual media of movies and television shows, school shootings generally and Columbine in particular have served as inspiration for musical artists across multiple genres. Rapper Eminem was one of the earliest to reference the April 20, 1999, shooting in his lyrics. The 2000 song "I'm Back" specifically mentioned Columbine, but the song was censored on all versions of the release (including the explicit lyrics copy) due to its timing related to the attack. Two other songs off the same album—"Remember Me" and "The Way I Am"—also referenced school shootings but did so more generally, without direct mention of Columbine. On his 2013 album, Eminem addressed the censorship of his early song in the lyrics of "Rap God," where he again directly referenced the attack, this time without it being blocked.

Other songs also have directly referenced the shooting or those involved in it. "The Real" by Childish Gambino (2010), "Yonkers" by Tyler, the Creator (2011), and "Broccoli" by DRAM (2016) each reference the Columbine shooting by name within their lyrics. Rapper Bones devoted his entire 2014 album

Teen Witch to different facets of the shooting and its perpetrators. Similarly, Ill Bill's song "Anatomy of a School Shooting" (2004) essentially recreates Columbine from the perspective of Shooter H. Conversely, however, the 2005 song "Cassie" by the band Flyleaf immortalized victim Cassie Bernall instead of focusing on the perpetrators. School shootings have been referenced more generally in other songs, such as Pearl Jam's "Jeremy" (1991), Alice Cooper's "Wicked Young Man" (2000), and P.O.D.'s "Youth of a Nation" (2001).

Arguably one of the most famous songs to be inspired by Columbine was the 2011 hit "Pumped Up Kicks" from the band Foster the People. Once considered a "perky pop ditty with just enough low-fi murkiness to make it hip" (Johnson, 2011, para. 3), the song drew considerable criticism for its chorus. Chronicling the preparation of a school shooter prior to his attack, the band repeatedly sings "All the other kids with the pumped up kicks/you better run, better run, outrun my gun/all the other kids with the pumped up kicks/you better run, better run, faster than my bullet" as the chorus. While the song enjoyed a considerable amount of success on industry charts, it was pulled from rotation the following year after the shooting at Sandy Hook Elementary School ("Pumped Up Kicks," 2012; Quan, 2012). Despite the pushback, the song had a personal meaning to the band—bassist Cubbie Fink's cousin attended Columbine and was present during the shooting (Quan, 2012).

While many artists seemingly capitalized off the popularity of Columbine and the broader phenomenon of school shootings, one instead was vilified for allegedly inspiring the perpetrators. Shock rocker Marilyn Manson became an object of contempt and vitriol when it was reported that the two Columbine perpetrators had listened to his music (France, 1999). The connection later proved to be false (Bell, 2012; Cullen, 2009; D'Angelo, 2001; Manson, 1999; Willis, 2015), but the damage had already been done. When Manson was scheduled to play in Denver as part of the Ozzfest concert series two years after the shooting, protests erupted (Walsh & Mazza, 2001); he ultimately pulled out of the show due to the widespread backlash (D'Angelo, 2001; Udo, 2016).

Part of the retaliation against Manson came in the wake of an op-ed he published in *Rolling Stone* just over two months after the shooting. In it, he wrote:

> When it comes down to who's to blame for the high school murders in Littleton, Colorado, throw a rock and you'll hit someone who's guilty. We're the people who sit back and tolerate children owning guns, and we're the ones who tune in and watch the up-to-the-minute details of what they do with them. I think it's terrible when anyone dies, especially if it is someone you know and love. But what is more offensive is that when these tragedies happen, most people don't really care any more than they would

about the season finale of *Friends* or *The Real World*. I was dumbfounded as I watched the media snake right in, not missing a teardrop, interviewing the parents of dead children, televising the funerals. Then came the witch hunt. (Manson, 1999, para. 4)

In many ways, Manson's op-ed called to task all that was wrong with how the media and society had handled the response to Columbine. Yet, for being outspoken, he became the new scapegoat in the absence of society placing the responsibility on the two perpetrators. A year later, Manson released the album *Holy Wood (In the Shadow of the Valley of Death)*, which again addressed the issue of the violence at Columbine and his purported role in it (France, 2009; Udo, 2016; Walters, 2000). After struggling for years to recreate the success he had before the shooting, Manson went on record as saying that Columbine and its associated backlash toward him had effectively destroyed his career (France, 2017; Petridis, 2017; Segarra, 2017; Willis, 2015).

Columbine Goes to (Off-)Broadway

In perhaps one of the more unconventional artistic expressions, several theater productions based upon the shooting have been introduced. One of the first was the production *columbinus*, written by P. J. Paparelli and Stephen Karam, which debuted in Washington, D.C., in 2005 before moving to New York City in 2006 (Hernandez, 2006; Reid, 2018). The "theatrical discussion," as its creators called it, drew inspiration from the Columbine shooters' diaries and home videos, as well as discussions with survivors, community leaders, and others affected by the tragedy (Hernandez, 2006; see also Isherwood, 2006; Reid, 2018). The overarching goal of the production was to try to answer the question of why the shooting had happened and why the cycle of violence surrounding these types of events rarely, if ever, changed (Hernandez, 2006; Isherwood, 2006; Reid, 2018). The play, which received several award nominations (Hernandez, 2006), later was updated after additional interviews with Columbine survivors around the 10-year anniversary (Reid, 2018). By 2008, the play had made its way to Chicago, with its most recent showing in 2018 (Reid, 2018).

A second production followed *columbinus* in 2009. Titled *The Columbine Project*, the production, written and directed by Paul Storiale, told the story of events before, during, and after April 20, 1999, from various perspectives, including those of the two perpetrators (BWW News Desk, 2014; Gans, 2009). Like other works based on the shooting, *The Columbine Project*'s script was based off interviews with survivors as well as the perpetrators' own writings (Gans, 2009). The play, which won numerous awards, originally opened in Los Angeles before moving to New York City, only to return to southern California in 2014 (BWW News Desk, 2014; Gans, 2009).

Two additional productions based on the shooting premiered in 2014. The first, opening in March, was titled *The Library*. Written by Scott Burns and directed by famed Hollywood producer Steven Soderbergh (who directed, among other movies, *Erin Brockovich*), the play was adapted from Cullen's (2009) book on the shooting (Horn, 2014). It starred actress Chloë Grace Moretz as Caitlin Gabriel, the main character who was injured in a school shooting but subsequently ostracized by her friends who believed that she had told the shooters the whereabouts of other students who subsequently were killed (Horn, 2014; Vanasco, 2014). As the play unfolds, Caitlin struggled not only to explain her experience to her parents, but also to the world as the media painted her in a different light (Rooney, 2014). As Vanasco (2014) points out in her review, "The play is almost about something else: about how people hold on to whatever version of a story is easiest for them to believe, or about how no one narrative can ever capture the messiness of a tragedy" (para. 6). Not only does this statement highlight the misguided narratives that developed after Columbine (see also Horn, 2014), but also of those that have surfaced after other school shootings.

The other production, *The Erlkings*, opened in November in New York City (Associated Press, 2014b; CNN Wire Service, 2014). Written by playwright Nathaniel Sam Shapiro, the play drew its name from a German poem that was found in one of the Columbine shooters' journals (Herbert, 2014; Warner, 2014). While the aforementioned plays largely drew inspiration outside of the two gunmen, *The Erlkings* was written specifically from their perspectives and includes language taken from their homework assignments, online chat logs, journals, and videos (Associated Press, 2014b; CNN Wire Service, 2014; Herbert, 2014; Warner, 2014). Despite pushback, Shapiro defended his choice of telling the Columbine story from the perpetrators' perspectives, saying that it would provide a greater understanding of why the shooting and other subsequent attacks happened (Herbert, 2014).

More Unintended Consequences

As has been discussed throughout this book, there are consequences for the constant attention, negative or otherwise, that has been given to the two perpetrators and their actions. This chapter only further supports the need to avoid glamorizing or romanticizing them. As Marilyn Manson (1999) aptly noted in this *Rolling Stone* op-ed,

> America puts killers on the cover of *Time* magazine, giving them as much notoriety as our favorite movie stars. From Jesse James to Charles Manson, the media, since their inception, have turned criminals into folk heroes. They just created two new ones when they plastered those dip-shits' [Shooter K and Shooter H] pictures on the front of every newspaper. Don't be surprised if every kid who gets pushed around has two new idols. (para. 2)

Coni Sanders (2014), daughter of Dave Sanders, who was murdered in the attack, shared similar concerns in her op-ed about Shapiro's play *The Erlkings*: "He [Shapiro] should have started by omitting the killers' identities, stripping them of the fame and notoriety they so desperately sought—the same notoriety that so many gunmen before and after Columbine wished to attain" (para. 8).

While there certainly is a value for utilizing artistic expression to provide another level of understanding of events like Columbine, it need not do so at the expense of continuing to elevate the statuses of the perpetrators. It is clear that other would-be assailants draw inspiration from these individuals and their attacks (see, generally, Chapter 10). Although there have been calls to limit such notoriety by the mainstream news media, such calls must be extended into popular entertainment. As Sanders (2014) astutely noted, continuing to promote these killers through any type of media, entertainment or otherwise, "sadly [will] only perpetuate our culture of violence and feed into society's larger fears about mass shootings" (para. 12). Therefore, it is important to tease out the lessons to be learned from events like Columbine separate from their perpetrators and focus solely on those that help—that is, continue to share only what information is needed to continue to move forward and grow.

CHAPTER THIRTEEN

Moving Beyond the Columbine Effect

Twenty years later, the Columbine and Jefferson County communities continue to heal and move forward from the events of April 20. Each fall, students enter the halls of Columbine High School for another year of learning, growing, and experiencing what the institution has to offer. They walk under

A view of the Columbine Memorial, looking down from Rebel Hill. (Author photo)

a quote that adorns the overhang just beyond the cafeteria: "Through These Halls Pass the Finest Kids in America, The Students of Columbine High School." The school continues to boast excellent academics, championship athletics, and a community that embodies the phrase former principal Frank DeAngelis used to rally his students after the shooting: "We are Columbine."

Adjacent to the school, over Rebel Hill in Clement Park—not far from where the media city set up to cover the shooting—sits a reminder of that day: the Columbine Memorial. With ground breaking on June 16, 2005, and the completion and dedication taking place on September 21, 2007, the memorial provides the community and visitors alike a place to "reflect on the impact and lessons learned from this tragedy" (Columbine Memorial Foundation, n.d.b.). In the heart of the memorial sits the Ring of Remembrance, where each of the 13 families has shared words about their loved ones—personal stories, quotes, or Bible verses—permanently etched in stone like the memories of the fallen (Crosby, 2018). At its center, inset into the carefully laid stones, is the memorial ribbon designed by Kyle Velasquez's parents, Al and Phyllis (Columbine Memorial Foundation, n.d.a.). Written on the ribbon are the words "Never Forgotten," a true testament to the events of that day and the people affected by it.

Just beyond the Ring of Remembrance on the edge of the memorial sits the Wall of Healing, which features quotes from students, teachers, parents, and first responders who were affected by the shooting, as well as then-President

The memorial ribbon designed by the parents of victim Kyle Velasquez sits at the heart of Columbine Memorial. (Author photo)

Bill Clinton, who offered remarks at the ground breaking, engraved on stones (Columbine Memorial Foundation, n.d.a.; Crosby, 2018). Each spring, the carefully selected flowers and trees bloom, showing perseverance after the long, hard, cold winter. In many ways, the spring awakening is perfectly symbolic of the recovery the community has navigated for the last 20 years.

A second tribute to the lives taken on April 20, 1999, the Columbine Memorial Garden, sits just 20 minutes from the Columbine Memorial in the Olinger Chapel Hill cemetery. Large, black granite crosses have been erected, each featuring the name and portrait of one of the 13 people whose lives were cut tragically short that day. Three of those individuals—students Rachel Scott and Corey DePooter and teacher Dave Sanders—also are buried in the same cemetery. Their headstones each have been flanked by flowers, teddy bears, and notes, not only from those who knew them but also those who never did but who come by, wanting to pay their respects. Similar tributes adorn the grave sites of Lauren Townsend, Cassie Bernall, Matthew Kechter, Kelly Fleming, Isaiah Shoels, Daniel Mauser, Kyle Velasquez, Steven Curnow, and Daniel Rohrbough, located across the Denver metropolitan area, and of John Tomlin in Waterford, Wisconsin, where he was laid to rest.

There is no doubt that Columbine left an indelible mark on both its community and the nation as a whole. In the immediate, intermediate, and long-term aftermath of the shooting, a number of lessons have been learned. These lessons have led to countless changes being made in a variety of areas in order to potentially prevent similar events and generally make schools safer. At the same time, it is equally clear that there is more work to be done.

What Have We Learned?

This book began with an inscription from the Wall of Healing at the Columbine Memorial, with a key focus on the latter part of the quote: "What have we learned?" In the last 20 years, there certainly have been times when it may have seemed like the answer was "nothing," as shooting after shooting has captured headlines on television screens and newspapers across the nation. Yet as Harris and Harris (2012) point out, events like Columbine are complex issues in need of multifaceted and multidimensional responses. Where the last 20 years have failed is that the focus has been on identifying a single key issue—often zeroing in on guns, mental health, or violent media (see Schildkraut & Muschert, 2013)—rather than considering Columbine and similar events as "perfect storms" of numerous factors. Thus, a key factor in answering the question "What have we learned?" is to recognize how much progress has been made in various areas and how these interrelated lessons have helped forge a new path in the understanding of school and mass violence, particularly when they are considered in conjunction with one another.

Columbine reshaped the protocols that dictate how police officers respond to school and mass shootings, as was discussed in Chapter 4 (see also Bates, 2017). The lessons learned on April 20, 1999, were immediately implemented by law enforcement departments across the nation, led in part by the efforts of the Los Angeles Police Department (Pampilio, 2014). What once was viewed as a crisis the SWAT team was required to handle has now shifted to a problem for patrol officers to address (Police Executive Research Forum, 2014). Today's police officers receive intense active shooter training, and when they arrive on scene, they no longer create a perimeter and wait for SWAT (Bates, 2017; Bryan, 2018). Instead, they enter the location with one goal: neutralize the threat (Police Executive Research Forum, 2014; Pampilio, 2014). Consequently, response times have been drastically reduced—the first officer at the 2012 Aurora, Colorado, movie theater shooting was on scene within 83 seconds (Noe, 2013). In other shootings, including Virginia Tech (2007) and Sandy Hook (2012), the quick arrival of law enforcement led the shooters to end their rampages, potentially mitigating the loss of additional lives (Pampilio, 2014). Where the Columbine perpetrators had control of the school for nearly 50 minutes, the majority of mass shootings since have ended in five minutes or less, and one-third are over even quicker (Blair & Schweit, 2014).

Due to the rapid police response, emergency medical services also have been able to gain entry to a scene more quickly—the very issue that led to Dave Sanders's death has evolved into a practice that has saved many other lives. In Aurora, for example, the first ambulance was on scene within three minutes, and all injured victims had been transported to area hospitals in under one hour (Noe, 2013). The outcome: every victim who left the scene alive that night survived (Noe, 2013). Improved medical training for police officers also has helped to increase survivability in school and mass shooting events (Police Executive Research Forum, 2014; Nichols, 2012).

Identifying threats before they become a school or mass shooting also has evolved since Columbine (see Chapter 5). Before the shooting, threats to bring guns to school and similar actions were not taken seriously (Pampilio, 2014). After the shooting, many schools adopted zero-tolerance strategies that went so far as suspending students for shaping chicken fingers into guns or pointing their hands in a similar manner at their classmates (e.g., Campbell, 2015; "Child suspended," 2001; Cuevas, 2014; Schworm & Anderson, 2014; see also Cornell, 2006). While these represent more extreme responses to these types of events (Pampilio, 2014), the fact remains that schools across the nation have taken the threat of violence in their buildings seriously and have acted. Like the changes in police practices, the adoption of threat assessment practices has led to an untold number of school-based rampages being avoided. Similarly, changes to school culture and the adoption of anonymous reporting practices also have led to an increase in the number of students who know about plots in advance coming forward (see, generally, Madfis, 2018).

Schools today continue to be one of the safest and most secure locations for children across the country (as discussed in Chapter 6). According to the 2017 Indicators of School Crime and Safety report, a joint effort between the U.S. Department of Education and the U.S. Department of Justice, just 1.7% of youth homicides (those students who were between the ages of 5 and 18) during the 2015–2016 school year occurred at school (Musu-Gillette et al., 2018). When homicide was combined with suicide, there was, on average, one event for every 1.9 million students enrolled in public schools across the nation (Musu-Gillette et al., 2018). The overall number of crime incidents continues to decline over time, as do nonfatal victimization rates of students at school. Further, the reported level of fear of harm or attack at school by students also continues to wane (Musu-Gillette et al., 2018).

Many of the lessons learned since Columbine have contributed to the declining crime rate in schools, and homicide occurrences more specifically. Today, more schools have active shooter plans than ever before (Bryan, 2018). Musu-Gillette and colleagues (2018) found that 92% of schools during the 2015–2016 academic year had a specific mandated training for a potential shooting, with 95% performing lockdown drills. Public schools also have continued to increase the presence of security staff, both in the form of school resource officers and sworn law enforcement personnel (Musu-Gillette et al., 2018). More than 90% of schools utilize controlled access to the building (e.g., locked or monitored doors, visitor check-in procedures) during school hours, and nearly three out of every four institutions employ an electronic notification system to alert students, faculty, and staff of an emergency within the school (Musu-Gillette et al., 2018). In sum, applying what was learned on April 20, 1999, continues to inform practices and protocols in schools and other institutions (including workplaces) nationwide.

Still More Lessons to Learn

At the same time, however, there remain identifiable opportunities for improvement with lessons that have gone unlearned since the shooting. For law enforcement personnel, training to respond to active shooter events must be a dynamic process that continues to develop over time. As police become more skilled at responding to mass shootings, so too will the perpetrators in carrying them out (see, generally, Duntley & Buss, 2011). With law enforcement arriving on scene more quickly, for example, the 2007 Virginia Tech shooter determined that he needed to buy more time—and subsequently chained all the doors to Norris Hall shut during his second shooting at the school (Virginia Tech Review Panel, 2007). Though police arrived on scene just five minutes after the shooting began, they could not make entry into the building for an additional five minutes, leaving the shooter with unrestricted access to victims (Nichols, 2012; Virginia Tech Review Panel, 2007). Consequently, law enforcement officers have received more training on breaching in the event that they were to face similar situations (see, for example, Blair, Nichols, Burns, & Curnutt, 2013).

School security is another area that, while improvements have been made, still provides opportunities for continued advancements of practices and protocols. Ironically, two of the areas where considerable room for improvement exists are both cost-effective and backed by evidence: locks on classrooms and anonymous reporting systems. Just two-thirds of schools, for instance, reported having locks on classroom doors that can be secured from the inside—a critical component to creating a barrier between shooters and their intended targets that has been proven to save lives and likely saved many during the Columbine shooting (Musu-Gillette et al., 2018). The inability to secure classrooms from the inside, however, has been found to be an issue during both the 2012 Sandy Hook Elementary School (Sandy Hook Advisory Commission, 2015; Sedensky, 2013) and 2018 Marjory Stoneman Douglas High School (Mazzei, 2018; Spencer, 2018) shootings. Similarly, despite the success of Safe2Tell, less than 44% of schools nationwide indicated that they had an anonymous threat reporting system (Musu-Gillette et al., 2018), a protocol that could undoubtedly facilitate increasing the number of averted rampages by providing early warnings of individuals for whom a threat assessment is needed.

As Pampilio (2014) points out, there is an additional lesson that went unlearned in the aftermath of Columbine: that "teen depression is real and a deadly problem" (para. 19). While Shooter H was typified as a psychopath or sociopath, Shooter K highlighted the issue of teen depression, a problem that affects millions of teenagers across the nation (see, generally, Cullen, 2009; Harter, Low, & Whitesell, 2003; Larkin, 2007). The National Institute of Mental Health (2017) estimates that more than three million adolescents between the ages of 12 and 17—representing nearly 13% of the U.S. population in this age group—suffered from at least one major depressive episode in 2016. These episodes are "marked by significant and pervasive feelings of sadness that are associated with suicidal thoughts and impair a young person's ability to concentrate or engage in normal activities" (Mental Health America, n.d.). Consequently, suicide among American youth also has been found to be on the rise (O'Donnell & Saker, 2018; Welch, 2017) and is currently the second leading cause of death among individuals between the ages of 10 and 24, behind accidents and unintentional injuries (Heron, 2017; Sullivan, Annest, Simon, Luo, & Dahlberg, 2015). Detecting and treating teen depression and suicidality would not only help to address the issue of school and mass shootings, but it also would help to prevent other problems faced by youth today, including teen pregnancy and drug and alcohol abuse (Cullen in Pampilio, 2014).

Moreover, factors that underlie events like Columbine, such as mental health (but also including abuse, violent media, toxic masculinity, the widespread availability of guns, and a culture of violence), also contribute to other, less severe forms of school violence, including assault, bullying, fighting, and sexual misconduct. Accordingly, more comprehensive identification and treatment of those with mental health issues and problems at home can help in reducing school violence as a whole and not just in the most extreme cases like school shootings. To this point, the role of the school psychologist and social worker has been underemphasized in comparison to surveillance technologies and other security measures; thus, a necessary remedy is that these individuals should be given more priority, particularly in the way of funding, to help identify students and troubled social dynamics earlier and intercede in productive ways. In sum, responses to school violence must extend beyond punitive disciplinary procedures and criminal justice-style surveillance and incorporate broad antiviolence efforts that are necessary to enhance the well-being of youth.

Finally, one of the most obvious lessons that has been overlooked is the way the media cover events like Columbine. As Cullen (2009) pointed out, there were many myths that arose in the initial coverage—and, even though they have long since been refuted, remain part of the cultural narrative of the event, even 20 years later (see also Pampilio, 2014). The role of the Trench Coat Mafia. The targeting of persons of color and athletes. The connection to Adolf Hitler's birthday and Marilyn Manson. These and other mythical narratives were propagated by the media, and each took on a life of its own that persists to this day (Cullen, 2009; Pampilio, 2014). The rush to break the story and "get it right" led to so many outlets getting it wrong (see also Chapter 3).

Moreover, the consequences of prioritizing the shooters over their victims linger to this day, as this trend has dominated media coverage since. The Columbine perpetrators have gone on to serve as inspiration for other shooters who model their own rampages after the pair (Chapter 10). In spite of this, the media continues to employ a format that spotlights new shooters, subsequently rewarding them for their actions and incentivizing the next killer. They publish manifestos and splash the name and image of the newest school or mass shooter across television screens and newspapers. No longer are only the Columbine shooters infamous, folk heroes, and household names—so too are many of their successors. Despite calls for changes in reporting and data to support such movements, the issues related to the coverage of school and mass shootings highlighted by how the media presented the Columbine story not only persist 20 years later, they have been exacerbated. A key to preventing these events from continuing to occur is altering the way they are covered by the media, and it is time for these organizations to change the narrative.

More broadly speaking, when assessing these areas individually or collectively, it is imperative that responses to school shootings like Columbine and other forms of mass violence not be conceived as existing in a vacuum. As noted in Chapter 3, Gladwell (2008) has asserted that "we learn more from extreme circumstances than anything else . . . [and] it's those who lie outside ordinary experience that have the most to teach us" (p. 6). Indeed, the lessons highlighted in this book have shown that there is much to be learned from events like Columbine. Yet, if we only consider such outliers as disconnected from other types of violence in schools (or, in the case of mass shootings, society more broadly), then we may miss opportunities to address other, more commonly occurring issues.

Where Do We Go from Here?

Today, just as 20 years ago on the morning after the shooting, it is clear that Columbine has changed the way people in the United States and world-wide view school and mass violence. The school's very name has become synonymous with a host of additional social problems, including (but certainly not limited to) youth crime and school violence. In the last two decades, it has become clear that many lessons have been learned that have improved our society and our responses to school and mass shootings. At the same time, it is clear that there remains more work to be done.

All too often, the outcry and demand for action after a mass shooting is short-lived. This may be due, at least in part, to "mass shooting fatigue," an unintended consequence of too many events too close together with too much media coverage. Simultaneously, it appears that many people also have become numb and desensitized to the news of events like Columbine, ultimately resigning themselves to the fact that nothing can be done and simply accepting mass shootings as a part of American society. Once this pessimism sets in, "not one more" becomes "add another one to the list." The shock felt by the nation after Columbine has long since waned.

Events like Columbine highlight the complex, multifaceted nature of the problem that is school and mass shootings. To expect or demand a "quick fix" to such an issue is not only pointless but irresponsible. Equally multidimensional responses are needed, utilizing the resources found throughout the country in disciplines including sociology, psychology, criminology and criminal justice, law, and social work (see also Harris & Harris, 2012). This requires an investment of time—the problem of mass violence in this nation did not appear overnight, and it will not be solved that quickly. At the same time, the expectations for remedy of this issue also must be realistic. We will never be able to completely rid this nation or this world of events like Columbine, but that does not mean that we should not work to reduce them (a feasible goal that can—and will—be achieved by building on the lessons highlighted in this book).

One of the most important ways we move forward from the milestone that is the 20th anniversary is to engage in a much-needed sustained and meaningful discourse about events like Columbine (Schildkraut, Elsass, & Muschert, 2015; see also Henry, 2000, 2009; Muschert, 2007a, 2010; Schildkraut & Muschert, 2013). Doing so, however, requires that we as a society reject these events as a problem that cannot be fixed or a common feature of our nation. It requires us to have conversations about what can be done not only in the immediate aftermath of a school or mass shooting, but in the ebb that is found between these events. It requires us to ask difficult questions—some that we may not even want answers to—and to hold others, such as our legislators, as well as ourselves, responsible for taking action.

We owe it to ourselves and our children to ask these questions so that future generations do not have to endure the same heartbreak and tragedy that so many communities to date have experienced. We owe it to the Columbine and Jefferson County communities to learn from their experiences and to do better (and continue to do better) moving forward. We owe it to the 13 people whose lives were taken that day—Cassie Bernall, Steven Curnow, Corey DePooter, Kelly Fleming, Matthew Kechter, Daniel Mauser, Daniel Rohrbough, Rachel Scott, Isaiah Shoels, John Tomlin, Lauren Townsend, Kyle Velasquez, and William "Dave" Sanders—to not let their deaths be in vain. We owe it to them and to the countless others affected by the shooting to ensure they and the lessons of April 20, 1999, are never forgotten.

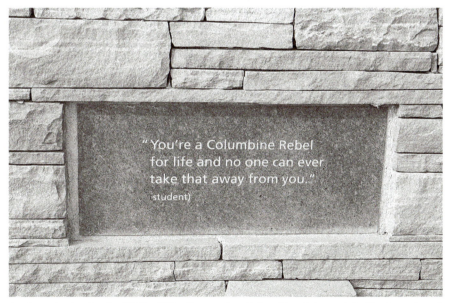

An inscription in the Wall of Healing at the Columbine Memorial. (Author photo)

References

A. 3697, 218th Leg., Reg. Sess. (N.J. 2018). A bill to repeal the Protection of Lawful Commerce in Arms Act, S. 2469, 114th Cong., 2nd Sess. (2016).

A&E. (2017). Attila the Hun biography. *Biography.com*. Retrieved from https://www.biography.com/people/attila-the-hun-9191831

Abramsky, S. (2016, August 9). The school-security industry is cashing in big on public fears of mass shootings. *The Nation*. Retrieved from https://www.thenation.com/article/the-school-security-industry-is-cashing-in-big-on-public-fears-of-mass-shootings/

Adams, C. (2016, May 4). May 4, 1970: Guardsmen open fire on Kent State protestors. *CBS News*. Retrieved from https://www.cbsnews.com/news/on-this-day-may-4-1970-guardsmen-open-fire-on-kent-state-protesters/

Addington, L. A. (2003). Students' fear after Columbine: Findings from a randomized experiment. *Journal of Quantitative Criminology, 19*(4), 367–387.

Addington, L. A. (2009). Cops and cameras: Public school security as a policy response to Columbine. *American Behavioral Scientist, 52*(10), 1426–1446.

Advanced Law Enforcement Rapid Response Training. (n.d.a.). *About ALERRT.* Retrieved from https://alerrt.org/page/about

Advanced Law Enforcement Rapid Response Training. (n.d.b.). *ALERRT active attack data.* Retrieved from http://activeattackdata.org/index.html

Advanced Law Enforcement Rapid Response Training. (n.d.c.). *Avoid. Deny. Defend.* Retrieved from http://www.avoiddenydefend.org/add.html

Advanced Law Enforcement Rapid Response Training. (n.d.d.). *Course catalog.* Retrieved from https://alerrt.org/Course-Catalog

Alfano, S. (2006, September 27). Cops: School shooting was "horrific." *CBS News*. Retrieved from https://www.cbsnews.com/news/cops-school-shooting-was-horrific/

Algar, S. (2016, July 22). New data show metal detectors are making schools safer. *New York Post*. Retrieved from https://nypost.com/2016/07/22/new-data-shows-metal-detectors-are-making-schools-safer/

Almeida, A. (2015, February 19). When schools simulate mass shootings. *The Atlantic*. Retrieved from https://www.theatlantic.com/education/archive/2015/02/when-schools-simulate-mass-shootings/385642/

Altheide, D. L. (2002). *Creating fear: News and the construction of crisis*. Hawthorne, NY: Aldine de Gruyter.

Altheide, D. L. (2009). The Columbine shooting and the discourse of fear. *American Behavioral Scientist, 52*(10), 1354–1370.

Altimari, D., & Wilson, J. (2013, December 4). On the six Newtown 911 calls, terror and pleas for help. *The Hartford Courant*. Retrieved from http://www.courant.com/news/connecticut/newtown-sandy-hook-school-shooting/hc-sandyhook-911-calls-released-20131204-story.html

Ames, M. (2007). *Going postal: Rage, murder, and rebellion in America*. London: Snowbooks.

Ariosto, D. (2012, August 26). Police: All Empire State shooting victims were wounded by officers. *CNN*. Retrieved from http://www.cnn.com/2012/08/25/justice/new-york-empire-state-shooting/

Armitage, R. (2017). Crime prevention through environmental design. In R. Wortley & M. Townsley (Eds.), *Environmental Criminology and Crime Analysis* (2nd ed., pp. 259–285). London: Routledge.

Arnowitz, N. W. (2014, February 14). Fake blood and blanks: Schools stage active shooter drills. *NBC News*. Retrieved from https://www.nbcnews.com/news/us-news/fake-blood-blanks-schools-stage-active-shooter-drills-n28481

Ascione, A. M. (1939). The federal firearms act. *St. John's Law Review, 13*(2), 437–446.

Assael, S. (1999, October). Rebels with a cause. *ESPN The Magazine*. Retrieved from http://www.espn.com/espn/news/story?page=Mag15rebelswithacause

Assault Weapons Ban and Law Enforcement Protection Act of 2003, H.R. 2038, 108th Cong., 1st Sess. (2003).

Assault Weapons Ban and Law Enforcement Protection Act of 2003, S. 1431, 108th Cong., 1st Sess. (2003).

Assault Weapons Ban and Law Enforcement Protection Act of 2005, H.R. 1312, 109th Cong., 1st Sess. (2005).

Assault Weapons Ban and Law Enforcement Protection Act of 2007, H.R. 1022, 110th Cong., 1st Sess. (2007).

Assault Weapons Ban of 2013, H.R. 437, 113th Cong., 1st Sess. (2013).

Assault Weapons Ban of 2013, S. 150, 113th Cong., 1st Sess. (2013).

Assault Weapons Ban of 2015, H.R. 4269, 114th Cong., 1st Sess. (2015).

Assault Weapons Ban of 2017, S. 2095, 115th Cong., 1st Sess. (2017).

Assault Weapons Ban of 2018, H.R. 5077, 115th Cong., 2nd Sess. (2018).

Assault Weapons Ban of 2018, H.R. 5087, 115th Cong., 2nd Sess. (2018).

Assault Weapons Ban Reauthorization Act of 2003, H.R. 3831, 108th Cong., 2nd Sess. (2004).

Assault Weapons Ban Reauthorization Act of 2003, S. 1034, 108th Cong., 1st Sess. (2003).

Assault Weapons Ban Reauthorization Act of 2004, S. 2109, 108th Cong., 2nd Sess. (2004).

Assault Weapons Ban Reauthorization Act of 2004, S. 2498, 108th Cong., 2nd Sess. (2004).

Assault Weapons Ban Reauthorization Act of 2005, S. 620, 109th Cong., 1st Sess. (2005).

Assault Weapons Ban Reauthorization Act of 2005, S. 645, 109th Cong., 1st Sess. (2004).

Assault Weapons Ban Reauthorization Act of 2008, H.R. 6257, 110th Cong., 2nd Sess. (2008).

Assault Weapons Ban Reauthorization Bill, H.R. 5099, 108th Cong., 2nd Sess. (2004).

Associated Press. (1989, January 18). Five children killed as gunman attacks a California school. *The New York Times*. Retrieved from https://www.nytimes.com/1989/01/18/us/five-children-killed-as-gunman-attacks-a-california-school.html

Associated Press. (2000, February 20). 2,000 mourn Columbine sweethearts. *Los Angeles Times*. Retrieved from http://articles.latimes.com/2000/feb/20/news/mn-895

Associated Press. (2001, June 10). New library at Columbine draws praise at unveiling. *The New York Times*. Retrieved from https://www.nytimes.com/2001/06/10/us/new-library-at-columbine-draws-praise-at-unveiling.html

Associated Press. (2006, February 8). Prosecutor discusses school shooting with Red Lake officials. *Farmers Independent*. Retrieved from https://news.google.com/newspapers?nid=1027&dat=20060208&id=5EplAAAAIBAJ&sjid=vJMNAAAAIBAJ&pg=2118,5968450&hl=en

Associated Press. (2007, April 18). Cho idolized Columbine killers. *The Denver Post*. Retrieved from https://www.denverpost.com/2007/04/18/cho-idolized-columbine-killers/

Associated Press. (2013, November 1). LAX shooting: Gunman kills TSA agent, injures 3. *The Hollywood Reporter*. Retrieved from https://www.hollywoodreporter.com/news/lax-shooting-gunman-kills-tsa-652525

Associated Press. (2014a, May 7). 22 states now challenging the constitutionality of NY Safe Act's ban on semi-automatic weapons. *Syracuse.com*. Retrieved from https://www.syracuse.com/news/index.ssf/2014/05/22_states_now_challenging_the_constitutionality_of_ny_safe_acts_ban_on_semi-auto.html

Associated Press. (2014b, October 7). Writer of Columbine shooters play: "We must acknowledge kinship with them." *The Guardian*. Retrieved from https://www.theguardian.com/us-news/2014/oct/07/columbine-high-school-play-erlkings-new-york-shooters

Associated Press. (2014c, October 7). Play about Columbine massacre to debut in NYC. *The New York Post*. Retrieved from https://nypost.com/2014/10/07/play-about-columbine-massacre-to-debut-in-nyc/

Associated Press. (2016, February 24). Columbine killer has cult of fans long after death. *The New York Post*. Retrieved from https://nypost.com/2016/02/24/columbine-killer-has-cult-of-fans-long-after-death/

Augé, K. (2009, April 18). Columbine: Memories at every turn. *The Denver Post*. Retrieved from https://www.denverpost.com/2009/04/18/columbine-mem ories-at-every-turn/

Austin, S. J. (2003, February). Lessons learned from the shootings at Columbine High School. In *The human side of school crises—A public entity risk institute symposium*. Alexandria, VA: Public Entity Risk Institute. Retrieved from https://www.schoolcounselor.org/asca/media/asca/Crisis/columbine.pdf

Bartlett/Chapman/Stockman Assault Weapon Ban Repeal Act, H.R. 698, 104th Cong., 1st Sess. (1995).

Bartlett/Stockman Assault Weapon Ban Repeal Act, H.R. 464, 104th Cong., 1st Sess. (1995).

Bates, A. (2017, April 20). Eighteen years after Columbine, what have we learned about spree shootings? *Cato Institute*. Retrieved from https://www.cato .org/blog/eighteen-years-after-columbine-what-have-we-learned-about -spree-shootings

Beauchamp, Z. (2018, May 18). A Santa Fe High School student says she expected to be shot at one day. *Vox*. Retrieved from https://www.vox.com/policy -and-politics/2018/5/18/17369098/santa-fe-high-school-shooting-texas -student-interview

Beaumont, H. (2015, February 24). *Inside the world of Columbine-obsessed Tumblr bloggers*. Retrieved from http://www.vice.com/read/speaking-to-columbiners -about-depression-suicide-and-the-halifax-shooting-plot-232

Beck, U. (1992). *Risk society: Towards a new modernity*. Newbury Park, CA: Sage.

Beck, U. (1999). *World risk society*. Malden, MA: Polity Press.

Bell, A. (1991). *The language of news media*. Oxford: Basil Blackwell Ltd.

Bell, C. (2012, May 10). Marilyn Manson thinks he's the most blamed person "in the history of music." *The Huffington Post*. Retrieved from http://www .huffingtonpost.com/2012/05/10/marilyn-manson-born-villain-most -blamed-person_n_1507130.html

Berger, R. R. (2002). Expansion of police powers in public schools and the van-ishing rights of students. *Social Policy, 29*(1–2), 119–130.

Bernard, T. (1999). Juvenile crime and the transformation of juvenile justice: Is there a juvenile crime wave? *Justice Quarterly, 16*(2), 337–356.

Bingham, J. (2009, March 13). Germany school shooting: Police foil second "high school plot." *The Telegraph*. Retrieved from https://www.telegraph .co.uk/news/4985876/Germany-school-shooting-Police-foil-second -high-school-plot.html

Birkland, T. A., & Lawrence, R. G. (2009). Media framing and policy change after Columbine. *American Behavioral Scientist, 52*(10), 1405–1425.

Blair, J. P., & Martaindale, M. H. (2013). *United States active shooter events from 2000 to 2010: Training and equipment implications*. San Marcos, TX: Advanced Law Enforcement Rapid Response Training (ALERRT). Retrieved from http:// www.acphd.org/media/372742/activeshooterevents.pdf

Blair, J. P., Nichols, T., Burns, D., & Curnutt, J. R. (2013). *Active shooter: Events and responses*. Boca Raton, FL: CRC Press.

Blair, J. P., & Schweit, K. W. (2014). *A study of active shooter incidents, 2000–2013*. Washington, D.C.: U.S. Department of Justice, Federal Bureau of Investigation. Retrieved from http://www.fbi.gov/news/stories/2014/sep tember/fbi-releases-study-on-active-shooter-incidents/pdfs/a-study-of -active-shooter-incidents-in-the-u.s.-between-2000-and-2013

Blake, A. (2017, July 6). TSA failed to detect 95 percent of prohibited items at Minneapolis airport: Report. *The Washington Times*. Retrieved from https://www.washingtontimes.com/news/2017/jul/6/tsa-failed-detect -95-percent-prohibited-items-minn/

Bondü, R., & Scheithauer, H. (2015). Narcissistic symptoms in German school shooters. *International Journal of Offender Therapy and Comparative Criminology, 59*(14), 1520–1535.

Bonin, L. (1999, May 25). Why the controversial finale of "Buffy" didn't air last night. *Entertainment Weekly*. Retrieved from http://ew.com/article/1999/05/25/why-controversial-finale-buffy-didnt-air-last-night/

Bort, R. (2017, April 22). Watching "Bowling for Columbine" with Michael Moore 18 years after the massacre. *Newsweek*. Retrieved from https://www.newsweek .com/michael-moore-bowling-columbine-screening-fear-america-587859

Borum, R., Cornell, D. G., Modzeleski, W., & Jimerson, S. J. (2010). What can be done about school shootings? A review of the evidence. *Educational Researcher, 39*(1), 27–37.

Borum, R., Fein, R., Vossekuil, B., & Berglund, J. (1999). Threat assessment: Defining and approach for evaluating risk of targeted violence. *Behavioral Sciences and the Law, 17*(3), 323–337.

Bradshaw, P. (2002, November 14). Bowling for Columbine—Review. *The Guardian*. Retrieved from https://www.theguardian.com/culture/2002/nov/15 /artsfeatures4

Brady Campaign Press Release. (2011, January 7). One million mental health records now in Brady background check system. *BradyCampaign.org*. Retrieved from http://bradycampaign.org/media/press/view/1336/ (link no longer active).

Brenan, M. (2017, October 16). Support for stricter gun laws edges up in U.S. *Gallup*. Retrieved from http://news.gallup.com/poll/220595/support-stricter -gun-laws-edges.aspx

Brener, N. D., Simon, T. R., Anderson, M., Barrios, L. C., & Small, M. L. (2002). Effect of the incident at Columbine on students' violence- and suicide-related behaviors. *American Journal of Preventive Medicine, 22*(3), 146–150.

Brooks, D. (2007, April 19). The mortality line. *The New York Times*. Retrieved from http://select.nytimes.com/2007/04/19/opinion/19brooks.html?hp

Brown, B., & Merritt, R. (2002). *No easy answers: The truth behind death at Columbine*. New York: Lantern Books.

Brucculieri, J., & Delbyck, C. (2016, January 25). These classic TV episodes about school shootings are more relevant than ever. *Huffington Post*. Retrieved from https://www.huffingtonpost.com/entry/school-shootings-on-tv_us _56a14986e4b076aadcc5c94b

Bryan, S. (2018, April 20). Columbine 19 years later: How far have we come? *Sun-Sentinel*. Retrieved from http://www.sun-sentinel.com/local/broward/fl-florida-school-shooting-columbine-lessons-learned-20180418-story.html

Buell, S. (2014, October 24). Arlington to adopt ALICE school crisis training. *The Arlington Advocate*. Retrieved from http://arlington.wickedlocal.com/article/20141024/NEWS/141027551

BulletBlocker. (n.d.). Bulletproof vest, protective safety clothing. *Bullet Blocker*. Retrieved from http://www.bulletblocker.com/

Bureau of Alcohol, Tobacco, and Firearms. (n.d.). National firearms act (NFA). Retrieved from http://www.atf.gov/firearms/nfa/

Burns, R., & Crawford, C. (1999). School shootings, the media, and public fear: Ingredients for a moral panic. *Crime, Law & Social Change, 32*(2), 147–168.

Buxton, R. (2014, November 20). Explaining hybristophilia: Why some people are sexually attracted to serial killers. *Huffington Post Live*. Retrieved from http://www.huffingtonpost.com/2014/11/20/hybristophilia-serial-killers_n_6194386.html

BWW News Desk. (2014, April 5). The Columbine Project returns to LA, now through 4/26. *Broadway World*. Retrieved from https://www.broadwayworld.com/los-angeles/article/THE-COLUMBINE-PROJECT-to-Return-to-LA-45-26-20140404

Calhoun, F. S., & Weston, S. W. (2003). *Contemporary threat management: A practical guide for identifying, assessing, and managing individuals of violent intent*. San Diego, CA: Specialized Training Services.

Callaway, D. W., Smith, E. R., Cain, J., Shapiro, G., Burnett, W. T., McKay, S. D., & Mabry, R. (2011). Tactical emergency casualty care (TECC): Guidelines for the provision of prehospital trauma care in high threat environments. *Journal of Special Operations Medicine, 11*(3), 104–122.

Campbell, A. (2015, March 6). 6-year-old suspended for pointing fingers in the shape of a gun. *Huffington Post*. Retrieved from https://www.huffingtonpost.com/2015/03/06/6-year-old-fingers-shape-of-gun-suspended_n_6813864.html

Carlson, D. K. (2001, March 5). Majority of parents think a school shooting could occur in their own community. *Gallup*. Retrieved from http://news.gallup.com/poll/1939/Majority-Parents-Think-School-Shooting-Could-Occur-Their-Community.aspx

Carlson, D. K. (2004, November 30). Americans softening on tougher gun laws? *Gallup*. Retrieved from http://news.gallup.com/poll/14185/Americans-Softening-Tougher-Gun-Laws.aspx

Carvalho, E. J. (2010). The poetics of a school shooter: Decoding political signification in Cho Seung-Hui's multimedia manifesto. *The Review of Education, Pedagogy, and Cultural Studies, 32*(4–5), 403–430.

Casella, R. (2003). The false allure of security technologies. *Social Justice, 30*(3), 82–93.

Cattafi, K. (2018, May 1). Police, fire, EMS (and even teachers) train together to care for mass casualties. *NorthJersey.com*. Retrieved from https://www

.northjersey.com/story/news/bergen/garfield/2018/05/01/rescue-training -brings-police-fire-ems-right-into-active-shooting-scenario/482019002/

CBC. (2015, April 18). Halifax shooting plot: Who are the "Columbiners"? *Huffington Post Canada*. Retrieved from http://www.huffingtonpost.ca/2015/02 /17/halifax-shooting-plot-columbiners_n_6696498.html

Centers for Disease Control. (2017). *2016 health and safe school environment district data* [Data file and codebook]. Retrieved from https://www.cdc.gov/healthyy outh/data/shpps/data.htm

Cerulo, K. (1998). *Deciphering violence: The cognitive structure of right and wrong.* New York: Routledge.

Chen, S. (2009, April 20). Debunking the myths of Columbine, 10 years later. *CNN*. Retrieved from http://www.cnn.com/2009/CRIME/04/20/columbine .myths/

Cheng, S. (2018, March 23). Here's how teen shows like "Degrassi" try to get school shootings right. *Buzzfeed News*. Retrieved from https://www .buzzfeednews.com/article/susancheng/school-shootings-tv-parkland -buffy-degrassi-greys-anatomy

Chermak, S. M. (1995). *Victims in the news: Crime and the American news media.* Boulder, CO: Westview Press.

Chick, M. (2007). *Statistics of handgun accuracy: A guide for target shooters.* West Conshohocken, PA: InfinityPublishing.com.

Child suspended for brandishing chicken. (2001, February 1). *Los Angeles Times.* Retrieved from http://articles.latimes.com/2001/feb/01/news/mn-19819

Chung, A. (2017, November 27). U.S. top court spurns challenge to Maryland assault weapons ban. *Reuters*. Retrieved from https://www.reuters.com /article/us-usa-court-guncontrol/u-s-top-court-spurns-challenge-to -maryland-assault-weapons-ban-idUSKBN1DR1SE

Chyi, H. I., & McCombs, M. E. (2004). Media salience and the process of framing: Coverage of the Columbine school shootings. *Journalism and Mass Communication Quarterly, 81*(1), 22–35.

Ciamacca, D. (2018, February 23). I was a Marine. Now I'm a teacher. Don't give me a gun. *People*. Retrieved from http://time.com/5172852/trump-guns-teachers-nra/

Clarke, R. V. (1997). *Situational crime prevention: Successful case studies* (2nd ed.). Albany, NY: Harrow and Heston.

Clary, G. (2014, March 12). Police: Maryland mall shooter was obsessed with Columbine. *CNN*. Retrieved from https://www.cnn.com/2014/03/12/justice /maryland-mall-shooting/index.html

Cloud, J. (2014, October 2). The bulletproof classroom: Armored whiteboards defend against school shootings. *Bloomberg Business*. Retrieved from http://www.bloomberg.com/bw/articles/2014-10-02/hardwires-armored -whiteboards-defend-against-school-shootings

Clouston, E., & Boseley, S. (2013, March 14). From the archive, 14 March 1996: Sixteen children killed in Dunblane massacre. *The Guardian*. Retrieved from https://www.theguardian.com/theguardian/2013/mar/14/dunblane -massacre-scotland-killing

CNN Wire Service. (2014, October 15). Off-Broadway play about Columbine High School shooting to debut in November. *Fox 6 Now*. Retrieved from https://fox6now.com/2014/10/15/off-broadway-play-about-columbine -high-school-shooting-to-debut-in-november/

Coccio, B. (2003, June 28). How they did it: The making of Zero Day. *Movie-Maker*. Retrieved from https://www.moviemaker.com/archives/series/how _they_did_it/zero-day-3015/

Cohen, B. C. (1963). *The press and foreign policy*. Princeton, NJ: Princeton University Press.

Columbine killer "God." (2006, November 22). *News 24*. Retrieved from https://www.news24.com/World/News/Columbine-killer-God-2006 1122

Columbine Memorial Foundation. (n.d.a.). *Design*. Retrieved from https://www .columbinememorial.org/?page_id=44

Columbine Memorial Foundation. (n.d.b.). *Overview*. Retrieved from https:// www.columbinememorial.org/?page_id=42

Columbine Review Commission. (2001). *The report of Governor Bill Owens' Columbine Review Commission*. Denver, CO: State of Colorado. Retrieved from http://trac.state.co.us/Documents/Reports%20and%20Publications/Col umbine_2001_Governor_Review_Commission.pdf

Columbine survivor's mother kills herself in pawn shop. (1999, October 23). *The Denver Post*. Retrieved from http://www.cnn.com/US/9910/23/columbine .suicide.01/

Conklin, J. (2002). *Why crime rates fell*. Upper Saddle River, NJ: Prentice Hall.

Connolly, C., & Harris, J. F. (2005, March 23). Rampage in Minn. mirrors other cases. *The Washington Post*. Retrieved from http://www.washingtonpost .com/wp-dyn/articles/A56147-2005Mar22.html

Connor, T. (2013, August 21). Bulletproof school supplies get low grades from safety experts. *NBC News*. Retrieved from http://www.nbcnews.com/ news/other/bulletproof-school-supplies-get-low-grades-safety-experts -f6C10963127

Consalvo, M. (2003). The monsters next door: Media construction of boys and masculinity. *Feminist Media Studies, 3*(1), 27–45.

Corcoran, L. (2015, May 14). Metal detectors: Boston's success story. *MassLive*. Retrieved from https://www.masslive.com/news/worcester/index.ssf/2015 /05/metal_detectors_in_schools_bos.html

Cornell, D. G. (2006). *School violence: Facts versus fears*. Mahwah, NJ: Lawrence Erlbaum Associates, Inc.

Cornell, D. G. (2013). The Virginia student threat assessment guidelines: An empirically supported violence prevention strategy. In N. Böckler, T. Seeger, P. Sitzer, & W. Heitmeyer (Eds.), *School shootings* (pp. 379–400). New York: Springer.

Cornell, D. G. (2015). Our schools are safe: Challenging the misperception that schools are dangerous places. *American Journal of Orthopsychiatry, 85*(3), 217–220.

Cornell, D. G., Sheras, P., Gregory, A., & Fan, X. (2009). A retrospective study of school safety conditions in high schools using the Virginia threat assessment guidelines versus alternative approaches. *American Psychological Association, 24*(2), 119–129.

Cornell, D. G., Sheras, P. L., Kaplan, S., McConville, D., Douglass, J., Elkon, A., . . . Cole, J. (2004). Guidelines for student threat assessment: Field-test findings. *School Psychology Review, 33*(4), 527–546.

Couvrette, P. (2006, September 15). Gunman was obsessed with Columbine shootings. *Deseret News.* Retrieved from https://www.deseretnews.com/article /645201695/Gunman-was-obsessed-with-Columbine-shootings.html

Cozens, P. (2011). Crime prevention through environmental design. In R. Wortley & L. Mazerolle (Eds.), *Environmental criminology and crime analysis* (pp. 153–177). London: Routledge.

Crepeau-Hobson, M. F., Filaccio, M., & Gottfried, L. (2005). Violence prevention after Columbine: A survey of high school mental health professionals. *Children and Schools, 27*(3), 157–165.

Crews, G. A., & Counts, M. R. (1997). *The evolution of school disturbance in America: Colonial times to modern day.* Westport, CT: Praeger.

Crosby, R. (2018, April 2). Columbine memorial a reminder of "how much was really lost then." *Las Vegas Review-Journal.* Retrieved from https://www. reviewjournal.com/crime/shootings/columbine-memorial-a-reminder -of-how-much-was-really-lost-then/

Cross, B. W., & Pruitt, S. W. (2013). Dark Knight Rising: The Aurora theater and Newtown school massacres and shareholder wealth. *Journal of Criminal Justice, 41*(6), 452–457.

Cuevas, M. (2014, March 4). 10-year-old suspended for making fingers into shape of gun. *CNN.* Retrieved from https://www.cnn.com/2014/03/04/us /ohio-boy-suspended-finger-gun/index.html

Cullen, D. (2004, April 20). The depressive and the psychopath: At least we know why the Columbine killers did it. *Slate.* Retrieved from http://www .slate.com/articles/news_and_politics/assessment/2004/04/the_depressive _and_the_psychopath.html

Cullen, D. (2009). *Columbine.* New York: Twelve.

Curiel, J. (2002, October 18). Moore captures U.S. zeitgeist/"Bowling for Columbine" explains violence. *San Francisco Chronicle.* Retrieved from https:// www.sfgate.com/entertainment/article/Moore-captures-U-S-zeitgeist -Bowling-for-2761485.php

D'Angelo, J. (2001, March 22). Marilyn Manson bows out of Denver Ozzfest date. *MTV News.* Retrieved from http://www.mtv.com/news/1442018/marilyn -manson-bows-out-of-denver-ozzfest-date/

Daniels, J. A., Buck, I., Croxall, S., Gruber, J., Kime, P., & Govert, H. (2007). A content analysis of news reports of averted school rampages. *Journal of School Violence, 6*(1), 83–99.

Daniels, J. A., Royster, T. E., & Vecchi, G. M. (2007). Barricaded hostage and crisis situations in schools: A review of recent incidents. *Proceedings of*

Persistently Safe Schools: The 2007 National Conference on Safe Schools and Communities. Retrieved from https://www.ncjrs.gov/pdffiles1/ojjdp/grants /226233.pdf?q=student-reports-of-bullying-results-from-the-2001 -school#page=75

Daniels, J. A., Volungis, A., Pshenishny, E., Gandhi, P., Winkler, A., Cramer, D. P., & Bradley, M. C. (2010). A qualitative investigation of averted school shooting rampages. *Counseling Psychologist, 38*(1), 69–95.

Darwin, C. (1906). *The Voyage of the Beagle*. New York: Dutton.

Davey, M. (2005, April 3). Inquiry on school attack may include 20 students. *The New York Times*. Retrieved from http://www.nytimes.com/2005/04/03 /us/inquiry-on-school-attack-may-include-20-students.html

Deacon, D. (2007). Yesterday's papers and today's technology: Digital newspaper archives and "push button" content analysis. *European Journal of Communications, 22*(1), 5–25.

Dean, C., Duggan, M., & Morin, R. (2016, December 15). Americans name the 10 most significant historic events of their lifetimes. *Pew Research Center for the People & the Press*. Retrieved from http://www.people-press. org/2016/12/15/americans-name-the-10-most-significant-historic -events-of-their-lifetimes/

DeAngelis, F. (2018). Foreword. In J. Schildkraut (ed.), *Mass shootings in America: Understanding the debates, causes, and responses* (pp. xi–xvii). Santa Barbara, CA: ABC-CLIO.

Dearing, J. (2018, February 26). School security systems industry—US market overview. *IHS Markit*. Retrieved from https://technology.ihs.com/600401 /school-security-systems-industry-us-market-overview

Deisinger, E. R. (2016). *Threat assessment in Virginia public schools: Model policies, procedures, and guidelines* (2nd ed.). Richmond, VA: Virginia Department of Criminal Justice Services. Retrieved from https://www .dcjs.virginia.gov/sites/dcjs.virginia.gov/files/publications/law-enforce ment/threat-assessment-model-policies-procedures-and-guidelinespdf .pdf

Deisinger, E. R., Randazzo, M. R., & Nolan, J. J. (2014). Threat assessment and management in higher education. In J. R. Meloy & J. Hoffman (Eds.), *International handbook of threat assessment* (pp. 107–125). New York, NY: Oxford University Press.

The Denver Post. (2000, April 16). Columbine timeline. *The Denver Post*. Retrieved from http://extras.denverpost.com/news/timeline.htm

The Denver Post. (2007, December 10). Guard's hands "didn't even shake" as she shot gunman. *The Denver Post*. Retrieved from https://www.denverpost .com/2007/12/10/guards-hands-didnt-even-shake-as-she-shot-gunman/

The Denver Post. (2009, April 18). Columbine: Where are they now. *The Denver Post*. Retrieved from https://www.denverpost.com/2009/04/18/columbine -where-they-are-now/

Deruy, E. (2015, December 2). The warning signs of a mass shooting. *The Atlantic*. Retrieved from https://www.theatlantic.com/politics/archive/2015/12 /the-warning-signs-of-a-mass-shooting/433527/

De Venanzi, A. (2012). School shootings in the USA: Popular culture as risk, teen marginality, and violence against peers. *Crime Media Culture, 8*(3), 261–278.

Dickinson, T. (2018, February 22). All-American killer: How the AR-15 became mass shooters' weapon of choice. *Rolling Stone*. Retrieved from https://www.rollingstone.com/politics/politics-features/all-american-killer-how-the-ar-15-became-mass-shooters-weapon-of-choice-107819/

Dietz, P. E. (1986). Mass, serial, and sensational homicides. *Bulletin of the New York Academy of Medicine, 62*(5), 477–491.

Dinkes, R., Cataldi, E. F., Lin-Kelly, W., & Snyder, T. D. (2007). *Indicators of school crime safety: 2007*. Washington, D.C.: U.S. Department of Education and U.S. Department of Justice.

District of Columbia v. Heller (2008). 554 U.S. 570.

Documents reveal more troubling details on FedEx facility shooter. (2014, October 10). *CBS 46*. Retrieved from http://www.cbs46.com/story/26521376/documents-reveal-more-troubling-details-on-fedex-facility-shooter

Doherty, M. (2016). From protective intelligence to threat assessment: Strategies critical to preventing targeted violence and the active shooter. *Journal of Business Continuity & Emergency Planning, 10*(1), 9–12.

Donohue, E., Schiraldi, V., & Ziedenberg, J. (1998, July). *School house hype: School shootings and the real risks kids face in America*. Washington, D.C.: Justice Policy Institute. Retrieved from http://www.justicepolicy.org/uploads/justicepolicy/documents/98-07_rep_schoolhousehype_jj.pdf

DontNameThem.org. (n.d.). *Don't name them (ALERRT at Texas State University)*. Retrieved from http://www.dontnamethem.org/

Doyle, S. (2017, October 3). If you don't think Stephen Paddock "fits the mass shooter profile," you haven't been paying attention. *ELLE*. Retrieved from https://www.elle.com/culture/career-politics/a12772832/stephen-paddock-las-vegas-mass-shooter-profile/

Dugan, A. (2012, December 20). Economy still top problem in U.S. but less so in the past. *Gallup*. Retrieved from http://news.gallup.com/poll/159434/economy-top-problem-less-past.aspx

Dunn, R. (2017, November 6). Toledo fire, police train together for active shooter. *The Blade*. Retrieved from http://www.toledoblade.com/Police-Fire/2017/11/06/Toledo-fire-police-train-together-for-active-shooter.html

Duntley, J. D., & Buss, D. M. (2011). Homicide adaptations. *Aggression and Violent Behavior, 16*(5), 399–410.

Dwyer, J., Flynn, K., & Fessenden, F. (2002, July 7). Fatal confusion: A troubled emergency response; 9/11 exposed deadly flaws in rescue plan. *The New York Times*. Retrieved from https://www.nytimes.com/2002/07/07/nyregion/fatal-confusion-troubled-emergency-response-9-11-exposed-deadly-flaws-rescue.html

Ebert, R. (2003, November 7). *Elephant*. Retrieved from https://www.rogerebert.com/reviews/elephant-2003

Edelstein, D. (2003, October 24). The kids in the hall: Gus Van Sant deconstructs Columbine in Elephant. *Slate*. Retrieved from http://www.slate.com/articles/arts/movies/2003/10/the_kids_in_the_hall.html

The Editors. (2018, February 23). Editorial: All the reasons it's a terrible idea to arm teachers. *The Weekly Standard.* Retrieved from https://www.weeklystandard.com/editorial-all-the-reasons-its-a-terrible-idea-to-arm-teachers/article/2011721

El Paso County Sheriff's Office. (2002). *Reinvestigation into the death of Daniel Rohrbough at Columbine High School on April 20, 1999: Executive summary.* Colorado Springs, CO: Author. Retrieved from http://news.findlaw.com/hdocs/docs/columbine/columbine41702shrfrpt.pdf

Entman, R. M. (2007). Framing bias: Media in the distribution of power. *Journal of Communication, 57*(1), 163–173.

Fabbri, W. P. (2014, September 29). FBI's view to improving survival in active shooter events. *Journal of Emergency Medical Services.* Retrieved from https://www.jems.com/articles/supplements/special-topics/when-time-matters-most/fbi-s-view-improving-survival-active-sho.html

Fast, J. (2008). *Ceremonial violence: A psychological explanation of school shootings.* New York: Overlook Press.

Federal Bureau of Investigation. (2018). *Developing emergency operations plans: A guide for businesses.* Washington, D.C.: U.S. Department of Justice. Retrieved from https://www.fbi.gov/file-repository/active-shooter-guide-for-businesses-march-2018.pdf/view

Federal Firearms Act of 1938. 15 U.S.C. §§ 901–909.

Fein, R. A., & Vossekuil, B. (1999). Assassination in the United States: An operational study of recent assassins, attackers, and near-lethal approaches. *Journal of Forensic Sciences, 44*(2), 321–333.

Fein, R. A., Vossekuil, B., & Holden, G. A. (1995). *Threat assessment: An approach to prevent targeted violence (Publication NCJ 155000).* Washington, D.C.: U.S. Department of Justice, Office of Justice Programs, National Institute of Justice. Retrieved from https://www.ncjrs.gov/pdffiles/threat.pdf

Fein, R. A., Vossekuil, B., Pollack, W. S., Borum, R., Modzeleski, W., & Reddy, M. (2002). *Threat assessment in schools: A guide to managing threatening situations and to creating safe school climates.* Washington, D.C.: U.S. Department of Education and U.S. Secret Service. Retrieved from http://www.cde.state.co.us/sites/default/files/documents/fedprograms/dl/ov_tiv_mtoi_threatassessment.pdf

Ferguson, C. J. (2014). Violent video games, mass shootings, and the Supreme Court: Lessons for the legal community in the wake of recent free speech cases and mass shootings. *New Criminal Law Review, 17*(4), 553–586.

Ferguson, C. J., Coulson, M., & Barnett, J. (2011). Psychological profiles of school shooters: Positive directions and one big wrong turn. *Journal of Police Crisis Negotiations, 11*(2), 141–158.

Ferguson, C. J., & Olson, C. K. (2014). Video game violence use among "vulnerable" populations: The impact of violent games on delinquency and bullying among children with clinically elevated depression or attention deficit symptoms. *Journal of Youth Adolescence, 43*(1), 127–136.

Fernandez, M., Turkewitz, J., & Bidgood, J. (2018, May 30). For "Columbiners," school shootings have a deadly allure. *The New York Times.* Retrieved from https://www.nytimes.com/2018/05/30/us/school-shootings-columbine.html

Ferner, M. (2014, February 13). Colorado Republican: It was actually 'a good thing' Aurora shooter had 100-round magazine. *Huffington Post.* Retrieved from https://www.huffingtonpost.com/2014/02/13/bernie-herpin-colorado-magazine_n_4781460.html

Ferraro, K. F. (1995). *Fear of crime: Interpreting victimization risk.* Albany: State University of New York Press.

Ferraro, K. F., & LaGrange, R. (1987). The measurement of fear of crime. *Sociological Inquiry, 57*(1), 70–101.

.50 Caliber BMG Regulation Act of 2004, A.B. 50, 2003-2004 Sess. (2004).

The Firearm Owners' Protection Act of 1986. 18 U.S.C. § 921.

Fletcher, T. (2016, June 22). Why solo-officer active shooter response should be trained. *PoliceOne.com.* Retrieved from https://www.policeone.com/police-products/firearms/training/articles/192578006-Why-solo-officer-active-shooter-response-should-be-trained/

Follman, M. (2015a, October 6). How the media inspires mass shootings. *Mother Jones.* Retrieved from https://www.motherjones.com/politics/2015/10/media-inspires-mass-shooters-copycats/

Follman, M. (2015b, December). Inside the race to stop the next mass shooter. *Mother Jones.* Retrieved from https://www.motherjones.com/politics/2015/10/mass-shootings-threat-assessment-shooter-fbi-columbine/

Follman, M., & Andrews, B. (2015, October 5). How Columbine spurned dozens of copycats: An obsession with the 1999 school shooting still fuels violent plots and attacks. *Mother Jones.* Retrieved from https://www.motherjones.com/politics/2015/10/columbine-effect-mass-shootings-copycat-data/

Forman, E. (2014, November 7). Danvers students to learn lockdown procedures. *The Salem News.* Retrieved from http://www.salemnews.com/news/local_news/danvers-students-to-learn-lockdown-procedures/article_b4a04ae4-72ab-521d-a52a-4a139b5453f7.html

Fox, J. A., & DeLateur, M. J. (2014). Mass shootings in America: Moving beyond Newtown. *Homicide Studies, 18*(1), 125–145.

Fox, J. A., Levin, J., & Fridel, E. (2019). *Extreme killing: Understanding serial and mass murder* (4th ed.). Thousand Oaks, CA: Sage.

France, L. R. (2009, April 20). Columbine left its indelible mark on pop culture. *CNN.* Retrieved from http://www.cnn.com/2009/SHOWBIZ/04/20/columbine.pop.culture/index.html

France, L. R. (2017, September 24). Marilyn Manson: Columbine massacre "destroyed" my career. *CNN.* Retrieved from https://www.cnn.com/2017/09/22/entertainment/marilyn-manson-columbine/index.html

Frankel, T. C. (2014, October 27). Can a wave of new inventions stop school shootings? *The Washington Post.* Retrieved from http://www.washington post.com/news/storyline/wp/2014/10/27/in-wake-of-school-shootings -a-flood-of-inventions-and-the-question-is-this-one-the-answer/

Frazzano, T. L., & Snyder, G. M. (2014). Hybrid targeted violence: Challenging conventional "active shooter" response strategies. *Homeland Security Affairs, 10.* Retrieved from https://www.hsaj.org/articles/253

Frymer, B. (2009). The media spectacle of Columbine: Alienated youth as an object of fear. *American Behavioral Scientist, 52*(10), 1387–1404.

Fuchs, C. (2005, April 6). Zero Day (2003). *Pop Matters.* Retrieved from https:// www.popmatters.com/zero-day-dvd-2496248835.html

Furedi, F. (2005). *Culture of fear: Risk-taking and the morality of low expectation.* New York: Continuum.

Gabriel, T. (2013, April 4). New gun restrictions pass the legislature in Maryland. *The New York Times.* Retrieved from https://www.nytimes.com/2013 /04/05/us/tighter-gun-rules-pass-the-maryland-legislature.html

Gagnon, J. C., & Leone, P. E. (2001). Alternative strategies for school violence prevention. *New Directions for Youth Development, 2001*(92), 101–125.

Gallup, G. (1999a, April 22). One-third of teenagers feel unsafe at school; one in six says weapons are a big problem in their school. *Gallup.* Retrieved from http://news.gallup.com/poll/3910/OneThird-Teenagers-Feel-Unsafe -School-One-Six-Says-Wea.aspx

Gallup, G. (1999b, May 20). Many teens report copycat-related problems at school in wake of Littleton shooting. *Gallup.* Retrieved from http://news .gallup.com/poll/3838/Many-Teens-Report-CopycatRelated-Problems -School-Wake-Little.aspx

Gans, A. (2009, August 9). *Columbine Project* opens Off-Broadway. *Playbill.* Retrieved from http://www.playbill.com/article/columbine-project-opens -off-broadway-com-163377

Gans, H. J. (1979). *Deciding what's news: A study of CBS Evening News, NBC Nightly News, Newsweek, and TIME.* New York, NY: Pantheon Books.

Garcia, C. A. (2003). School safety technology in America: Current use and perceived effectiveness. *Criminal Justice Policy Review, 14*(1), 30–54.

Garcia-Bernardo, J., Qi, H., Shultz, J. M., Cohen, A. M., Johnson, N. F., & Dodds, P. S. (2017). Social media affects the timing, location, and severity of school shootings. Retrieved from http://arxiv.org/pdf/1506.06305.pdf

Garfield, L. (2018, March 25). These $20,000 bulletproof shelters for classrooms can withstand shooters and Category 5 hurricanes. *Business Insider.* Retrieved from https://www.businessinsider.com/shelter-in-place-designs -ballistic-shelters-for-classrooms-2018-3

Gastic, B. (2011). Metal detectors and feeling safe at school. *Education and Urban Society, 43*(4), 486–498.

Gibbs, N., & Roche, T. (1999, December 20). The Columbine tapes. *TIME.* Retrieved from http://www.time.com/time/magazine/article/0,9171,992873,00.html

Giffords Law Center to Prevent Gun Violence. (n.d.a.). *Assault weapons.* Retrieved from http://lawcenter.giffords.org/gun-laws/policy-areas/hardware-ammu nition/assault-weapons/

Giffords Law Center to Prevent Gun Violence. (n.d.b.). *Tiahrt amendments.* Retrieved from http://lawcenter.giffords.org/gun-laws/federal-law/other -laws/tiahrt-amendments/

Giffords Law Center to Prevent Gun Violence. (2017a). *Assault weapons in Connecticut.* Retrieved from http://lawcenter.giffords.org/assault-weapons-in -connecticut/

Giffords Law Center to Prevent Gun Violence. (2017b). *Assault weapons in Hawaii.* Retrieved from http://lawcenter.giffords.org/assault-weapons-in-hawaii/

Giffords Law Center to Prevent Gun Violence. (2017c). *Assault weapons in Maryland.* Retrieved from http://lawcenter.giffords.org/assault-weapons-in-maryland/

Giffords Law Center to Prevent Gun Violence. (2017d). *Assault weapons in Massachusetts.* Retrieved from http://lawcenter.giffords.org/assault-weapons -in-massachusetts/

Giffords Law Center to Prevent Gun Violence. (2017e). *Assault weapons in New Jersey.* Retrieved from http://lawcenter.giffords.org/assault-weapons-in-new -jersey/

Giffords Law Center to Prevent Gun Violence. (2017f). *Assault weapons in New York.* Retrieved from http://lawcenter.giffords.org/assault-weapons-in-new -york/

Gill, M. (2014). *How offenders say they get around security measures: Why they say it is easy.* Keynote presented at ASIS International Middle East Security Conference, Dubai, United Arab Emirates.

Gillespie, M. (1999, April 30). Americans have very mixed opinions about blame for Littleton shootings. *Gallup.* Retrieved from http://news.gallup.com /poll/3889/Americans-Very-Mixed-Opinions-About-Blame-Littleton -Shootings.aspx

Gillespie, M. (2000, April 20). One in three say it is very likely that Columbine-type shootings could happen in their community. *Gallup.* Retrieved from http://www.gallup.com/poll/2980/One-Three-Say-Very-Likely-Columbi neType-Shootings-Could.aspx

Gladwell, M. (2008). *Outliers: The story of success.* New York, NY: Back Bay Books.

Goffman, E. (1974). *Frame analysis: An essay on the organization of experience.* Cambridge: Harvard University Press.

Goldstein, D. (2018, May 22). Why campus shootings are so shocking: School is the "safest place" for a child. *The New York Times.* Retrieved from https:// www.nytimes.com/2018/05/22/us/safe-school-shootings.html

Golgowski, N. (2018, February 21). Sales of bulletproof backpacks rise, but they're unlikely to do much good. *Huffington Post.* Retrieved from https:// www.huffingtonpost.com/entry/bulletproof-backpack-sales-rise_us _5a8d8ce1e4b03414379c2cf1

Goodrum, S., & Woodward, W. (2016). *Report on the Arapahoe High School shooting: Lessons learned on information sharing, threat assessment, and systems integrity.* Boulder, CO: University of Colorado Center for the Study and Prevention of Violence. Retrieved from https://www.colorado.edu/cspv/publications/AHS-Report/Report_on_the_Arapahoe_High_School_Shooting_FINAL.pdf

Gottlieb, C. (1999, April 25). TV bloopers Littleton lessons: The problem with live, unfiltered coverage. *The Chicago Tribune,* p. 19. Retrieved from http://www.chicagotribune.com/news/ct-xpm-1999-04-25-9904250283-story.html

Graber, D. (1980). *Crime news and the public.* Chicago, IL: University of Chicago Press.

Graber, D. A. (2006). *Mass media and American politics* (7th ed.). Washington, D.C.: CQ Press.

Green, M. W. (1999). *The appropriate and effective use of security technologies in U.S. schools.* Washington, D.C.: National Institute of Justice. Retrieved from https://www.ncjrs.gov/school/state.html

Greenberg, S. (2007). Active shooters on college campuses: Conflicting advice, roles of the individual and first responder, and the need to maintain perspective. *Disaster Medicine and Public Health Preparedness, 1*(S1), S57–S61.

Greenblatt, M. (2012, September 30). TSA lets loaded guns past security, on to planes. *ABCNews.* Retrieved from http://abcnews.go.com/US/tsa-lets-loaded-guns-past-security-planes/story?id=17358872

Grimaldi, J. V., & Horwitz, S. (2010, October 24). Industry pressure hides gun traces, protects dealers from public scrutiny. *The Washington Post.* Retrieved from http://www.washingtonpost.com/wp-dyn/content/article/2010/10/23/AR2010102302996.html

Grossman, D., & Christensen, L. (2012). *On combat: The psychology and physiology of deadly conflict in war and peace* (3rd ed.). Mascoutah, IL: Warrior Science Publications.

Gruenewald, J., Pizarro, J., & Chermak, S. (2009). Race, gender, and the newsworthiness of homicide incidents. *Journal of Criminal Justice, 37*(3), 262–272.

The Gun Control Act of 1968. 18 U.S.C. § 44.

Gun Show Accountability Act, H.R. 902, 106th Cong., 1st Sess. (1999).

Gun Show Accountability Act, H.R. 1903, 106th Cong., 1st Sess. (1999).

Gun Show Accountability Act, S. 443, 106th Cong., 1st Sess. (1999).

Gun Show Background Check Act of 2001, S. 767, 107th Cong., 1st Sess. (2001).

Gun Show Background Check Act of 2002, H.R. 4034, 107th Cong., 2d Sess. (2001).

Gun Show Background Check Act of 2003, H.R. 260, 108th Cong., 1st Sess. (2003).

Gun Show Background Check Act of 2008, S. 2577, 110th Cong., 2d Sess. (2008).

Gun Show Background Check Act of 2009, S. 843, 111th Cong., 1st Sess. (2009).

Gun Show Background Check Act of 2011, S. 35, 112th Cong., 1st Sess. (2011).

Gun Show Background Check Act of 2013, S. 22, 113th Cong., 1st Sess. (2013).

Gun Show Loophole Closing Act of 2003, S. 1807, 108th Cong., 1st Sess. (2003).

Gun Show Loophole Closing Act of 2004, H.R. 3832, 108th Cong., 2d Sess. (2004).

Gun Show Loophole Closing Act of 2005, H.R. 3540, 108th Cong., 1st Sess. (2005).

Gun Show Loophole Closing Act of 2007, H.R. 96, 110th Cong., 1st Sess. (2007).

Gun Show Loophole Closing Act of 2009, H.R. 2324, 111th Cong., 1st Sess. (2009).

Gun Show Loophole Closing Act of 2011, H.R. 591, 112th Cong., 1st Sess. (2011).

Gun Show Loophole Closing Act of 2013, H.R. 141, 113th Cong., 1st Sess. (2013).

Gun Show Loophole Closing Act of 2015, H.R. 2380, 114th Cong., 1st Sess. (2015).

Gun Show Loophole Closing Act of 2017, H.R. 1612, 115th Cong., 1st Sess. (2017).

Gun Show Loophole Closing and Gun Law Enforcement Act of 2001, H.R. 2377, 107th Cong., 1st Sess. (2001).

Gun Show Loophole Closing and Gun Law Enforcement Act of 2001, S. 890, 107th Cong., 1st Sess. (2001).

Gun Violence Prevention and Reduction Act of 2013, H.R. 2910, 113th Cong., 1st Sess. (2013).

Haga, C. (2012, December 17). Woman lives with horrors of 2005 Red Lake shootings, brought back by new tragedy. *Grand Forks Herald*. Retrieved from https://www.grandforksherald.com/news/2185456-woman-lives -horrors-2005-red-lake-shootings-brought-back-new-tragedy

Haider-Markel, D. P., & Joslyn, M. R. (2001). Gun policy, opinion, tragedy, and blame attribution: The conditional influence of issue frames. *Journal of Politics, 63*(2), 520–543.

Halsey, A., III. (2015, June 3). Why the TSA catches your water bottle, but guns and bombs get through. *The Washington Post*. Retrieved from http://www .washingtonpost.com/local/trafficandcommuting/why-the-tsa-catches -your-water-bottle-but-guns-and-bombs-get-through/2015/06/03 /7e0596fc-0a07-11e5-95fd-d580f1c5d44e_story.html

Hamblin, J. (2018, February 18). What are active-shooter drills doing to kids? *The Atlantic*. Retrieved from https://www.theatlantic.com/health/archive /2018/02/effects-of-active-shooter/554150/

Hamel, L., Firth, J., & Brodie, M. (2015, July 1). Kaiser health tracking poll: Late June 2015 – A special focus on the Supreme Court Decision. *Henry J. Kaiser Family Foundation*. Retrieved from https://www.kff.org/health-reform /poll-finding/kaiser-health-tracking-poll-late-june-2015-a-special-focus -on-the-supreme-court-decision/

Hamilton, M. (2017, July 31). Congressman seeks to void SAFE Act with new federal bill. *Albany Times Union*. Retrieved from https://www.timesunion

.com/7day-state/article/Congressman-seeks-to-void-SAFE-Act-with
-new-bill-11720471.php

Hamilton, W. L. (1999, May 6). How suburban design is failing teenagers. *The New York Times*. Retrieved from http://www.nytimes.com/1999/05/06 /garden/how-suburban-design-is-failing-teen-agers.html

Hankin, A., Hertz, M., & Simon, T. (2011). Impacts of metal detector use in schools: Insights from 15 years of research. *Journal of School Health, 81*(2), 100–106.

Hansen, M. (2018, February 27). There are ways to make schools safer and teachers stronger – but they don't involve guns. *The Brookings Institution*. Retrieved from https://www.brookings.edu/blog/brown-center-chalk-board/2018/02/27/there-are-ways-to-make-schools-safer-and-teachers-stronger-but-they-dont-involve-guns/

Hardwire. (n.d.). *Bulletproof whiteboards*. Retrieved from https://www.hardwirellc .com/collections/bulletproof-whiteboards

Hardy, D. T. (1986). The Firearm Owners' Protection Act: A historical and legal perspective. *Cumberland Law Review, 17*, 585–681.

Hari, J. (2004, January 15). The cult of Eric and Dylan. *The Independent*. Retrieved from https://www.independent.co.uk/news/world/americas/the-cult-of -eric-and-dylan-73697.html

Harrington, R. (2018, April 3). What you should do in an active-shooter situation—remember "Run, Hide, Fight." *Business Insider*. Retrieved from https://www.businessinsider.com/what-is-run-hide-fight-what-should -you-do-if-theres-an-active-shooter-2016-11

Harris, J. M., & Harris, R. B. (2012). Rampage violence requires a new type of research. *American Journal of Public Health, 102*(6), 1054–1057.

Harter, S., Low, S. M., & Whitesell, N. R. (2003). What have we learned from Columbine: The impact of the self-system on suicidal and violent ideation among adolescents. *Journal of School Violence, 2*(3), 3–26.

Hastings, D. (2018, May 30). Active shooter drills in preschools: The new normal. *Inside Edition*. Retrieved from https://www.insideedition.com/active -shooter-drills-preschool-new-normal-43766

H.B. 15, 2000 Assemb., Reg. Sess. (Ky. 2000).

H.B. 199, 53rd Leg., Reg. Sess. (Utah 2000).

H.B. 444, 55th Leg., Reg. Sess. (Idaho 2000).

H.B. 663, 55th Leg., Reg. Sess. (Idaho 2000).

H.B. 905, 2000 Assemb., Reg. Sess. (Va. 2000).

Hellgren, M. (2012, August 30). Accused Perry Hall HS gunman's Facebook page lists Columbine shooters as inspiration; victim's father has social media warning. *CBS Baltimore*. Retrieved from https://baltimore.cbslocal.com /2012/08/30/baltimore-co-community-comes-together-as-investigation -into-perry-hall-high-shooting-continues/

Hempel, A. G., Meloy, J. R., & Richards, T. C. (1999). Offender and offense characteristics of a nonrandom sample of mass murderers. *Journal of the American Academy of Psychiatry and the Law, 27*(2), 213–225.

Henry, S. (2000). What is school violence? An integrated definition. *Annals of the American Academy of Political and Social Science, 567*, 16–29.

Henry, S. (2009). School violence beyond Columbine: A complex problem in need of an interdisciplinary analysis. *American Behavioral Scientist, 52*(9), 1246–1265.

Herbert, G. (2014, November 4). Columbine shooting victim's daughter slams NY play written from killers' perspectives. *Syracuse.com*. Retrieved from https://www.syracuse.com/news/index.ssf/2014/11/columbine_shooting_play_erklings_killers_perspective_ny.html

Hernandez, E. (2006, May 5). Columbine revisited in Off-Broadway's *columbinus*, starting May 5. *Playbill*. Retrieved from http://www.playbill.com/article/columbine-revisited-in-off-broadways-columbinus-starting-may-5-com-132390

Heron, M. (2017). Deaths: Leading causes for 2015. *National Vital Statistics Report, 66*(5). Hyattsville, MD: National Center for Health Statistics. Retrieved from https://www.cdc.gov/nchs/data/nvsr/nvsr66/nvsr66_05.pdf

Hess, A. (2017, November 13). This Florida school is selling $120 bulletproof panels to put in kids' backpacks. *CNBC*. Retrieved from https://www.cnbc.com/2017/11/13/a-florida-school-is-selling-bulletproof-panels-for-kids-backpacks.html

Hesterman, J. (2015). *Soft target hardening: Protecting people from attack*. Boca Raton, FL: CRC Press.

Hewitt, B. (1999, May 3). Archive: Sorrow and outrage. *People*. Retrieved from https://people.com/archive/cover-story-sorrow-and-outrage-vol-51-no-16/

Hill, E. W. (2013). *The cost of arming schools: The price of stopping a bad guy with a gun*. Retrieved from http://cua6.urban.csuohio.edu/publications/hill/ArmingSchools_Hill_032813.pdf

Hinman, D. L., & Cook, P. E. (2001). A multi-disciplinary team approach to threat assessment. *Journal of Threat Assessment, 1*(1), 17–33.

Holl, J. (2006, May 19). Man sentenced to 32-year prison term in mall shooting. *The New York Times*. Retrieved from https://www.nytimes.com/2006/05/19/nyregion/19cnd-mall.html

Home-Assembled Firearms Restriction Act of 2015, H.R. 376, 114th Cong., 1st Sess. (2015).

Hong, J. S., Cho, H., Allen-Meares, P., & Espelage, D. L. (2011). The social ecology of the Columbine High School shootings. *Children and Youth Services Review, 33*(6), 861–868.

Horn, J. (2014, April 24). "The Library" rewrites the book on Columbine. *Los Angeles Times*. Retrieved from http://www.latimes.com/entertainment/movies/moviesnow/la-et-mn-library-steven-soderbergh-hbo-20140424-story.html

Hough, M. (1987). Offenders' choice of target: Findings from victim surveys. *Journal of Quantitative Criminology, 3*(4), 355–369.

Hsu, T. (2018, March 4). Threat of shootings turns school security into a growth industry. *The New York Times*. Retrieved from https://www.nytimes.com

/2018/03/04/business/school-security-industry-surges-after-shootings
.html

Husser, J., Usry, K., Anderson, D., & Covington, C. (2018). What North Carolina
teachers think about guns in schools. *ELON POLL*. Retrieved from
https://www.elon.edu/e/CmsFile/GetFile?FileID=1245

Hussey, K., & Rojas, R. (2018, April 1). Remington's bankruptcy stalls ruling in
Sandy Hook families' suit. *The New York Times*. Retrieved from https://
www.nytimes.com/2018/04/01/nyregion/remington-sandy-hook-shooting
.html

Imported Assault Weapons Ban of 2016, H.R. 4748, 114th Cong., 2nd Sess. (2016).

Ingraham, C. (2016, June 12). Assault rifles are becoming mass shooters' weapon
of choice. *The Washington Post*. Retrieved from https://www.washington
post.com/news/wonk/wp/2016/06/12/the-gun-used-in-the-orlando
-shooting-is-becoming-mass-shooters-weapon-of-choice/?utm_term=.
e9029bb3d3f8

Ingraham, C. (2018, February 27). For the first time since Columbine, most
Americans believe mass shootings can be stopped. *The Washington Post*.
Retrieved from https://www.washingtonpost.com/news/wonk/wp/2018
/02/27/for-the-first-time-since-columbine-most-americans-believe
-mass-shootings-can-be-stopped/

Ingram, C. (1989, May 19). Assault gun ban wins final vote: Deukmejian's promised approval would make it 1st such U.S. law. *Los Angeles Times*.
Retrieved from http://articles.latimes.com/1989-05-19/news/mn-112_1
_assault-weapons-ban-military-style-assault-types-of-semiautomatic
-rifles

International Association of Chiefs of Police. (2013). *Tactical emergency medical
training for law enforcement personnel*. Retrieved from http://www.theiacp
.org/ViewResult?SearchID=2310

International Association of Chiefs of Police. (2018). *Active shooter*. Alexandria,
VA: IACP Law Enforcement Policy Center. Retrieved from http://www
.theiacp.org/model-policy/wp-content/uploads/sites/6/2018/04/Active
ShooterPaper2018.pdf

International Association of Fire Chiefs. (n.d.). *IAFC position: Active shooter and
mass casualty terrorist events*. Retrieved from https://www.iafc.org/topics
-and-tools/resources/resource/iafc-position-active-shooter-and-mass
-casualty-terrorist-events

International Association of Fire Fighters. (n.d.). *IAFF position statement: Active
shooter events*. Retrieved from http://www.acphd.org/media/372823/iaff
_active_shooter_position_statement.pdf

International Public Safety Association. (2017). *The International Public Safety
Association's rescue task force best practices guide*. Retrieved from https://
www.joinipsa.org/resources/Documents/International%20Public%20
Safety%20Association%20Rescue%20Task%20Force%20Best%20Prac
tices%20Guide%20October%202017.pdf

Isherwood, C. (2006, May 23). "Columbinus": Exploring the evil that roams a high school's halls. *The New York Times*. Retrieved from https://www.nytimes.com/2006/05/23/theater/reviews/23colu.html

Ivanson, A. (2015, October 6). Firefighters, police partner for active shooter training. *Wane.com*. Retrieved from https://www.wane.com/news/local-news/firefighters-police-partner-for-active-shooter-training/1071806621

Jacobs, L. M., Rotondo, M., McSwain, N., Fabbri, W. P., Eastman, A., Butler, F. K., Sinclair, J., . . . Kamin, R. (2013b). Active shooter and intentional mass casualty events: The Hartford Consensus II. *Bulletin of the American College of Surgeons, 98*(9), 35–39.

Jacobs, L. M., Wade, D. S., McSwain, N. E., Butler, F. K., Fabbri, W. P., Eastman, A. L., . . . Burns, K. L. (2013a). The Hartford consensus: THREAT, a medical disaster preparedness concept. *Journal of the American College of Surgeons, 217*(5), 947–953.

James v. Meow Media, Inc., 300 F. 3d 683 (2002).

Janofsky, M. (2000, February 15). In sandwich shop, 2 more Columbine students are killed. *The New York Times*. Retrieved from https://www.nytimes.com/2000/02/15/us/in-sandwich-shop-2-more-columbine-students-are-killed.html

Jefferson County Sheriff's Office. (1999). *Columbine documents: JC-001-025923 through JC-001-026859.* Golden, CO: Jefferson County Sheriff's Office. Retrieved from https://schoolshooters.info/sites/default/files/JCSO%2025%2C923%20-%2026%2C859.pdf

Jefferson County Sheriff's Office. (2000). *Columbine High School: Columbine investigative materials.* Golden, CO: Jefferson County Public Information Department. Retrieved from http://edition.cnn.com/SPECIALS/2000/columbine.cd/Pages/TOC.htm

Jeffery, C. R. (1971). *Crime prevention through environmental design.* Beverly Hills, CA: Sage.

Johnson, I. M. (1999). School violence: The effectiveness of a school resource officer program in a Southern city. *Journal of Criminal Justice, 27*(2), 173–193.

Johnson, K. (2017, November 9). Texas church shooting: Background check breakdown highlights federal gun records problem. *USA Today*. Retrieved from https://www.usatoday.com/story/news/politics/2017/11/09/texas-church-shooting-background-check-breakdown-highlights-federal-gun-record-problems/847947001/

Johnson, K., & Frosch, D. (2007, December 11). Police tie Colorado church shootings to one gunman. *The New York Times*. Retrieved from http://www.nytimes.com/2007/12/11/us/11churches.html

Johnson, M. (2014, December 30). VAS implementing ALICE safety plan. *Vernon County Broadcaster*. Retrieved from http://lacrossetribune.com/vernonbroadcaster/news/local/vas-implementing-alice-safety-plan/article_dbe8a8ad-8fa9-5653-bce4-8f75f6104771.html

Johnson, O., Carlson, P., Murphy, B., Flory, D., Lankford, B., & Wyllie, D. (2016). Preparing civilians to survive an active shooter event. *Journal of Law Enforcement, 5*(2), 1–13.

Johnson, S. (2011, October 3). Dark meaning of bubble-gum pumped up kicks is tough to chew. *Chicago Tribune.* Retrieved from http://articles.chicagotribune.com/2011-10-03/entertainment/ct-ent-1004-foster-lyrics-20111004_1_school-shooting-pop-music-song

Jones, J. M. (2001, September 4). Parents not overly concerned about school environments for their children. *Gallup.* Retrieved from http://news.gallup.com/poll/4843/Parents-Overly-Concerned-About-School-Environments-Their-Children.aspx

Jones, J. M. (2006, October 17). Parent concern about children's safety at school on the rise. *Gallup.* Retrieved from http://news.gallup.com/poll/25021/parent-concern-about-childrens-safety-school-rise.aspx

Jones, J. M. (2017, August 17). Parental fear about school safety back to pre-Newtown level. *Gallup.* Retrieved from http://news.gallup.com/poll/216308/parental-fear-school-safety-back-pre-newtown-level.aspx

Jones, J. M. (2018, March 14). U.S. preference for stricter gun laws highest since 1993. *Gallup.* Retrieved from http://news.gallup.com/poll/229562/preference-stricter-gun-laws-highest-1993.aspx

Juvonen, J. (2001). *School violence: Prevalence, fears, and prevention.* Retrieved from https://www.rand.org/content/dam/rand/pubs/issue_papers/2006/IP219.pdf

Kalish, R., & Kimmel, M. S. (2010). Suicide by mass murder: Masculinity, aggrieved entitlement, and rampage school shootings. *Health Sociology Review, 19*(4), 451–464.

Kaplan, T. (2013, January 15). Sweeping limits on guns become law in New York. *The New York Times.* Retrieved from https://www.nytimes.com/2013/01/16/nyregion/tougher-gun-law-in-new-york.html

Karas, B. (2009, August 21). Man obsessed with Columbine convicted of murder. *CNN.* Retrieved from http://www.cnn.com/2009/CRIME/08/21/north.carolina.castillo.trial/index.html

Kasler v. Lockyer, 2 P.3d 581 (Cal. 2000).

Kass, J. (2010, April 15). Media coverage of the Columbine shootings. *The Denver Post.* Retrieved from https://www.denverpost.com/2010/04/15/media-coverage-of-the-columbine-shootings/

Kellner, D. (2003). *Media spectacle.* London: Routledge.

Kellner, D. (2008a). *Guys and guns amok: Domestic terrorism and school shootings from the Oklahoma City bombing to the Virginia Tech massacre.* Boulder, CO: Paradigm Publishers.

Kellner, D. (2008b). Media spectacle and the "Massacre at Virginia Tech." In B. Agger & T. W. Luke (Eds.), *There is a gunman on campus* (pp. 29–54). Lanham, MD: Rowan & Littlefield Publishers, Inc.

Keyes, J. M. (2018, July). *SRP/SRM train the trainer.* Workshop presentation at The Briefings: A National School Safety Symposium, Westminster, CO.

Khomami, N. (2017, April 13). Russia could have done more to prevent Beslan school siege, court finds. *The Guardian*. Retrieved from https://www.the guardian.com/world/2017/apr/13/russia-could-have-done-more-to -prevent-beslan-school-siege-court-finds

Kiefer, H. M. (2005, April 5). Public: Society powerless to stop school shootings. *Gallup*. Retrieved from http://news.gallup.com/poll/15511/Public-Society -Powerless-Stop-School-Shootings.aspx

Kiilakoski, T., & Oksanen, A. (2011a). Cultural and peer influences on homicidal violence: A Finnish perspective. *New Directions for Youth Development, 2011*(129), 31–42.

Kiilakoski, T., & Oksanen, A. (2011b). Soundtrack of the school shootings: Cultural script, music and male rage. *Young, 19*(3), 247–269.

Kimmel, M. S., & Mahler, M. (2003). Adolescent masculinity, homophobia, and violence: Random school shootings, 1982-2001. *American Behavioral Scientist, 46*(10), 1439–1458.

Kissner, J. (2016). Are active shootings temporally contagious? An empirical assessment. *Journal of Police and Criminal Psychology, 31*(1), 48–58.

Kleck, G. (2009). Mass shootings in schools: The worst possible case for gun control. *American Behavioral Scientist, 52*(10), 1447–1464.

Klein, N. (2007). *Shock doctrine*. New York: Picador.

Klinger, A., & Klinger, A. (2018). 30 days since Parkland: School-based violent incidents and threats from Feb 15th–Mar 16th. *The Educator's School Safety Network*. Retrieved from https://static1.squarespace.com/static/55674 542e4b074aad07152ba/t/5aba8598562fa76217664d9f/1522173337463 /fact+sheet-+30+days+of+data+since+parkland.Educator%27s.School .Safety.Network.+www.eSchoolSafety.org.pdf

Knoll, J. L., & Meloy, J. R. (2014). Mass murder and the violent paranoid spectrum. *Psychiatric Annals, 44*(5), 236–243.

Kocieniewski, D., & Gately, G. (2006, October 3). Man shoots 11, killing 5 girls, in Amish school. *The New York Times*. Retrieved from https://www.nytimes .com/2006/10/03/us/03amish.html

Kupchik, A. (2010). *Homeroom security: School discipline in an age of fear*. New York: NYU Press.

Kupchik, A., & Bracy, N. L. (2009). The news media on school crime and violence: Constructing dangerousness and fueling fear. *Youth Violence and Juvenile Justice, 7*(2), 136–155.

Kupchik, A., Brent, J. J., & Mowen, T. J. (2015). The aftermath of Newtown: More of the same. *British Journal of Criminology, 55*(6), 1115–1130.

KUSA Staff. (2017, May 10). 17 years later, murder of two teens in Subway restaurant still unsolved. *9News*. Retrieved from https://www.9news.com /article/news/crime/17-years-later-murder-of-two-teens-in-subway -restaurant-still-unsolved/438110665

Kwak, H., Lee, C., Park, H., & Moon, S. (2010). *What is Twitter, a social network or news media?* Paper presented at the International World Wide Web

Conference, Raleigh, NC. Retrieved from http://www.ambuehler.ethz.ch /CDstore/www2010/www/p591.pdf

Langer, G. (2015, October 2). Mass shootings like Umpqua lift support for gun control, but not for long. *ABC News*. Retrieved from https://abcnews .go.com/Politics/mass-shootings-umpqua-lift-support-gun-control-long /story?id=34202609

Langford, C. (2018, July 11). Texas high school upgrades security after shooting. *Courthouse News Service*. Retrieved from https://www.courthousenews .com/texas-high-school-upgrades-security-after-shooting/

Langman, P. (2009). Rampage school shooters: A typology. *Aggression and Violent Behavior, 14*(1), 79–86.

Langman, P. (2015). *School shooters: Understanding high school, college, and adult perpetrators*. Lanham, MD: Rowman & Littlefield.

Langman, P. (2017). Role models, contagions, and copycats: An exploration of the influence of prior killers on subsequent attacks. *SchoolShooters.info*. Retrieved from https://schoolshooters.info/sites/default/files/role_models _3.1.pdf

Lankford, A., & Madfis, E. (2018). Don't name them, don't show them, but report everything else: A pragmatic proposal for denying mass killers the attention they seek and deterring future offenders. *American Behavioral Scientist, 62*(2), 260–279.

Lankford, A., & Tomek, S. (2017). Mass killings in the United States from 2006 to 2013: Social contagion or random clusters? *Suicide and Life-Threatening Behavior*. doi:10.1111/sltb.12366

Lansat, M. (2018, July 27). 10 items that show how much US school shootings have changed back-to-school shopping. *Business Insider*. Retrieved from https://www.businessinsider.com/us-school-shootings-have-changed -back-to-school-shopping-2018-7

Lardieri, A. (2017, November 9). TSA fails most tests in undercover operation. *U.S. News and World Report*. Retrieved from https://www.usnews.com /news/national-news/articles/2017-11-09/tsa-fails-most-tests-in-under cover-operation

Large Capacity Ammunition Feeding Device Act of 2013, H.R. 138, 113th Cong., 1st Sess. (2013).

Large Capacity Ammunition Feeding Device Act of 2013, S. 33, 113th Cong., 1st Sess. (2013).

Larkin, R. W. (2007). *Comprehending Columbine*. Philadelphia: Temple University Press.

Larkin, R. W. (2009). The Columbine legacy: Rampage shootings as political acts. *American Behavioral Scientist, 52*(9), 1309–1326.

LaRowe, A., & Raible, M. (2017, April 1). All visitors must sign in. *School Planning & Management*. Retrieved from https://webspm.com/Articles/2017/04/01 /School-Visitors.aspx

Las Vegas Metropolitan Police Department. (2018). *LVMPD preliminary investigative report: 1 October/mass casualty shooting*. Las Vegas, NV: Author.

Retrieved from https://www.lvmpd.com/en-us/Documents/1_October
_FIT_Report_01-18-2018_Footnoted.pdf

Lawrence, R. (2007). *School crime and juvenile justice* (2nd ed.). New York: Oxford
University Press.

Lawrence, R. G., & Birkland, T. A. (2004). Guns, Hollywood, and criminal justice: Defining the school shootings problem across public arenas. *Social
Science Quarterly, 85*(5), 1193–1207.

Leary, M. R., Kowalski, R. M., Smith, L., & Phillips, S. (2003). Teasing, rejection,
and violence: Case studies of the school shootings. *Aggressive Behavior,
29*(3), 202–214.

Leavy, P., & Maloney, K. P. (2009). American reporting of school violence and
"people like us": A comparison of newspaper coverage of the Columbine
and Red Lake school shootings. *Critical Sociology, 35*(2), 273–292.

Lemonick, M. D. (2002, April 29). Germany's Columbine. *TIME*. Retrieved from
http://content.time.com/time/magazine/article/0,9171,234133,00.html

Lendon, B. (2010, October 26). "Blast boxers" aim to curb "life-changing" wounds.
CNN. Retrieved from http://news.blogs.cnn.com/2010/10/26/blast-boxers
-aim-to-curb-life-changing-wounds/

Levin, J., & Madfis, E. (2009). Mass murder at school and cumulative strain: A
sequential model. *American Behavioral Scientist, 52*(9), 1227–1245.

Levkulich, J. (2014, November 26). "Panic button" provides instant response at
schools. *WYTV 33 News*. Retrieved from http://panic-button-for-commu
nities.maiyimai.shop/52fJ9XmAEJc/_Panic_button_provides_instant
_response_at_schools/

Lewin, T. (1999, May 2). Terror in Littleton: The teenage culture; Arizona high
school provides glimpse inside cliques' divisive webs. *The New York Times*.
Retrieved from http://www.nytimes.com/1999/05/02/us/terror-littleton
-teen-age-culture-arizona-high-school-provides-glimpse-inside.html
?pagewanted=all&src=pm

Lewis, T. (2003). The surveillance economy of post-Columbine schools. *The
Review of Education, Pedagogy, and Cultural Studies, 25*(4), 335–355.

Lickel, B., Schmader, T., & Hamilton, D. L. (2003). A case of collective responsibility: Who else was to blame for the Columbine High School shootings? *Personality and Social Psychology Bulletin, 29*(2), 194–204.

Lindberg, N., Oksanen, A., Sailas, E., & Kaltiala-Heino, R. (2012). Adolescents
expressing school massacre threats online: Something to be extremely worried about? *Child and Adolescent Psychiatry and Mental Health, 6*(1), 39–46.

Lipschultz, J. H., & Hilt, M. L. (2011). Local television coverage of a mall shooting: Separating facts from fiction in breaking news. *Electronic News, 5*(4),
197–214.

Lohman, J. (2006). *School security technologies*. Hartford, CT: Office of Legislative
Research. Retrieved from https://www.cga.ct.gov/2006/rpt/2006-R-0668.
htm

Ma, A. (2018, May 8). Anxiety over shootings bolsters $2.7 billion school secur-
ity industry. *Marketplace*. Retrieved from https://www.marketplace.org

/2018/05/08/education/anxiety-over-shootings-bolsters-27-billion-school
-security-industry

Madfis, E. (2014a). *The risk of school rampage: Assessing and preventing threats of school violence.* New York: Palgrave Macmillan.

Madfis, E. (2014b). Averting school rampage: Student intervention amid a persistent code of silence. *Youth Violence and Juvenile Justice, 12*(3), 229–249.

Madfis, E. (2018). Insight from averted mass shootings. In J. Schildkraut (Ed.), *Mass shootings in America: Understanding the debates, causes, and responses* (pp. 79–84). Santa Barbara, CA: ABC-CLIO.

Madison, L. (2011, January 20). Poll: Americans remain split on gun control. *CBS News.* Retrieved from https://www.cbsnews.com/news/poll-americans
-remain-split-on-gun-control/

Maguire, B., Sandage, D., & Weatherby, G. A. (1999). Crime stories as television news: A content analysis of national big city and small-town newscasts. *Journal of Criminal Justice and Popular Culture, 7*(1), 1–14.

Maguire, B., Weatherby, G. A., & Mathers, R. A. (2002). Network news coverage of school shootings. *The Social Science Journal, 39*(3), 465–470.

Mandatory Gun Show Background Check Act, H.R. 2122, 106th Cong., 1st Sess. (1999).

Manson, M. (1999, June 24). Columbine: Whose fault is it? *Rolling Stone.* Retrieved from https://www.rollingstone.com/culture/culture-news/columbine-whose
-fault-is-it-232759/

Mapp v. Ohio, 367 U.S. 643 (1961).

Markey, P. M., Markey, C. N., & French, J. E. (2014). Violent video games and real-world violence: Rhetoric versus data. *Psychology of Popular Media Culture.* Retrieved from https://www.apa.org/pubs/journals/features/ppm
-ppm0000030.pdf

Martaindale, M. H., & Blair, J. P. (2019). *The evolution of active shooter response training protocols.* Manuscript submitted for publication.

Martaindale, M. H., Sandel, W. L., & Blair, J. P. (2017). Active-shooter events in the workplace: Findings and policy implications. *Journal of Business Continuity & Emergency Planning, 11*(1), 6–20.

Matthews, Z. (2018, April 17). Local police departments join for active-shooter training. *The Eagle-Tribune.* Retrieved from http://www.eagletribune.com
/news/merrimack_valley/local-police-departments-join-for-active
-shooter-training/article_1850fdf3-b427-5c38-b8fb-1f29b00bd2c5.html

May, D. C., Fessel, S. D., & Means, S. (2004). Predictors of principals' perceptions of school resource officer effectiveness in Kentucky. *American Journal of Criminal Justice, 29*(1), 75–93.

Mayer, M. J., & Leone, P. E. (1999). A structural analysis of school violence and disruption: Implications for creating safer schools. *Education and Treatment of Children, 22*(3), 333–356.

Mayo, B. (2018, May 23). Pittsburgh rescue task forces: How city police, firefighters and paramedics are training to save lives while active threats are

underway. *Pittsburgh's Action News 4*. Retrieved from http://www.wtae
.com/article/pittsburgh-rescue-task-forces-how-city-police-firefighters
-and-paramedics-are-training-to-save-lives-while-active-threats-are-under
-way/20889946

Mazzei, P. (2018, April 24). Parkland gunman carried out rampage without
entering a single classroom. *The New York Times*. Retrieved from https://
www.nytimes.com/2018/04/24/us/parkland-shooting-reconstruction
.html

McCarthy, J. (2015, August 25). Three in 10 U.S. parents worry about child's
safety at school. *Gallup*. Retrieved from http://news.gallup.com/poll/184853
/three-parents-worry-child-safety-school.aspx

McCombs, M. E. (1997). Building consensus: The news media's agenda-setting
roles. *Political Communication, 14*(4), 433–443.

McCombs, M. E. (2005). A look at agenda-setting: Past, present and future. *Journalism Studies, 6*(4), 543–557.

McCombs, M. E., & Shaw, D. L. (1972). The agenda-setting function of mass
media. *Public Opinion Quarterly, 36*(2), 176–187.

McCormack, D. (2012, December 14). Murdered principal's haunting pictures of
Sandy Hook children practicing their evacuation drill – just days before
massacre. *Daily Mail*. Retrieved from http://www.dailymail.co.uk/news
/article-2248426/Connecticut-massacre-Heart-breaking-pictures-Sandy
-Hook-Elementary-School-just-days-shooting.html

McDevitt, J., & Panniello, J. (2005). *National assessment of school resource officer
programs: Survey of students in three large new SRO programs*. Washington,
D.C.: U.S. Department of Justice. Retrieved from https://www.ncjrs.gov
/pdffiles1/nij/grants/209270.pdf

McDonald v. Chicago, 130 S. Ct. 3020 (2010).

McGee, J. P., & DeBernardo, C. R. (1999). The classroom avenger: A behavioral
profile of school-based shootings. *The Forensic Examiner, 8*(5/6), 16–18.

McMillin, S. (2009, April 18). Getting teens to talk may be key to secure schools.
The Gazette. Retrieved from http://gazette.com/getting-teens-to-talk-may
-be-key-to-secure-schools/article/51999

Mechem, C. C., Bossert, R., & Baldini, C. (2015). Rapid assessment medical support (RAMS) for active shooter incidents. *Prehospital Emergency Care,
19*(2), 213–217.

Meenach, D. (2015, April 30). Military use of chest seals and tourniquets: Lessons for EMS. *EMS1.com*. Retrieved from https://www.ems1.com/ems
-products/Bleeding-Control/articles/2165377-Military-use-of-chest-seals
-and-tourniquets-Lessons-for-EMS/

Meindl, J. N., & Ivy, J. W. (2017). Mass shootings: The role of the media in promoting generalized imitation. *American Journal of Public Health, 107*(3),
368–370.

Meloy, J. R. (2014). The seven myths of mass murder. *Violence and Gender, 1*(3),
102–104.

Meloy, J. R., Hempel, A. G., Gray, B. T., Mohandie, K., Shiva, A., & Richards, T. C. (2004). A comparative analysis of North American adolescent and adult mass murderers. *Behavioral Sciences and the Law, 22*(3), 291–309.

Meloy, J. R., Hempel, A. G., Mohandie, K., Shiva, A. A., & Gray, B. T. (2001). Offender and offense characteristics of a nonrandom sample of adolescent mass murderers. *Journal of the American Academy of Child and Adolescent Psychiatry, 40*(6), 719–728.

Meloy, J. R., & Hoffmann, J. (Eds.). (2014). *International handbook of threat assessment*. New York: Oxford University Press.

Meloy, J. R., Hoffman, J., Roshdi, K., & Guldimann, A. (2014). Some warning behaviors discriminate between school shooters and other students of concern. *Journal of Threat Assessment and Management, 1*(3), 203–211.

Meloy, J. R., Mohandie, K., Knoll, J. L., & Hoffmann, J. (2015). The concept of identification in threat assessment. *Behavioral Sciences and the Law, 33*(2–3), 213–237.

Meloy, J. R., & O'Toole, M. E. (2011). The concept of leakage in threat assessment. *Behavioral Sciences and the Law, 29*(4), 513–527.

Meloy, J. R., Sheridan, L., & Hoffmann, J. (2008). Public figure stalking, threats, and attacks: The state of the science. In J. R. Meloy, L. Sheridan, & J. Hoffman (Eds.), *Stalking, threatening, and attacking public figures* (pp. 3–34). New York, NY: Oxford University Press.

Mental Health America. (n.d.). *2017 state of mental health in America—Youth data*. Retrieved from http://www.mentalhealthamerica.net/issues/2017-state -mental-health-america-youth-data

Meyers, M. (1997). *News coverage of violence against women: Engendering blame*. Thousand Oaks, CA: Sage.

Miller v. Texas, 153 U.S. 535 (1894).

Ministry of Justice. (2009). *Jokela school shooting on 7 November 2007: Report of the investigation commission*. Helsinki: Finland: Ministry of Justice, Finland. Retrieved from https://schoolshooters.info/sites/default/files/Jokela%20 School%20Shooting%20Official%20Report.pdf

Mink, T. (2006). *Sheriff Ted Mink's statement regarding Columbine tapes*. Golden, CO: Jefferson County Sheriff's Office.

Monroe, R. (2012, October 5). *The killer crush: The horror of teen girls, from Columbiners to Beliebers*. Retrieved from https://www.theawl.com/2012/10/the -killer-crush-the-horror-of-teen-girls-from-columbiners-to-beliebers/

Moore, D. W. (2001a, March 26). Americans divided on whether school shootings can be prevented. *Gallup*. Retrieved from http://news.gallup.com /poll/1867/Americans-Divided-Whether-School-Shootings-Can-Prevented .aspx

Moore, D. W. (2001b, April 5). Americans look to parents to stop school shootings. *Gallup*. Retrieved from http://news.gallup.com/poll/1828/Americans -Look-Parents-Stop-School-Shootings.aspx

Moore, M. H., Petrie, C. V., Braga, A. A., & McLaughlin, B. L. (Eds.). (2003). *Deadly lessons: Understanding lethal school violence*. Washington, D.C.: The National Academies Press.

Moreno, I. (2018, June 24). Gunshot detection technology coming to Wisconsin schools. *US News & World Report*. Retrieved from https://www.usnews .com/news/healthiest-communities/articles/2018-06-24/gunshot -detection-technology-coming-to-wisconsin-schools

Morrison, G. B. (2006). Deadly force programs among larger police departments. *Police Quarterly, 9*(3), 331–360.

Mueck, R. (2017, September 20). Active shooter incidents: The rescue task force concept. *Domestic Preparedness*. Retrieved from https://www.domesticpre paredness.com/healthcare/active-shooter-incidents-the-rescue-task-force -concept/

Murphy, B. (2017, July). *Firsthand experience of the Sikh temple shooting*. Paper presented at The Briefings: A National School Safety Symposium, Little-ton, CO.

Muschert, G. W. (2002). *Media and massacre: The social construction of the Colum-bine story* (Unpublished doctoral dissertation). University of Colorado at Boulder, Boulder, CO.

Muschert, G. W. (2007a). Research in school shootings. *Sociology Compass, 1*(1), 60–80.

Muschert, G. W. (2007b). The Columbine victims and the myth of the juvenile superpredator. *Youth Violence and Juvenile Justice, 5*(4), 351–366.

Muschert, G. W. (2009). Frame-changing in the media coverage of a school shooting: The rise of Columbine as a national concern. *The Social Science Journal, 46*(1), 164–170.

Muschert, G. W. (2010). School shootings. In M. Herzog-Evans (ed.), *Transna-tional criminology manual, volume 2* (pp. 73–89). Nijmegen, Netherlands: Wolf Legal Publishing.

Muschert, G. W., & Carr, D. (2006). Media salience and frame changing across events: Coverage of nine school shootings, 1997–2001. *Journalism and Mass Communication Quarterly, 83*(4), 747–766.

Muschert, G. W., Henry, S., Bracy, N. L., & Peguero, A. A. (Eds.). (2014). *Respond-ing to school violence: Confronting the Columbine Effect*. Boulder, CO: Lynne Rienner Publishers.

Muschert, G. W., & Larkin, R. W. (2007). The Columbine High School shoot-ings. In S. Chermak & F. Y. Bailey (Eds.), *Crimes and trials of the century* (pp. 253–266). Westport, CT: Praeger.

Muschert, G. W., & Peguero, A. A. (2010). The Columbine Effect and school anti-violence policy. *Research in Social Problems and Public Policy, 17*, 117–148.

Muschert, G. W., & Ragnedda, M. (2010). Media and violence control: The fram-ing of school shootings. In W. Heitmeyer, H. G. Haupt, S. Malthaner, & A. Kirschner (Eds.), *The control of violence in modern society: Multidisciplin-ary perspectives, from school shootings to ethnic violence* (pp. 345–361). New York, NY: Springer Publishing.

Muschert, G. W., & Schildkraut, J. (2015). School shootings. In H. Montgomery (Ed.), *Oxford bibliographies in childhood studies*. New York: Oxford Univer-sity Press.

Musu-Gillette, L., Zhang, A., Wang, K., Zhang, J., Kemp, J., Diliberti, M., & Oudekerk, B. A. (2018). *Indicators of school crime safety: 2017.* Washington, D.C.: U.S. Department of Education and U.S. Department of Justice.

Nance, J. (2014). School surveillance and the Fourth Amendment. *Wisconsin Law Review, 2014*(1), 79–137.

Nasopharyngeal Airway (NPA). (n.d.). *Oxford medical education.* Retrieved from http://www.oxfordmedicaleducation.com/clinical-skills/procedures /nasopharyngeal-airway/

National Firearms Act of 1934. 26 U.S.C. § 53.

National Institute of Mental Health. (2017). *Major depression.* Retrieved from https://www.nimh.nih.gov/health/statistics/major-depression.shtml

National School Safety and Security Services. (n.d.). *School metal detectors.* Retrieved from http://www.schoolsecurity.org/trends/school-metal-detectors/

The National School Shield Task Force. (2013). *The report of the National School Shield Task Force.* Retrieved from https://www.nraschoolshield.org/media /1844/summary-report-of-the-national-school-shield-task-force.pdf

Nedzel, N. E. (2014). Concealed carry: The only way to discourage mass school shootings. *Academic Questions, 27*(4), 429–435.

Neighborhood Security Act, H.R. 5100, 108th Cong., 2nd Sess. (2004).

Neuman, Y., Assaf, D., Cohen, Y., & Knoll, J. L. (2015). Profiling school shooters: Automatic text-based analysis. *Frontiers in Psychiatry, 6.* doi:10.3389/fpsyt .2015.00086

Newman, K. S. (2006). School shootings are a serious problem. In S. Hunnicutt (Ed.), *School shootings* (pp. 10–17). Farmington Hills, MI: Greenhaven Press.

Newman, K. S., & Fox, C. (2009). Repeat tragedy: Rampage shootings in American high schools and college settings, 2002–2008. *American Behavioral Scientist, 52*(9), 1286–1308.

Newman, K. S., Fox, C., Harding, D. J., Mehta, J., & Roth, W. (2004). *Rampage: The social roots of school shootings.* New York, NY: Basic Books.

Newman, O. (1972). *Defensible space: Crime prevention through urban design.* New York, NY: Macmillan.

Newman, O. (1973). *Defensible space: People and design in the violent city.* London: Architectural Press.

Newport, F. (1999a, May 21). Teenagers and adults differ on causes, cures for Columbine-type situations. *Gallup.* Retrieved from http://news.gallup .com/poll/3835/Teenagers-Adults-Differ-Causes-Cures-ColumbineType -Situations.aspx

Newport, F. (1999b, June 16). Americans support wide variety of gun control measures. *Gallup.* Retrieved from http://news.gallup.com/poll/3775/Amer icans-Support-Wide-Variety-Gun-Control-Measures.aspx

Newport, F. (2001, April 20). Americans say the family is the starting point for preventing another Columbine. *Gallup.* Retrieved from http://news.gallup .com/poll/1783/Americans-Say-Family-Starting-Point-Preventing-Another -Columbine.aspx

Newport, F. (2006, October 4). Before recent shootings, most parents not worried about school safety. *Gallup.* Retrieved from http://news.gallup.com/poll/24844/Before-Recent-Shootings-Most-Parents-Worried-About-School-Safety.aspx

Nichols, T. (2012, October 4). How 5 active shooter incidents have changed police training. *PoliceOne.com.* Retrieved from https://www.policeone.com/active-shooter/articles/6002951-How-5-active-shooter-incidents-have-changed-police-training/

Nicholson, K. (2000, August 22). Teen who sent Columbine threat via 'Net is freed. *The Denver Post.* Retrieved from http://extras.denverpost.com/news/col0822a.htm

Nicholson, K. (2007, April 18). Cho: Killers at Columbine "martyrs." *The Denver Post.* Retrieved from https://www.denverpost.com/2007/04/18/cho-killers-at-columbine-martyrs/

Nicoletti, J. (2017, July). *Threat assessment and threat management: Current considerations and practices.* Paper presented at The Briefings: A National School Safety Symposium, Littleton, CO.

NICS Improvement Amendments Act of 2007, H.R. 2640, 110th Cong., 1st Sess. (2007).

Noe, G. (2013). *Lessons from the Century 16 theatre shooting.* Retrieved from https://www.google.com/url?sa=t&rct=j&q=&esrc=s&source=web&cd=14&cad=rja&uact=8&ved=0CDEQFjADOApqFQoTCLTE9d6xgMcCFYGBDQodHqcAzQ&url=http%3A%2F%2Ficma.org%2FDocuments%2FDocument%2FDocument%2F305481&ei=Yc24VfSPIIGDNp7OgugM&usg=AFQjCNETsLCPtI7R9x18VeQbZ83O1KmF5w&sig2=VooqkGgRGkZ_PJJ6B7NFNQ&bvm=bv.98717601,d.eXY

NoNotoriety.com. (n.d.). *No Notoriety: No name. No photo. No Notoriety.* Retrieved from https://nonotoriety.com/

Noonan, K. (2018, July 15). Why Shotspotter, Inc. soared 170% in the first half of 2018. *The Motley Fool.* Retrieved from https://www.fool.com/investing/2018/07/15/why-shotspotter-inc-soared-170-in-the-first-half-o.aspx

Norman, J. (2016, June 15). How high will terrorism concerns rise, how long will they last? *Gallup.* Retrieved from http://news.gallup.com/poll/192713/high-terrorism-concerns-rise-long-last.aspx

O'Donnell, J., & Saker, A. (2018, March 19). Teen suicide is soaring. Do spotty mental health and addiction treatment share blame? *USA Today.* Retrieved from https://www.usatoday.com/story/news/politics/2018/03/19/teen-suicide-soaring-do-spotty-mental-health-and-addiction-treatment-share-blame/428148002/

Office of Community Policing Services. (n.d.a.). *2014 COPS hiring program awards.* Retrieved from https://cops.usdoj.gov/pdf/2014AwardDocs/CHP/CHP-2014-Announcement-9-24-14.pdf

Office of Community Policing Services. (n.d.b.). *2015 COPS hiring program awards.* Retrieved from https://cops.usdoj.gov/pdf/2015AwardDocs/chp/CHP_Award_List.pdf

Office of Community Policing Services. (n.d.c.). *2016 COPS hiring program awards.* Retrieved from https://cops.usdoj.gov/pdf/2016AwardDocs/chp/Award _List_Reapportionment.pdf

Office of Community Policing Services. (n.d.d.). *2017 COPS hiring program awards.* Retrieved from https://cops.usdoj.gov/pdf/2017AwardDocs/chp /Detailed_Award_List.pdf

Office of Community Policing Services. (2017). *Fact sheet: 2017 COPS hiring program.* Retrieved from https://cops.usdoj.gov/pdf/2017AwardDocs/chp/Post _Award_Fact_Sheet.pdf

Ogle, J. P., Eckman, M., & Leslie, C. A. (2003). Appearance cues and the shootings at Columbine High: Construction of a social problem in the print media. *Sociological Inquiry, 73*(1), 1–27.

Oksanen, A., Hawdon, J., & Räsänen, P. (2014). Glamorizing rampage online: School shooting fan communities on YouTube. *Technology in Society, 39,* 55–67.

Oksanen, A., Nurmi, J., Vuori, M., & Räsänen, P. (2013). Jokela: The social roots of a school shooting tragedy in Finland. In N. Böckler, T. Seeger, P. Sitzer, & W. Heitmeyer (Eds.), *School shootings: International research, case studies, and concepts for prevention* (pp. 189–215). New York, NY: Springer.

Olinger, D., & Devlin, N. H. (2000, May 6). Song only clue to student's despair. *The Denver Post.* Retrieved from http://extras.denverpost.com/news/col0506 .htm

Olinger, D., Robinson, M., & Simpson, K. (1999, October 23). Victim's mother commits suicide. *The Denver Post.* Retrieved from http://extras.denverpost.com/news/shot1023.htm

Ortiz, E. (2018, March 14). 3 students injured when California high school teacher fires gun during safety course. *NBC News.* Retrieved from https://www.nbcnews.com/news/us-news/3-students-injured-when-california -high-school-teacher-fires-gun-n856481

Osborne, M., & Dredze, M. (2014). *Facebook, Twitter and Google Plus for breaking news: Is there a winner?* Paper presented at the International AAAI Conference on Weblogs and Social Media, Ann Arbor, MI. Retrieved from http:// homepages.inf.ed.ac.uk/miles/papers/icwsm14.pdf

O'Toole, M. E. (2000). *The school shooter: A threat assessment perspective.* Quantico, VA: Critical Incident Response Group, FBI Academy, National Center for the Analysis of Violent Crime. Retrieved from https://www.fbi.gov /file-repository/stats-services-publications-school-shooter-school-shooter

Page, S., & Icsman, M. (2018, March 22). Poll: For Columbine generation, gun violence is a defining fear. *USA Today.* Retrieved from https://www.usato day.com/story/news/2018/03/22/poll-columbine-generation-gun-violence -defining-fear/441446002/

Pampilio, N. (2014). What have we learned from the deadly Columbine High School shooting? *Legacy.com.* Retrieved from http://www.legacy.com/news /culture-and-trends/article/columbine-15-years-later

Pappas, S. (2012, July 23). Mass shootings: Why it's so hard to predict who will snap. *Live Science*. Retrieved from https://www.livescience.com/21787 -predicting-mass-shootings.html

Park County Office of Emergency Management. (2006). *Platte Canyon High School shooting: After action report*. Park County, CO: Office of Emergency Management. Retrieved from https://hazdoc.colorado.edu/bitstream/handle /10590/4940/C021451.pdf?sequence=1

Paton, N. E. (2012). Media participation of school shooters and their fans. In G. W. Muschert & J. Sumiala (Eds.), *School shootings: Mediatized violence in a global age* (pp. 203–230). Bingley, United Kingdom: Emerald Publishing Group Limited.

Paul, A. (2018, March 4). Active shooter protocols have changed over the years. *Corvallis Gazette-Times*. Retrieved from https://www.gazettetimes.com/news /active-shooter-protocols-have-changed-over-the-years/article_a2027e64 -68d8-5e13-8cc2-6652b225c6a8.html

Paulsen, D. (2003). Murder in black and white: The newspaper coverage of homicide in Houston. *Homicide Studies, 7*(3), 289–317.

Payne, A. (2014, December 10). New school administrators receive active shooter training. *MetroNews*. Retrieved from http://wvmetronews.com/2014/12/10 /new-school-administrators-receive-active-shooter-training/

Payne, S. R. T., & Elliott, D. S. (2011). Safe2Tell®: An anonymous, 24/7 reporting system for preventing school violence. *New Directions in Youth Development, 2011*(129), 103–111.

Pearce, J. D., & Goldstein, S. (2015). Not just for SWAT teams: The importance of training officers in tactical emergency medicine. *The Police Chief, 82*. Retrieved from http://www.policechiefmagazine.org/not-just-for-swat-teams -the-importance-of-training-officers-in-tactical-emergency-medicine/

Pennsylvania Department of Education. (2018). *Targeted grant – School police officer: Request for application*. Harrisburg, PA: Author. Retrieved from https:// www.education.pa.gov/Documents/K-12/Safe%20Schools/Safe%20 Schools%20Targeted%20Grants/2018-2019/2018-2019%20School%20 Police%20Officer.pdf

Perumean-Chaney, S. E., & Sutton, L. M. (2013). Students and perceived safety: The impact of school security measures. *American Journal of Criminal Justice, 38*(4), 570–588.

Peterson, B. (2014, November 30). "Lockdown" vs. "silent safety drill": The school security language debate. *The Boston Globe*. Retrieved from http:// www.bostonglobe.com/ideas/2014/11/30/lockdown-silent-safety-drill -the-school-security-language-debate/v30JvvEZR8T2R8dARoGG2H /story.html#

Peterson, R. L., Larson, J., & Skiba, R. (2001). School violence prevention: Current status and policy recommendations. *Law & Policy, 23*(3), 345–371.

Petridis, A. (2017, September 21). "Columbine destroyed my entire career": Marilyn Manson on the perils of being the lord of darkness. *The Guardian*.

Retrieved from https://www.theguardian.com/music/2017/sep/21/columbine
-destroyed-my-entire-career-marilyn-manson-on-the-perils-of-being-the
-lord-of-darkness

Petrosino, A. J., Fellow, S., & Brensilber, D. (1997). Convenient victims: A
research note. *Criminal Justice Policy Review, 8*(4), 405–420.

Pew Research Center for the People & the Press. (1998a, April 3). *Democratic
congressional chances helped by Clinton ratings; Jonesboro compels news audiences.* Retrieved from http://www.people-press.org/1998/04/03/democratic
-congressional-chances-helped-by-clinton-ratings/

Pew Research Center for the People & the Press. (1998b, June 15). *Compared to
1994, voters not so angry, not so interested.* Retrieved from http://www.people
-press.org/1998/06/15/voters-not-so-angry-not-so-interested/

Pew Research Center for the People & the Press. (1999, December 28). *Columbine
shooting biggest news draw of 1999.* Retrieved from http://people-press.org
/report/48/columbine-shooting-biggest-news-draw-of-1999

Pew Research Center for the People & the Press. (2000, April 19). *A year after
Columbine public looks to parents more than schools to prevent violence.*
Retrieved from http://www.people-press.org/2000/04/19/a-year-after-col
umbine-public-looks-to-parents-more-than-schools-to-prevent-violence/

Pew Research Center for the People & the Press. (2007a, April 23). *Little boost for
gun control or agreement on causes.* Retrieved from http://www.people
-press.org/2007/04/23/little-boost-for-gun-control-or-agreement-on
-causes/

Pew Research Center for the People & the Press. (2007b, April 25). *Widespread
interest in Virginia Tech shootings, but public paid closer attention to Columbine.* Retrieved from http://people-press.org/report/322/widespread-interest
-in-virginia-tech-shootings

Pew Research Center for the People & the Press. (2009, November 11). *Fort Hood
shootings top interest, coverage.* Retrieved from http://www.people-press
.org/2009/11/11/fort-hood-shootings-top-interest-coverage/

Pew Research Center for the People & the Press. (2010, March 23). *Public divided
over state, local laws banning handguns.* Retrieved from http://www.people
-press.org/2010/03/23/public-divided-over-state-local-laws-banning
-handguns/

Pew Research Center for the People & the Press. (2011, January 18). *Arizona
rampage dominates public's news interest.* Retrieved from http://www.people
-press.org/2011/01/18/arizona-rampage-dominates-publics-news-interest/

Pew Research Center for the People & the Press. (2012a, July 23). *Colorado shootings capture public's interest.* Retrieved from http://www.people-press.org
/2012/07/23/colorado-shootings-capture-publics-interest/

Pew Research Center for the People & the Press. (2012b, December 17). *Public
divided over what Newtown signifies.* Retrieved from http://www.people
-press.org/2012/12/17/public-divided-over-what-newtown-signifies/

Pew Research Center for the People & the Press. (2013, September 23). *Blame for
both sides as possible government shutdown approaches.* Retrieved from http://

www.people-press.org/2013/09/23/blame-for-both-sides-as-possible
-government-shutdown-approaches/

Pew Research Center for the People & the Press. (2017, June 22). *Public views about guns*. Retrieved from http://www.people-press.org/2017/06/22/public-views-about-guns/#total

Phone system, "panic buttons" failed during deadly LAX shooting. (2014, February 27). *RT*. Retrieved from http://rt.com/usa/phone-panic-systems-failed-lax-092/

Pierce, N. (2002, November 13). Bowling for Columbine (2002). *BBC*. Retrieved from http://www.bbc.co.uk/films/2002/10/28/bowling_for_columbine_2002_review.shtml

Pioneer Press. (2015, March 17). 10 years after Red Lake shootings, memories still haunt. *Twin Cities Pioneer Press*. Retrieved from https://www.twincities.com/2015/03/17/10-years-after-red-lake-shootings-memories-still-haunt/

Police Executive Research Forum. (2014). *Critical issues in policing series: The police responses to active shooter incidents*. Washington, D.C.: Police Executive Research Forum. Retrieved from http://www.policeforum.org/assets/docs/Critical_Issues_Series/the%20police%20response%20to%20active%20shooter%20incidents%202014.pdf

Pollack, W. S., Modzeleski, W., & Rooney, G. (2008). *Prior knowledge of potential school-based violence: Information students learn may prevent a targeted attack*. Washington, D.C.: United States Secret Service and United States Department of Education. Retrieved from https://rems.ed.gov/docs/DOE_BystanderStudy.pdf

Pons, P. T., Jerome, J., McMullen, J., Manson, J., Robinson, J., & Chapleau, W. (2015). The Hartford Consensus on active shooters: Implementing the continuum of prehospital trauma response. *The Journal of Emergency Medicine, 49*(6), 878–885.

Powers, A. (1999, April 25). The nation: The stresses of youth, the strains of its music. *The New York Times*. Retrieved from http://www.nytimes.com/1999/04/25/weekinreview/the-nation-the-stresses-of-youth-the-strains-of-its-music.html

Pratt, T. C., & Turanovic, J. J. (2016). Lifestyle and routine activity theories revisited: The importance of "risk" to the study of victimization. *Victims & Offenders, 11*(3), 335–354.

Prendergast, A. (2015, February 2). Columbine killers' basement tapes destroyed. *Westword*. Retrieved from http://www.westword.com/news/columbine-killers-basement-tapes-destroyed-6283043

Protection of Lawful Commerce in Arms Act, S. 397, 109th Cong., 1st Sess. (2005).

"Pumped Up Kicks" & Newtown: Foster the People's song pulled from radio after school shootings. (2012, December 19). *Huffington Post*. Retrieved from http://www.huffingtonpost.com/2012/12/19/pumped-up-kicks-newtown-foster-the-people-school-shooting_n_2329503.html

Quan, D. (2012, December 21). Band talks "Pumped Up Kicks" post school shooting. *CNN*. Retrieved from http://marquee.blogs.cnn.com/2012/12 /21/foster-the-people-school-shooting/

Quinton, S. (2018, March 16). To prevent suicides and school shootings, more states embrace anonymous tip lines. *The Pew Charitable Trusts*. Retrieved from http://www.pewtrusts.org/en/research-and-analysis/blogs/stateline /2018/03/16/to-prevent-suicides-and-school-shootings-more-states-embrace -anonymous-tip-lines

Rasmussen, C., & Johnson, G. (2008). The ripple effect of Virginia Tech: Assessing the nationwide impact on campus safety and security policy and practice. *Midwestern Higher Education Compact*. Retrieved from http://files .eric.ed.gov/fulltext/ED502232.pdf

Rawdon, S. (2014, December 1). Parent group to donate 3007 door barricades. *Licking County News*. Retrieved from http://www.thisweeknews.com/con tent/stories/lickingcounty/news/2014/12/01/southwest-licking-parent -group-to-donate-307-door-barricades.html

Ray, M. (2011). Fox News Channel. *Encyclopedia Britannica*. Retrieved from https://www.britannica.com/topic/Fox-News-Channel

Raymond, N. (2018, April 6). U.S. judge upholds Massachusetts assault weapons ban. *Reuters*. Retrieved from https://www.reuters.com/article/us-usa-guns -massachusetts/u-s-judge-upholds-massachusetts-assault-weapons-ban -idUSKCN1HD2CW

Rayner, G. (2008, September 23). Finnish school shooting: How killer "calmly" picked off his victims. *The Telegraph*. Retrieved from https://www.tele graph.co.uk/news/worldnews/europe/finland/3068671/Finnish-school -shooting-how-killer-calmly-picked-off-his-victims.html

The Rebels Project. (2017). *Home*. Retrieved from http://therebelsproject.org/

Reddy, M., Borum, R., Berglund, J., Vossekuil, B., Fein, R., & Modzeleski, W. (2001). Evaluating risk for targeted violence in schools: Comparing risk assessment, threat assessment, and other approaches. *Psychology in the Schools, 38*(2), 157–172.

Reese, S. D. (2007). The framing project: A bridging model for media research revisited. *Journal of Communication, 57*(1), 148–154.

Reid, D. (2002, October 25). "I'm trying to connect the dots between the local violence and the global violence," says director Michael Moore of his new film, "Bowling for Columbine." *Sacramento Bee*. Retrieved from https:// web.archive.org/web/20080908062845/http://www.bowlingforcolumbine .com/reviews/2002-10-25-sacra.php

Reid, K. (2018, May 7). Review: "Columbinus" at Steppenwolf: As shootings continue, this play gets more difficult to watch. *Chicago Tribune*. Retrieved from http://www.chicagotribune.com/entertainment/theater/reviews/ct -ent-columbinus-steppenwolf-0508-story.html

Reinhart, R. J. (2018, January 23). In the news: School shootings. *Gallup*. Retrieved from http://news.gallup.com/poll/226202/news-school-shootings.aspx

Reinwald, C. (2014, June 10). Muscatine teachers' invention could save your child's life. *WQAD 8.* Retrieved from http://wqad.com/2014/06/10/mus catine-teachers-invention-could-save-your-childs-life/

Reisman, N. (2018, January 16). 5 years of SAFE Act and gun control still triggers heated debate. *Spectrum News.* Retrieved from http://spectrumlocal news.com/nys/capital-region/politics/2018/01/16/new-york-safe -act-5-years

Remarks from the NRA press conference on Sandy Hook school shooting, delivered on December 21, 2012 (Transcript). *The Washington Post.* Retrieved from https://www.washingtonpost.com/politics/remarks-from-the-nra -press-conference-on-sandy-hook-school-shooting-delivered-on-dec -21-2012-transcript/2012/12/21/bd1841fe-4b88-11e2-a6a6-aabac85e8036 _story.html?utm

Rescue Essentials. (n.d.). *Hemostatics.* Retrieved from https://www.rescue-essentials .com/hemostatics-1/

Ripley, A. (2008). *The unthinkable: Who survives when disaster strikes—And why.* New York, NY: Three Rivers Press.

Roberts, J. (2004, May 18). Communication breakdown on 9/11. *CBS News.* Retrieved from https://www.cbsnews.com/news/communication-break-down-on-9-11/

Robertson, T. (2006, January 30). Prosecutor: Dozens knew school shooter's plan. *Minnesota Public Radio.* Retrieved from http://news.minnesota.pub licradio.org/features/2006/01/30_robertsont_redlake/?refid=0

Robinson, M. B. (2011). *Media coverage of crime and criminal justice.* Durham, NC: Carolina Academic Press.

Rock, A. (2018, March 2). Experts: Hurricane-proof glass prevented more deaths in Parkland shooting. *Campus Safety.* Retrieved from https://www .campussafetymagazine.com/safety/hurricane-proof-glass-fla-school -shooting/

Rocque, M. (2012). Exploring school rampage shootings: Research, theory, and policy. *The Social Science Journal, 49*(3), 304–313.

Rogers, L. (2018, March 26). Sign of the times: Officers, EMTs gather for active shooter training. *Hometown Life.* Retrieved from https://www.hometown-life.com/story/news/2018/03/26/sign-times-officers-emts-gather-active -shooter-training/424439002/

Rooney, D. (2014, January 16). Steven Soderbergh to direct Off-Broadway play starring Chloe Grace Moretz. *The Hollywood Reporter.* Retrieved from https://www.hollywoodreporter.com/news/steven-soderbergh-direct-broad way-play-671668

Roper Center for Public Opinion Research. (n.d.). *Shootings, guns and public opinion.* Retrieved from https://ropercenter.cornell.edu/shootings-guns-public -opinion/

Rose, V. (2013). Weapons banned as assault weapons. *OLR Research Report.* Retrieved from https://www.cga.ct.gov/2013/rpt/2013-R-0241.htm

Rostker, B. D., Hanser, L. M., Hix, W. M., Jensen, C., Morral, A. R., Ridgeway, G., & Schell, T. L. (2008). *Evaluation of the New York City Police Department firearm training and firearm-discharge review process.* Santa Monica, CA: The RAND Corporation. Retrieved from http://www.nyc.gov/html/nypd/downloads/pdf/public_information/RAND_FirearmEvaluation.pdf

Russell, L. (2013, August 25). Photos: Bulletproof products for urban survival. *CNN.* Retrieved from https://www.cnn.com/2013/08/25/us/bulletproof-products/index.html

Ryan, J. (1999, April 23). "Buffy" slayed by school massacre. *E! News.* Retrieved from https://www.eonline.com/news/38063/buffy-slayed-by-school-massacre

Saad, L. (1999, April 23). Public views Littleton tragedy as sign of deeper problems in country. *Gallup News.* Retrieved from http://www.gallup.com/poll/3898/public-views-littleton-tragedy-sign-deeper-problems-country.aspx

Saad, L. (2006, August 31). One in four parents concerned about child's safety at school. *Gallup.* Retrieved from http://news.gallup.com/poll/24337/One-Four-Parents-Concerned-About-Childs-Safety-School.aspx

Saad, L. (2007, May 2). Americans skeptical about preventing Virginia Tech-like incidents. *Gallup.* Retrieved from http://news.gallup.com/poll/27430/Americans-Skeptical-About-Preventing-Virginia-TechLike-Incidents.aspx

Saad, L. (2009, April 8). Before recent shootings, gun-control support was fading. *Gallup.* Retrieved from http://news.gallup.com/poll/117361/Recent-Shootings-Gun-Control-Support-Fading.aspx

Saad, L. (2012, December 28). Parents' fear for children safety at school rises slightly. *Gallup.* Retrieved from http://news.gallup.com/poll/159584/parents-fear-children-safety-school-rises-slightly.aspx

Saad, L. (2017a, April 20). Gallup vault: Columbine a sign of systemic US problems. *Gallup.* Retrieved from http://news.gallup.com/vault/208808/gallup-vault-columbine-sign-systemic-problems.aspx

Saad, L. (2017b, October 17). American widely support tighter regulations on gun sales. *Gallup.* Retrieved from http://news.gallup.com/poll/220637/americans-widely-support-tighter-regulations-gun-sales.aspx

Sacco, V. F. (2005). *When crime waves.* Thousand Oaks, CA: Sage.

Safe2Tell. (n.d.a.). *Data 2 report: 2016–2017.* Retrieved from https://safe2tell.org/sites/default/files/u18/End%20of%20Year%202016-2017%20Data2Report.pdf

Safe2Tell. (n.d.b.). *About us: History.* Retrieved from https://safe2tell.org/?q=history

Sanchez, R. (1998, May 23). Educators pursue solutions to violence crisis; as deadly sprees increase, schools struggle for ways to deal with student anger. *The Washington Post,* A12.

Sanders, C. (2014, November 3). Columbine play's bad lessons. *New York Post.* Retrieved from https://nypost.com/2014/11/03/columbine-plays-bad-lessons/

Sanders v. Acclaim Entertainment, Inc., 188 F. Supp. 2d 1264 (2002).

Sandy Hook Advisory Commission. (2015). *Final report of the Sandy Hook Advisory Committee.* Hartford, CT: Sandy Hook Advisory Committee. Retrieved from http://www.shac.ct.gov/SHAC_Final_Report_3-6-2015.pdf

S.B. 23, 1999-2000, Reg Sess. (Cal. 2000).

S.B. 211, 414th Assemb., Reg Sess. (Md. 2000).

S.B. 548, 218th Leg., Reg. Sess. (N.J. 2018).

S.B. 6206, 56th Leg., Reg Sess. (Wash. 2000).

Schachter, K. (2018, March 4). Execs: Fear of terror attacks fuels demand for window security film. *Newsday.* Retrieved from https://www.newsday.com/business/chb-industries-window-security-film-1.17007086

Scharrer, E., Weidman, L. M., & Bissell, K. L. (2003). Pointing the finger of blame: News media coverage of popular-culture culpability. *Journalism & Communication Monographs, 5*(2), 49–98.

Scheufele, D. A., & Tewksbury, D. (2007). Framing, agenda setting, and priming: The evolution of three media effects models. *Journal of Communication, 57*(1), 9–20.

Schildkraut, J. (2012a). Media and massacre: A comparative analysis of the reporting of the 2007 Virginia Tech shootings. *Fast Capitalism, 9*(1). Retrieved from http://www.uta.edu/huma/agger/fastcapitalism/9_1/schildkraut9_1.html

Schildkraut, J. (2012b). The remote is controlled by the monster: Issues of mediatized violence and school shootings. In G. W. Muschert & J. Sumiala (Eds.), *School shootings: Mediatized violence in a global age* (pp. 231–254). Bingley, United Kingdom: Emerald Publishing Group Limited.

Schildkraut, J. (2014). *Mass murder and the mass media: An examination of the media discourse on U.S. rampage shootings, 2000-2012* (Unpublished doctoral dissertation). Texas State University, San Marcos, TX.

Schildkraut, J. (2016). Mass murder and the mass media: understanding the construction of the social problem of mass shootings in the U.S. *Journal of Qualitative Criminal Justice and Criminology, 4*(1), 1–41.

Schildkraut, J., & Elsass, H. J. (2016). *Mass shootings: Media, myths, and realities.* Santa Barbara, CA: Praeger.

Schildkraut, J., Elsass, H. J., & Meredith, K. (2018). Mass shootings and the media: Why all events are not created equal. *Journal of Crime and Justice, 41*(3), 223–243.

Schildkraut, J., Elsass, H. J., & Muschert, G. W. (2016). Satirizing mass murder: What many think, yet few will say. In L. Eargle and A. Esmail (Eds.), *Gun violence in American society: Crime, justice, and public policy* (pp. 233–255). Lanham, MD: University Press of America.

Schildkraut, J., Elsass, H. J., & Stafford, M. C. (2015). Could it happen here? Moral panics, school shootings, and fear of crime among college students. *Crime, Law and Social Change, 63*(1–2), 91–110.

Schildkraut, J., Formica, M. K., & Malatras, J. (2018). *Can mass shootings be stopped? To address the problem, we must better understand the phenomenon*

(Policy brief). Retrieved from http://rockinst.org/wp-content/uploads/2018/05/5-22-18-Mass-Shootings-Brief.pdf

Schildkraut, J., & Hernandez, T. C. (2014). Laws that bit the bullet: A review of legislative responses to school shootings. *American Journal of Criminal Justice, 39*(2), 358–374.

Schildkraut, J., & Muschert, G. W. (2013). Violent media, guns, and mental illness: The three ring circus of causal factors for school massacres, as related in media discourse. *Fast Capitalism, 10*(1). Retrieved from http://www.uta.edu/huma/agger/fastcapitalism/10_1/schildkraut10_1.html

Schildkraut, J., & Muschert, G. W. (2014). Media salience and the framing of mass murder in schools: A comparison of the Columbine and Sandy Hook school massacres. *Homicide Studies, 18*(1), 23–43.

Schneider, T. (2001). New technologies for school security. *National Clearinghouse for Educational Facilities.* Retrieved from https://scholarsbank.uoregon.edu/xmlui/bitstream/handle/1794/3368/digest145.pdf?sequence=1

Schneider, T. (2010). School securities technologies. *National Clearinghouse for Educational Facilities.* Retrieved from http://files.eric.ed.gov/fulltext/ED507917.pdf

Schoetz, D., & Goldman, R. (2007, November 13). Online, teens "idolized" Columbine killers. *ABC News.* Retrieved from https://abcnews.go.com/Technology/story?id=3848474&page=1

School gunman stole police pistol, vest. (2005, March 23). *CNN.* Retrieved from http://www.cnn.com/2005/US/03/22/school.shooting/

School Safety Infrastructure Council. (2014). *Report of the school safety infrastructure council: Revised and updated to June 27, 2014.* Danbury, CT: School Safety Infrastructure Council. Retrieved from http://das.ct.gov/images/1090/ssic_final_draft_report.pdf

Schuman, H., & Rodgers, W. L. (2004). Cohorts, chronology, and collective memory. *Public Opinion Quarterly, 68*(2), 217–254.

Schuman, H., & Scott, J. (1989). Generations and collective memories. *American Sociological Review, 54*(3), 359–381.

Schuppe, J. (2018, May 20). Schools are spending billions on high-tech security. But are students any safer? *NBC News.* Retrieved from https://www.nbcnews.com/news/us-news/schools-are-spending-billions-high-tech-security-are-students-any-n875611

Schwartz, H. L., Ramchand, R., Barnes-Proby, D., Grant, S., Jackson, B. A., Leuschner, K., . . . Saunders, J. (2016). *The role of technology in improving K–12 school safety.* Santa Monica, CA: The RAND Corporation. Retrieved from https://www.rand.org/pubs/research_reports/RR1488.html

Schworm, P., & Anderson, T. (2014, November 19). Milford fifth-grader punished over pretend gun. *Boston Globe.* Retrieved from https://www.bostonglobe.com/metro/2014/11/19/fifth-grader-suspended-for-pointing-imaginary-gun-his-hand/l7MqowzO5yEP5yb4IFXemN/story.html

Scott, A. O. (2002, October 11). Film review: Seeking a smoking gun in U.S. violence. *The New York Times.* Retrieved from https://www.nytimes.com

/2002/10/11/movies/film-review-seeking-a-smoking-gun-in-us-violence
.html

Scott, J. (2018, March 14). Are more schools looking at window film as a viable option? *Window Film Magazine.* Retrieved from https://www.windowfilm mag.com/2018/03/are-more-schools-looking-at-window-film-as-a -viable-option/

Second Amendment Restoration and Protection Act of 1998, H.R. 4137, 105th Cong., 2nd Sess. (1998).

Sedensky, S. J. (2013). *Report of the State's Attorney for the judicial district of Danbury on the shootings at Sandy Hook Elementary School and 36 Yoga-nanda Street, Newtown, Connecticut on December 14, 2012.* Danbury, CT: Office of the State's Attorney, Judicial District of Danbury. Retrieved from http://health-equity.lib.umd.edu/4223/1/Sandy_Hook_Final_Report .pdf

Seelye, K. Q. (1999, May 20). Campaigns find all talk turns to Littleton. *The New York Times.* Retrieved from http://www.nytimes.com/1999/05/20/us /campaigns-find-all-talk-turns-to-littleton.html

Segarra, L. M. (2017, September 22). Marilyn Manson: "Columbine destroyed my entire career." *TIME.* Retrieved from http://time.com/4954072/marilyn -manson-columbine-shooting-career/

Shepard, A. C. (2000). *The Columbine shooting: Live television coverage.* Retrieved from http://www.columbia.edu/itc/journalism/j6075/edit/readings/colum bine.html

Shoup, C. (2018, April 18). Police training: What comes next after school shoot-ing. *Freemont News Messenger.* Retrieved from https://www.thenews-mes senger.com/story/news/local/2018/04/18/police-training-active-school -shooting/528633002/

Sideras, J. (2011, January 17). Tension pneumothorax: Identification and treat-ment. *EMS1.com.* Retrieved from https://www.ems1.com/ems-products /medical-equipment/airway-management/articles/957467-Tension -Pneumothorax-Identification-and-treatment/

Silver, J., Simons, A., & Craun, S. (2018). *A study of the pre-attack behaviors of active shooters in the United States between 2000 and 2013.* Washington, D.C.: Fed-eral Bureau of Investigation, U.S. Department of Justice. Retrieved from https://www.fbi.gov/file-repository/pre-attack-behaviors-of-active-shooters -in-us-2000-2013.pdf

Simons, A., & Meloy, J. R. (2017). Foundations of threat assessment and manage-ment. In V. B. Van Hasselt & M. L. Bourke (Eds.), *Handbook of behavioral criminology* (pp. 627–644). Cham, Switzerland: Springer International Publishing AG.

Singh, R. (1999). Gun politics in America: Continuity and change. *Parliamentary Affairs, 52*(1), 1–18.

Slinger, A. (2014, December 5). Southwest Licking schools order firefighter-designed safety device for every classroom. *WSYX-ABC 6.* Retrieved from https://www.youtube.com/watch?v=5LJdAPXp5os

Smith, E. R., & Delaney, J. B. (2013, December 1). Supporting paradigm change in EMS' operational medical response to active shooter events. *Journal of Emergency Medical Services, 38*(12), 48–55.

Smith, E. R., Iselin, B., & McKay, S. (2009). Toward the sound of shooting. *JEMS: A Journal of Emergency Medical Services, 34*(12), 48–55.

Snell, C., Bailey, C., Carona, A., & Mebane, D. (2002). School crime policy changes: The impact of recent highly-publicized school crimes. *American Journal of Criminal Justice, 26*(2), 269–285.

Soothill, K., & Grover, C. (1997). A note on computer searches of newspapers. *Sociology, 31*(3), 591–596.

Soraghan, M. (2000). Colorado after Columbine: The gun debate. *State Legislatures, 26*(6), 14–21.

Spencer, J. W. (2011). *The paradox of youth violence.* Boulder, CO: Lynne Rienner Publishing.

Spencer, T. (2018, April 24). Investigators: School design contributed to Parkland massacre. *Florida Today.* Retrieved from https://www.floridatoday .com/story/news/2018/04/24/investigators-school-design-contributed -parkland-massacre/546961002/

Spicer, B. (2013, October 23). 11 components of a secure school front entrance. *Campus Safety Magazine.* Retrieved from https://www.campussafetymag azine.com/safety/11-components-of-a-secure-school-front-entrance/

Springhall, J. (1999). Violent media, guns, and moral panics: The Columbine High School massacre, 20 April 1999. *Paedagogica Historica, 35*(3), 621–641.

S. Rep. No. 82, 75th Cong. 1st Sess. 2 (1937).

SSRS. (2018). *CNN February 2018.* Glen Mills, PA: Author. Retrieved from http:// cdn.cnn.com/cnn/2018/images/02/25/rel3a.-.trump,.guns.pdf

Stein, S., & Cherkis, J. (2014, June 16). With school shootings routine, parents turn to bulletproof backpacks, child clothing. *Huffington Post.* Retrieved from http://www.huffingtonpost.com/2014/06/16/school-shootings_n _5497428.html

Steinhauser, P. (2012, August 9). CNN poll: Gun control opinions following shootings. *CNN Politics.* Retrieved from http://politicalticker.blogs .cnn.com/2012/08/09/cnn-poll-gun-control-opinions-in-wake-of -shootings/

Strauss, V. (2012, December 19). Michelle Rhee: "Guns have no place in schools." *The Washington Post.* Retrieved from https://www.washingtonpost.com /news/answer-sheet/wp/2012/12/19/michelle-rhee-guns-have-no-place -in-schools/

Stretesky, P. B., & Hogan, M. J. (2001). Columbine and student perceptions of safety: A quasi-experimental study. *Journal of Criminal Justice, 29*(5), 429–443.

Sullivan, E. M., Annest, J. L., Simon, T. R., Luo, F., & Dahlberg, L. L. (2015). Suicide trends among persons aged 1024 years—United States, 19942012. *Morbidity and Mortality Weekly Report, 64*(8), 201–205.

Sumiala, J., & Tikka, M. (2011a). Imagining globalized fears: School shooting videos and circulation of violence on YouTube. *Social Anthropology/ Anthropologie Sociale, 19*(3), 254–267.

Sumiala, J., & Tikka, M. (2011b). Reality on circulation: School shootings, ritualised communication, and the dark side of the sacred. *ESSACHESS: Journal for Communication Studies, 4*(8), 145–159.

Surette, R. (2015). *Media, crime, & criminal justice: Images and reality* (5th ed.). Pacific Grove, CA: Brooks/Cole Publishing Company.

Swenson, K., & Schmidt, S. (2018, Feburary 15). "I'm not really shocked": Florida high school prepared for the worst. Then it happened. *The Washington Post*. Retrieved from https://www.washingtonpost.com/news/morning-mix/wp/2018/02/15/im-not-really-shocked-florida-high-school-prepared-for-the-worst-then-it-happened/

Tankard, J. W. (2001). The empirical approach to the study of media framing. In S. D. Reese, O. H. Gandy, & A. E. Grant (Eds.), *Framing public life: Perspectives on media and our understanding of the social world* (pp. 95–106). Mahwah, NJ: Lawrence Erlbaum.

Thomas, P., Levine, M., Cloherty, J., & Date, J. (2014, October 7). Columbine shootings' grim legacy: More than 50 school attacks, plots. *ABC News*. Retrieved from https://abcnews.go.com/US/columbine-shootings-grim-legacy-50-school-attacks-plots/story?id=26007119

Tiahrt Restrictions Repeals Act, H.R. 661, 113th Cong., 1st Sess. (2013).

Tiahrt Restrictions Repeals Act, H.R. 1449, 114th Cong., 1st Sess. (2015).

Tiahrt Restrictions Repeals Act, H.R. 5271, 115th Cong., 2nd Sess. (2018).

TIME. (1999a, May 3). *Columbine murders—May 3, 1999*. Retrieved from http://content.time.com/time/covers/0,16641,19990503,00.html

TIME. (1999b, December 20). *Columbine tapes—December 20, 1999*. Retrieved from http://content.time.com/time/covers/0,16641,19991220,00.html

To Better Regulate the Transfer of Firearms at Gun Shows, H.R. 109, 106th Cong., 1st Sess. (1999).

To Better Regulate the Transfer of Firearms at Gun Shows, H.R. 3833, 105th Cong., 2nd Sess. (1998).

To Better Regulate the Transfer of Firearms at Gun Shows, H.R. 4442, 105th Cong., 2nd Sess. (1998).

To Better Regulate the Transfer of Firearms at Gun Shows, S. 2527, 105th Cong., 2nd Sess. (1998).

Tonso, K. L. (2009). Violent masculinities as tropes for school shooters: The Montréal massacre, the Columbine attack, and rethinking schools. *American Behavioral Scientist, 52*(9), 1266–1285.

Toppo, G. (2018, February 22). "Generation Columbine" has never known a world without school shootings. *USA Today*. Retrieved from https://www.usatoday.com/story/news/2018/02/22/generation-columbine-has-never-known-world-without-school-shootings/361656002/

Touré, M. (2018, March 9). Use of metal detectors in New York City schools under scrutiny amid Parkland shooting. *Observer*. Retrieved from http://observer.com/2018/03/metal-detectors-nyc-public-schools/

Towers, S., Gomez-Lievano, A., Khan, M., Mubayi, A., & Castillo-Chavez, C. (2015). Contagion in mass killings and school shootings. *PLOS One, 10*: e0117259. Retrieved from https://doi.org/10.1371/journal.pone.0117259

Travis, S. (2018, June 4). Metal detectors among 100 safety measures recommended as a result of Parkland shooting. *Sun Sentinel*. Retrieved from http://www.sun-sentinel.com/local/broward/parkland/florida-school-shooting/fl-florida-school-shooting-safety-report-20180604-story.html

Trump, K. S. (2001). *2001 NASRO school resource officer survey*. Boynton Beach, FL: National School Safety and Security Services. Retrieved from http://www.schoolsecurity.org/resources/2001NASROsurvey%20NSSSS.pdf

Turner, J. T., & Gelles, M. (2003). *Threat assessment: A risk management approach*. New York, NY: Routledge.

Twemlow, S. W., Fonagy, P., Sacco, F. C., O'Toole, M. E., & Vernberg, E. (2002). Premeditated mass shootings in schools: Threat assessment. *Journal of American Academy of Child and Adolescent Psychiatry, 41*(4), 475–477.

Udo, T. (2016, July 28). Marilyn Manson: The story of Holy Wood (In the Shadow of the Valley of Death). *Metal Hammer*. Retrieved from https://www.loudersound.com/features/marilyn-manson-story-behind-holy-wood

United States v. Miller, 307 U.S. 174 (1939).

Urist, J. (2014, November 20). The architecture of loss: How to redesign after a school shooting. *The Atlantic*. Retrieved from https://www.theatlantic.com/education/archive/2014/11/the-architecture-of-loss-how-to-redesign-after-a-school-shooting/382952/

U.S. Const. amend. II.

U.S. Department of Education. (2007). *Issue brief: Public school practices for violence prevention and reduction: 2003–04*. Washington, D.C.: National Center for Education Statistics.

U.S. Department of Justice. (2014). *Department of Justice awards hiring grants for law enforcement and school safety officers*. Retrieved from https://www.justice.gov/opa/pr/department-justice-awards-hiring-grants-law-enforcement-and-school-safety-officers

U.S. Department of Labor, Bureau of Labor Statistics. (n.d.). Inflation calculator. Retrieved from http://www.bls.gov/data/inflation_calculator.htm

U.S. News and World Report. (n.d.). *Columbine high school*. Retrieved from https://www.usnews.com/education/best-high-schools/colorado/districts/jefferson-county-school-district-no-r-1/columbine-high-school-4206

Vanasco, J. (2014, April 19). Soderbergh's "The Library" takes the blood out of a school shooting. *New York Public Radio*. Retrieved from https://www.wnyc.org/story/theater-review-school-shooting-library/

van Dijk, T. A. (1988). *News analysis: Case studies of international and national news in the press*. Hillsdale, NJ: Lawrence Erlbaum Associates, Publishers.

Vann, M. (2018, May 24). Parkland families sue gun manufacturer and dealer, citing complicity. *NBC News*. Retrieved from https://www.nbcnews.com/news/us-news/parkland-families-sue-gun-manufacturer-dealer-citing-complicity-n877146

Verger, R. (2014, April 17). Newsweek rewind: 15 years after Columbine, a nation still asks "why?" *Newsweek*. Retrieved from http://www.newsweek

.com/newsweek-rewind-15-years-after-columbine-nation-still-asks-why
-246535

Verlinden, S., Hersen, M., & Thomas, J. (2000). Risk factors in school shootings. *Clinical Psychology Review, 20*(1), 3–56.

Victor, D. (2018, February 17). Mass shooters are all different. Except for one thing: Most are men. *The New York Times.* Retrieved from https://www.nytimes.com/2018/02/17/us/mass-murderers.html

Vila, B. J., & Morrison, G. B. (1994). Biological limits to police combat handgun shooting accuracy. *American Journal of Police, 13*(1), 1–30.

Vila, H. (2018, March 1). The children of guns: The Columbine generation & the way of war. *The Policy.* Retrieved from https://thepolicy.us/the-children-of-guns-the-columbine-generation-the-way-of-war-878693a153d

Violent Crime Control and Law Enforcement Act of 1994, H.R. 3355, 103d Cong., 2nd Sess. (1994).

Virginia Tech Review Panel. (2007). *Mass shootings at Virginia Tech April 16, 2007: Report of the review panel.* Arlington, VA: Governor's Office of the Commonwealth of Virginia. Retrieved from https://scholar.lib.vt.edu/prevail/docs/April16ReportRev20091204.pdf

Visram, T. (2018, July 2). School security is a rapidly growing business. *CNN Money.* Retrieved from https://money.cnn.com/2018/07/02/news/companies/school-shooting-security/index.html

Vossekuil, B., Fein, R. A., Reddy, M., Borum, R., & Modzeleski, W. (2004). *The final report and findings of the Safe School Initiative: Implications for the prevention of school attacks in the United States.* Washington, D.C.: U.S. Secret Service and U.S. Department of Education. Retrieved from https://www2.ed.gov/admins/lead/safety/preventingattacksreport.pdf

Walsh, S., & Mazza, E. (2001, June 21). Protests in Denver over Marilyn Manson gig. *ABC News.* Retrieved from http://abcnews.go.com/Entertainment/story?id=104105&page=1&singlePage=true

Walters, B. (2000, November 23). Holy Wood (In the Shadow of the Valley of Death). *Rolling Stone.* Retrieved from https://www.rollingstone.com/music/music-album-reviews/holy-wood-in-the-shadow-of-the-valley-of-death-248081/

Warner, R. (2014, November 10). Controversial new play comes from Columbine shooters' perspectives. *Colorado Public Radio News.* Retrieved from http://www.cpr.org/news/story/controversial-new-play-comes-columbine-shooters-perspectives

Warr, M. (2000). Fear of crime in the United States: Avenues for research and policy. In D. Duffee (Ed.), *Measurement and analysis of crime: Criminal justice 2000.* Washington, D.C.: US Department of Justice, Office of Justice Programs.

The Warren Commission. (1964). *Report of the Warren Commission on the assassination of President Kennedy* (1st ed.). New York, NY: McGraw-Hill Book Co.

Washington Post-ABC News Poll. (n.d.). *Washington post politics.* Retrieved September 4, 2013, from http://www.washingtonpost.com/wp-srv/politics/polls/postabcpoll_20121216.html

Watkins, M. (2016, July 26). The armed civilian who helped stop UT's tower sniper 50 years ago. *Texas Tribune.* Retrieved from https://apps.texastribune.org/guns-on-campus/allen-crum-helped-stop-ut-tower-shooter-charles-whitman/

Weatherby, G. A., Luzzo, E., & Zahm, S. (2016). Infamous killers, forgotten victims: A content analysis of print media coverage of three major school shootings. *International Journal of Forensic Sciences, 1*(1), 1–12.

Weaver, D. H. (2007). Thoughts on agenda setting, framing, and priming. *Journal of Communication, 57*(1), 142–147.

Webb, R. (2018, March 1). Stopping school shootings: Is Colorado's "Safe2Tell" hotline a solution? *Center on Media Crime and Justice at John Jay College.* Retrieved from https://thecrimereport.org/2018/03/01/stopping-school-shootings-colorados-safe2tell-hotline-offers-roadmap/

Welch, A. (2017, November 21). What's behind the rise in youth suicides? *CBS News.* Retrieved from https://www.cbsnews.com/news/suicide-youth-teens-whats-behind-rise/

Welch, C. (2011, January 6). Slain assistant principal sent student home because of trespass charge. *CNN.* Retrieved from http://www.cnn.com/2011/CRIME/01/06/nebraska.school.shooting/index.html

Welk, B. (2018, July 12). 15 top grossing documentaries at the box office, from "Monkey Kingdom" to "Sicko" (photos). *The Wrap.* Retrieved from https://www.thewrap.com/top-grossing-documentaries-box-office/

Weller, R. (2000, May 5). Student's suicide leaves Columbine to grieve again. *The Guardian.* Retrieved from https://www.theguardian.com/world/2000/may/06/6

Welsh-Huggins, A. (2015, July 25). School safety: Experts disapprove of new classroom locks. *The Columbus Dispatch.* Retrieved from http://www.dispatch.com/content/stories/local/2015/07/25/experts-disapprove-of-new-classroom-locks.html

White, S., & Meloy, J. R. (2017, September 20). *Threat assessments 101: Understanding the red flags of workplace violence* [Webinar]. Retrieved from https://vimeo.com/234743780

Wigley, S., & Fontenot, M. (2009). Where media turn during crises: A look at information subsidies and the Virginia Tech Shootings. *Electronic News, 3*(2), 94–108.

Wike, T. L., & Fraser, M. W. (2009). School shootings: Making sense of the senseless. *Aggression and Violent Behavior, 14*(3), 162–169.

Willis, J. (2015, June 24). Marilyn Manson says Columbine school shooting "shut down my career." *Entertainment Tonight.* Retrieved from http://www.etonline.com/news/166762_marilyn_manson_says_columbine_shootings_ruined_his_career/

Winn, Z. (2017, October 4). NYC school safety agents find 328 weapons in 3 months. *Campus Safety Magazine*. Retrieved from https://www.campussa fetymagazine.com/safety/nyc-school-safety-agents-find-328-weapons -in-3-months/

Winn, Z. (2018, April 27). The pros and cons of installing metal detectors in schools. *Campus Safety Magazine*. Retrieved from https://www.campussa fetymagazine.com/safety/metal-detectors-in-schools/

Witkin, G. (2012, April 16). On anniversary of Virginia Tech shooting, law to close loophole hasn't accomplished much. *iWatchNews.org*. Retrieved from https://www.publicintegrity.org/2012/04/16/8660/anniversary-virginia -tech-shooting-law-close-loophole-hasnt-accomplished-much

WNYC. (2015, September 16). *Data news: Metal detectors in NYC high schools by the numbers*. Retrieved from http://datanews.tumblr.com/post/12922164 1847/metal-detectors-in-nyc-high-schools-by-the-numbers

Wood, M. (2016, June 15). Why "Run, Hide, Fight" is flawed. *PoliceOne.com*. Retrieved from https://www.policeone.com/active-shooter/articles/19062 1006-Why-Run-Hide-Fight-is-flawed/

WRIC Newsroom. (2018, June 15). Virginia schools receive grant for more security, resource officers. *ABC 8 News*. Retrieved from https://www.wric.com /news/virginia-news/virginia-schools-receive-grant-for-more-security -resource-officers/1240694955

Wright, M. (2018, February 21). Facebook deletes pages glorifying Columbine shooters after survivor says they could inspire other shootings. *The Telegraph*. Retrieved from https://www.telegraph.co.uk/news/2018/02/21/face book-deletes-pages-glorifying-columbine-shooters-survivor/

YouGov Staff. (2012, July 25). After Aurora: Little change in opinions about gun control measures. *YouGov*. Retrieved from https://today.yougov.com/top ics/politics/articles-reports/2012/07/25/after-aurora-little-change-opinions -about-gun-cont

Youth Gun Crime Enforcement Act of 1999, H.R. 1768, 106th Cong., 1st Sess. (1999).

Youth Gun Crime Enforcement Act of 1999, S. 995, 106th Cong., 1st Sess. (1999).

Yurkevich, V. (2017, March 28). This designer clothing line is stylish . . . and bulletproof. *CNN*. Retrieved from https://money.cnn.com/2017/03/27/tech nology/caballero-bulletproof-clothing/index.html

Zimring, F. (2001). *Continuity and change in the American gun debate*. Boalt Hall: UC Berkeley. Retrieved from http://escholarship.org/uc/item/42n784rt

Index

About the Authors

Jaclyn Schildkraut, PhD, is associate professor of criminal justice at the State University of New York (SUNY) at Oswego. Her research interests include mass/school shootings, homicide trends, mediatization effects, moral panics, and crime theories. She is the coauthor of *Mass Shootings: Media, Myths, and Realities* (with H. Jaymi Elsass) and editor of *Mass Shootings in America: Understanding the Debates, Causes, and Responses*. She has published in numerous journals, including *Homicide Studies*; *American Journal of Criminal Justice*; *Journal of Qualitative Criminal Justice & Criminology*; *Journal of Crime and Justice*; *Crime, Law and Social Change*; and *Criminology, Criminal Justice, Law & Society*, as well as in other journals and edited volumes.

Glenn W. Muschert, PhD, is professor of sociology at Khalifa University of Science and Technology in Abu Dhabi (UAE). He earned a BS in international studies from Drexel University (USA) and a PhD in sociology from the University of Colorado, Boulder (USA). His previous appointments include professor of sociology and social justice studies and faculty affiliate in comparative media studies at Miami University (USA). He has also served temporary appointments at Purdue University (USA) and Erzincan University (Turkey). His research interests lie in the intersection of crime and deviance, digital sociology, and media studies. He has edited numerous academic volumes and journal special issues and has written numerous journal articles and chapters in academic volumes in the fields of sociology, criminology, and media studies.